The Architecture Concept Book

The
Architecture
Concept
Book

JAMES TAIT

565 illustrations

Thames & Hudson

First published in 2018 in the United States of America
by Thames & Hudson Inc., 500 Fifth Avenue, New York,
New York 10110

www.thamesandhudsonusa.com

Library of Congress Control Number 2017945403

ISBN 978-0-500-29413-0

Printed and bound in China by C&C Offset Printing Co. Ltd.

CONTENTS

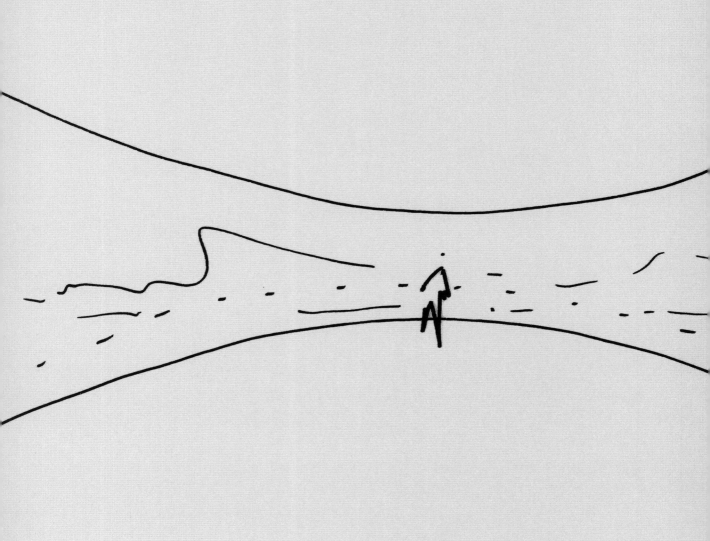

INTRODUCTION

Concept

A concept is often thought of as an abstracted idea; a symbolic representation of more complex and explicative detail. 'Concept' derives from the Latin *conceptum*, meaning 'something conceived'. The term should not be viewed as purely an abstract headline, though, but as something more universal: it is the reason for being of any object, entity or product created by human endeavour and thought. Any oeuvre – be it a work of art, music or literature – has been conceived by the human mind to some degree to bring about its creation. The concept is the reason for its existence; the oeuvre the tangible manifestation of the original idea.

Concept in architecture

The term 'concept' is often misused in architecture. There are 'concept architects' – those whose dreams are destined to remain on paper, too grandiose or underdeveloped to be realized at a particular point in time. Then there is the generalized term of 'conceptual architecture', referring to projects created but not built, intended to stir up reaction by their ambitiousness or provocativeness (political, social or formal). Finally, there is the 'concept stage' of a design, where most student projects remain: a sketch of a project designed with nominal wall thicknesses, notional structure and assumed site constraints.

Yet these terms are misleading. Their current usage in architecture suggests a disconnection between the idea and the built reality – but this need not be the case. The two should not be separate entities; a building should be the physical manifestation of the original concept. The concept, then, for architects, should be the reason to build. We must always have a reason to build.

The specific and the universal

These reasons to build can be both specific and universal. Specific concepts arise from the unique conditions and environment of a particular project. These can be related to the brief: the use of the building, the needs of its users, the opportunities of the site, how the building will respond to the topography or neighbouring buildings, and what it will accentuate about the existing physical conditions. Or they might relate to the political and social context: whether it reflects or rails against prevailing attitudes, and how it will improve local social conditions. Specific concepts are posed as solutions to the challenges inherent in any brief, site or environment, and can be fed into universal concepts.

Universal concepts transcend transient project conditions. They are timeless, embodying aspects of architecture that have always been, and will continue to be. For example, how architecture shapes the ways in which we interact with each other, how life plays out in space; the perpetual search for beauty in all its forms through the manipulation of proportion, scale and form; the honesty of our architecture, how we build it with truth and integrity; and how architecture harnesses and accentuates light, the giver of life.

These concepts, the specific and the universal, must be present in our minds at all stages of the design process. Without them each step becomes dulled, stunted, until all we have designed is a building – not architecture. Architecture has the concept at its core; a building need not. Yet often architects create only buildings. Buildings that do not reflect the capacity they have to be informed and enriched by the concept – to become architecture.

Conception to completion

The word 'architect' comes from the Ancient Greek words *archi* ('chief') and *tekton* ('builder'). The term reflects the cultural and social conditions from which it came: an era in which architects' ambitions and knowledge were equal to their practical abilities and experience. Today, however, this seems a narrow and erroneous definition of the role of the architect and the practice of architecture. Most architects today could not claim to be chiefs, or even builders. We struggle to assert ourselves in a tumultuous and complex world ruled by market forces and fleeting fashions. We build in an insular and abstract way, often removed from practicalities – or worse, without overriding concepts or beliefs. Our ways of working can struggle to keep up with our dreams, and sometimes the dreams aren't even there.

Our architecture should be created with the reason for its creation at its core. Great ideas undeveloped or poorly executed hold more weight than bad ideas (or indeed something with no central idea) well realized.[1] No amount of wilful form finding, fashion following, flashy presentation, intricate modelling, effusive promotional text or expensive materials can disguise a bad or absent idea. However, a sketch of a good idea, of a reason to build, will endure. Yet this is only half of the solution. We must also learn how to carry our concepts forward to the physical reality of our buildings: buildings that address the disconnection between architecture and the forces that shape it; between utopianism and pragmatism within the profession. Buildings that become architecture by the successful realization of the original concept. Think before you design, at every stage of the design process – whether it is the first sketches of a city-wide masterplan, or a construction drawing of a façade detail. Think about how you are being true to the original concept.

Introduction

The Architecture Concept Book

This book is structured in four sections, representing the steps of the architectural design process from conception to completion:

1 — ASSESSING
In this chapter we observe and assess our surrounding environments to extrapolate the salient points for architecture.

2 — ANALYSING
Here we review our modus operandi within the world, and consider how architects can improve.

3 — ASSEMBLING
Here we review and reinterpret the key elements of built architecture, from the floor to the roof.

4 — AUGMENTING
In this chapter we study the tricks used (such as colour, scale and contrast) to elevate our buildings from good to great.

The Architecture Concept Book proposes ways of formulating and developing strategies that will make our buildings better, shape our spaces and further the architect's influence in the creation of architecture by learning from the wider world, challenging our existing practices, and elevating the concept above all else. We must always think before we design. We must always have a reason to build.

PUBLIC SQUARE PROPOSAL
La Praza do Berbés, Vigo, Spain, J. Tait

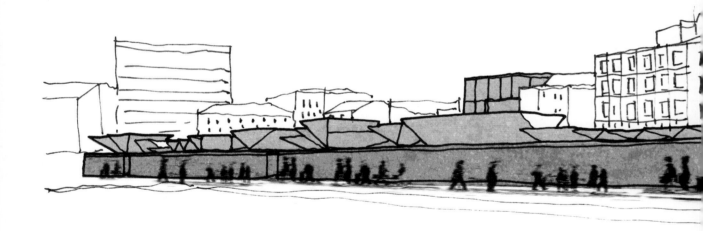

Introduction

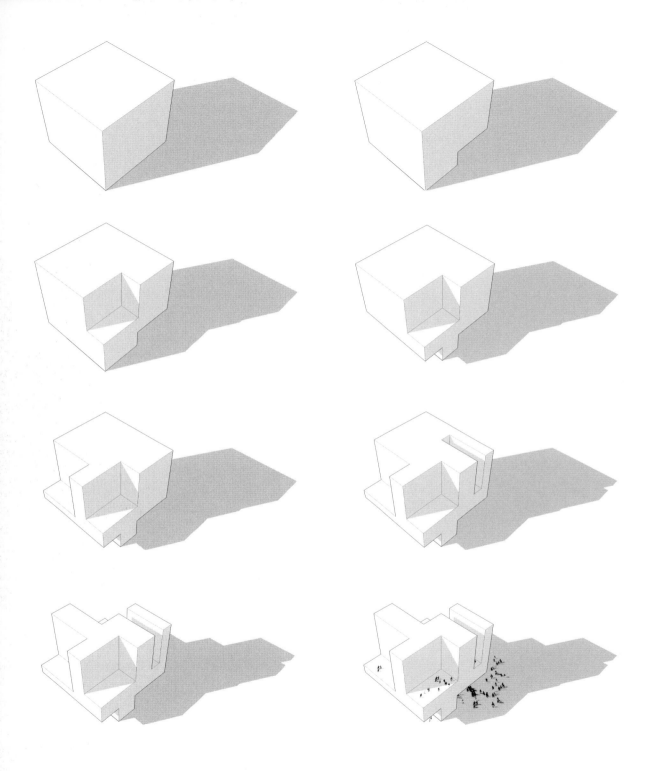

FROM NOTHING TO SOMETHING
Cube to concept: a study in subtraction

Introduction

1
ASSESS

WONDER

Spaces of numen

wonder, *noun*
Germanic – origin unknown
1. The feeling or emotion of amazement,
astonishment or admiration caused by
something that is strange, remarkable
and unfamiliar.
2. The object or instigator of this feeling
of amazement and astonishment.

Wonder in architecture – spaces and buildings that provoke an emotional response through their form, scale and detail – is often associated with religious buildings. Temples, shrines, cathedrals, mosques and synagogues, for example, embody the 'divine creative act' of a higher power, as expressed by theologian Rudolf Otto: 'A mystical awe ... that creature-feeling as personal nothingness and submergence before the awe-inspiring object directly experienced.'[1] Otto relates this to the omnipresence of a higher power that engenders numinous feelings.

Numen and the sublime

This concept of the numinous is related to the philosophical concept of the sublime. Originated by Edmund Burke and developed by Immanuel Kant, the sublime can be best described in its relationship to beauty. In the words of Kant: 'the sublime moves, the beautiful charms'.[2] The sublime is something to be experienced; beauty is merely to be looked at. Kant characterizes the sublime as mountain peaks, raging storms, tall shadowy trees, the night sky and depictions of hell. Conversely, the beautiful was defined by valleys and meadows, grazing flocks, daytime skies and depictions of Elysium. The sublime possesses a mysteriousness and darkness that fascinates.

The sublime, unlike the numinous, is unrelated to religious experience, deriving instead from concepts of infinity, and powerlessness against nature – yet the outcome is the same: awe in the face of a higher power. These similarities are further elaborated by Otto in relation to architecture: 'In the arts nearly everywhere the most effective means of representing the numinous is the sublime. This is especially true of architecture in which it would appear to have first been realised.'[3]

Numen and architecture

The megalithic age, the period of awakening that Otto refers to, prior to Christianity and monotheism in general, is manifest in the monumental construction of Stonehenge, 'where numen was localised, preserved and stored in solid presence by magic', or in the imposing magnitude of the pyramids of ancient Egypt, whose builders 'had numen throbbing in the soul like a mechanical reflex'. These ancient structures, while in some sense spiritual, are not religious buildings. Their capacity for invoking feelings of wonder is undisputed, though – like the many examples of numen (or the sublime) in nature.

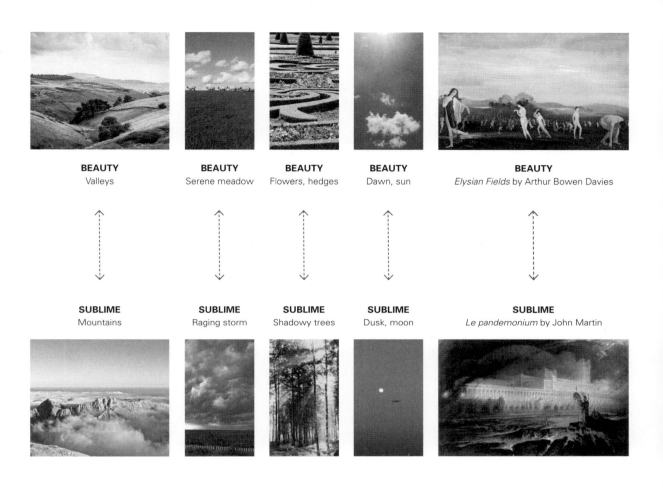

BEAUTY
Valleys

BEAUTY
Serene meadow

BEAUTY
Flowers, hedges

BEAUTY
Dawn, sun

BEAUTY
Elysian Fields by Arthur Bowen Davies

SUBLIME
Mountains

SUBLIME
Raging storm

SUBLIME
Shadowy trees

SUBLIME
Dusk, moon

SUBLIME
Le pandemonium by John Martin

It is true that some religious architecture does not inspire feelings of the numinous or the sublime, just as some non-religious architecture does. It is not the purpose of a building that engenders feelings of awe, but rather the experiential effects harnessed by its design. But what are the architectural components capable of inspiring such feelings? How can we create spaces of wonder?

Rational and irrational

Otto divides the characteristics of numen into the indirect and the direct, described by Kant as rational and irrational aspects of the sublime. The rational, indirect aspect is the *a priori* knowledge deduced from reason, independent of human experience and manifest in concepts of absoluteness, necessity and substance. In contrast, the irrational, direct aspect of numen is related to the present and ephemeral world of human reactions and 'sensuous feeling'.[4] These concepts can be applied to the creation of numinous, sublime buildings and spaces. The indirect, rational elements are the fixed, silent attributes of building and space: form, scale and detail; the direct and irrational relate to the transient experience of a building: light, silence and void.

IMPOSSIBLE SCALE
Pyramids, Giza, Hemiunu, 2580–2560 BC

IMPOSSIBLE ENGINEERING
Duomo, Florence, Filippo Brunelleschi, 1436

IMPOSSIBLE LOOP
CCTV, Beijing, OMA, 2008

STRANGENESS CARVED
Rock formation, Utah; Temple, Angkor Wat

STRANGENESS BRANCHED
Dragon tree, Socotra; Wells Cathedral, 1306
(Chapter House)

STRANGENESS WINGED
Glass-winged butterfly; Philips Pavilion,
Le Corbusier and Iannis Xenakis, 1958

Form

A numinous building must challenge the 'bounds of our understanding by dynamic or mathematic greatness'.[5]

— Impossibility

The building must display a technical genius that is hard to comprehend, almost beyond human capability. This quality is reflected in the sheer scale of human effort and ingenuity required to construct the Pyramids of Giza, for example, the gravity-defying engineering of Brunelleschi's Duomo in Florence, or the illogical contortions of OMA's 'three-dimensional cranked loop'[6] CCTV building in Beijing. By pushing the realms of possibility these structures appear almost otherworldly, unattainable by a mere mortal.

— Strangeness

Strangeness in form exhibits a 'peculiar dual character',[7] which is both 'daunting, and yet singularly attracting'.[8] By its strangeness an object is imprinted more vividly on the mind. This can be seen in chimney-like rock formations in Utah, or the tortured limbs of the dragon tree of West Africa, or the transparency of the glass-winged butterfly found across the Americas. The quality of strangeness is also evident in architecture, from the stepped temples of Cambodia built by the Khmer, to the Gothic fan vaults of Wells Cathedral, or the free-wheeling concrete expression at Le Corbusier's

1 — Assess

INFINITE SPACE Night sky

INFINITE SPACE Desert, Inner Mongolia

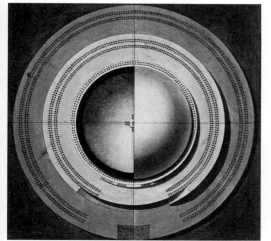

COLLECTIVE SCALE   **COLLECTIVE SCALE**

COLLECTIVE SCALE
Above: Cénotaphe de Newton, Étienne-Louis Boullée, 1784; Centre: Chogha Zanbil Ziggurat, Iran, 1250 BC; Centre, right: Fujisankei Communications Group Headquarters, Tokyo, Kenzo Tange, 1996

INDIVIDUAL SCALE
Above, left: Recessed alcove, medieval castle; Above, centre: Japanese house design, Toyama Memorial Museum, Japan; Above, right: 'Thinking pod', Scottish Parliament, EMBT, 2004

Expo '58 for Philips Pavilion. All of these manmade structures possess a beautiful, sublime strangeness – similar to examples found in nature.

Scale

The second aspect of the rational and indirect manifestation of numen is scale. Otto describes as numinous 'potent manifestations of magnitude in spatial extent':[9] magnitude meaning not only largeness of space, but also potency or intensity of space. These two opposing scales, the vast and the concentrated, create two experiences of the numinous – collective and individual.

— *Collective scale*

Magnitude of space engenders numen in the communal sense; a collective purpose beyond that of the individual. Massive scale invokes concepts of infinite space and, conversely, the finiteness of humankind and its creations. This is evident in the endless black of a night sky or the vast nothingness of the Mongolian Desert, for example – they will always be there regardless of human presence. This same quality can be found in the ancient ziggurats of Babylon, or Étienne-Louis Boullée's giant cenotaph to Newton, or the gargantuan proposals of the Japanese Metabolists. These structures rise above their surroundings to transcend any perception of human scale and become something other, something greater than the individual.

DETAIL Intricacy

DETAIL Repetition

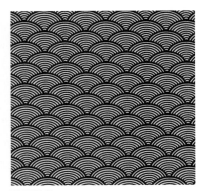

DETAIL Pattern

INFINITY Nature

INFINITY Nature

INFINITY Nature

— *Individual scale*

A small space can also comfort and nurture an inhabitant such that they experience numen or the sublime. Otto describes the humble submergence of private devotion, which exalts the mind.[10] By decreasing the scale of a space we need not decrease its potency. The ideal space for an individual numinous experience would comprise:

- *access to daylight* – to remind one of the giver of life, the Sun
- *views out to nature or cityscape* – to recognize the individual's place in the wider context of nature and humankind
- *comfort* – to allow for a variety of seating arrangements for different states of contemplation
- *richness of material* – simple, un-gilded but high-quality materials to reflect the importance of the space
- *correct proportions* – too large and the space becomes unwelcoming, too small and it becomes uncomfortable.

These aspects can be found in the scalability of traditional Japanese tea houses, which expand and contract according to use and the need for privacy; the recessed alcoves of medieval castles, which provided reflective space as a refuge from their great halls and dining rooms; or the protruding think-pods of Enric Miralles's Scottish Parliament Building, which provide space for contemplation.

DETAIL
Top, left: Frontispiece, Diamond Sutra, China; Top, centre: Terracotta Army, Xi'an, China; Top, right: Traditional Japanese wave pattern

INFINITY
Above, left: Fractals of a Romanesco broccoli; Above, centre: Honeycomb; Above, right: Zebra stripes

1 — Assess

INFINITY Built

INFINITY Built

MATERIAL AND DETAIL

The distinction between spaces for common assembly or private contemplation is one of scale. This ability of scale to provoke wonder is achieved in building design by ensuring that the correct scale is chosen for the particular space. Not vast enough, and collective numen will not be inspired; not small enough, and individual numen will not be found.

Detail

Otto describes the detail of numinous art and architecture as possessing 'an unusual richness and depth', creating 'impressions of the magical'.[11] The magic inherent in the detail of ancient Chinese and Japanese art, for example, is achieved through its intricacy, repetition and colour. Similarly, numen and the sublime are manifest in the detail of a building in two ways: infinity and perception.

— *Suggestions of infinity*

Through pattern and repetition, a sense of infinity and futility in the face of a higher power can be fostered. Endless repetition, with subtle incremental variation, is abundant in nature: the intricate fractals of a Romanesco broccoli, the limitless regularity of honeycomb or the stark pattern of a zebra's hide. In architecture, the abstraction of repetition invokes the feeling that the building is not the product of a single human mind. This is evidenced in the countless carvings of ancient Egyptian façades to the seemingly endless mullions of a Miesian office block. Both create a sense of infinity through multiplicity.

LIGHT Pool   **LIGHT** Shaft   **LIGHT** Dappled   **LIGHT** Opalescent

LIGHT Pool   **LIGHT** Shaft   **LIGHT** Dappled   **LIGHT** Opalescent

— *Affecting perception through detail*

By paying attention to detail, the architect can add to the experience of the building and control the message it conveys to inhabitants. This can be achieved through attention to material qualities and how they combine, the concepts embodied in the detail, and how the details relate to the overall form and scale of the building. This is true of religious buildings, where elements such as stained-glass windows, marble fonts, velvet curtains and intricate carvings combine to add to the overall sense of magnitude. Similarly, in grand public buildings, qualities of colour, luxuriousness of materials, and attention to junctions (how different materials join) combine to achieve the same effect.

Yet form, scale and detail do not invoke the numinous or sublime on their own. For this they must be interwoven with the transient, experiential factors of architecture – direct aspects of numen, described by Otto as light, silence and void.

Light

Light is the first and most important aspect of direct numen. Light exalts us, while darkness humbles us; numen resides in the conflict between these two opposites. As Otto describes, 'darkness must be enhanced by contrast, the mystical begins with semi-darkness'.[12] Examples abound in nature: a pool of light in a clearing in a forest, a shaft illuminating the depths of a cave, dappled light on waves, or the ethereal opalescence of fog.

Top, left to right: Clearing in a forest; canyon; moonlight on sea; fog. Above, left to right: Olympiastadion, Berlin, March and Speer, 1936; Jatiyo Sangsad Bhaban, Dhaka, Louis I. Kahn, 1982; L'Institute du Monde Arabe, Paris, Jean Nouvel, 1987; Nelson-Atkins Museum of Art, Kansas City, Steven Holl, 2007

MONUMENTAL SILENCE Salk Institute, California, Louis I. Kahn, 1965

Numinous buildings too allow for pools of light illuminating a space from above, shafts of light pouring through windows, dappled light broken by screens and gratings, or opalescent light filtered and softened by screens – all made apparent by darkness. In architecture as in nature a magical, awesome effect is created by the contrast between light and dark.

Interior lighting levels are increasingly dictated by legislation, describing the exact levels required for a particular function, and more concerned with health and safety than the quality of light and space and the requirement for contrasting darkness. However, as creators of space we must embrace the role darkness plays in our appreciation and experience of light. Buildings are quickened and stirred by light. Concentrated light brings an energy and mysteriousness to sublime forms and massive or small spaces, and clarity to detail.

Silence

The second element of direct numen is defined by Otto as silence; not the silence imposed in a library or church, but rather a 'spontaneous reaction to the feeling of the actual numen praesens'.[13] There are two stages to the presence of silence in architecture – *provision* for silence, ensuring our designs provide the perfect environment, which then allows for the physical urge to be silent, the *reaction*.

— *Provision of silence*

Silence – and its opposite, sound – is one of the most overlooked aspects of architecture. Architects think about how a building and its constituent parts look – form, proportions, quality of materials, colour; and how they feel – the cold sheen of a metal door handle, the smoothness of polished concrete, the dimpled roughness of brick. We associate buildings with particular smells, too – our childhood swimming pools laden with chemicals, the aroma of a leather booth in a café, or the scent of wildflowers from an adjacent garden. Yet sound is rarely considered in relation to the design of space, except in a practical sense.

Silence can indeed be designed for, with triple-glazed windows to block out external noise, or soundproof doors and partitions to limit noise from adjoining rooms and corridors, or acoustically absorbent materials on walls and ceilings. Yet these elements tend to be considered only if they are written into a brief for technical or functional reasons; the provision for silence for experiential rather than practical reasons is rarely a priority.

Sound may be invisible, but it is a building material just as much as brick, wood or glass. With the increasing pace and clamour of modern life and its soundtrack, architects could do worse than provide spaces of refuge within buildings; spaces of silence for silence's sake.

— *The power of silence*

Juhani Pallasmaa has defined architecture as the 'art of petrified silence'.[14] This is a powerful analogy. Take a tree trunk, for example: silent in nature until it is interrupted by the violent roar of the chainsaw, then the dull thud of being shunted into a lorry, and after that the sawmill, then again the dull thud, and nailed, hammered and jointed into place, to finally become silent again in architecture. Architecture returns materials to their natural acoustic state – silence is inherent in the materials we use to define and enclose space.

Pallasmaa elaborates: 'A powerful architectural experience silences all external noise, it focuses our attention on our very existence … of our fundamental solitude.'[15] Silence in architecture fosters the sense of the numinous, often through interaction with that other direct source of numen – light.

Louis Kahn has described silence as 'lightless; darkless' … the 'ambient soul',[16] a deep presence within us. He puts the experience of architecture before programmatic or technical concerns. When silence is introduced to light, the interaction between the two creates a kind of ambient threshold, an experiential entrance, to inspiration and numen.

Void

Otto stipulates one final means of direct numen – the void. Using the example of the 'laying out and grouping of buildings' of ancient Chinese architecture he describes the 'silent amplitude' of the enclosed spaces, courtyards and vestibules.[17]

Voids in architecture can be found at three varying scales: at an urban level (best depicted in Giambattista Nolli's plan of Rome, where it is manifest in paths, roads, public squares and parks); at a building level in the form of courtyards, light wells and atria; and in individual rooms with roof lights, loggia and apses. A void creates a space of light and silence. Light reveals the void, and silence inhabits it. It is pure space, devoid of

URBAN VOID
Nuova Pianta di Roma,
Giambattista Nolli, 1748

BUILDING VOID
Light well, Glasgow School
of Art (Reid Building), UK,
Steven Holl, 2014

INDIVIDUAL VOID
Stair, Weissenhof Estate,
Stuttgart, Germany,
Le Corbusier, 1927

1 — Assess

programmatic function. Of course, voids can be functional – breakout spaces, lift shafts, service voids and so on – but in a numinous sense their primary purpose should be to contrast with solid mass just as light in architecture contrasts with darkness. The void accentuates mass and solidity, while mass defines the void – preventing it becoming simply a vacuum. It is a space which, by subtraction, allows light, silence and numen in.

Non-functional voids, however, like all the other forms of numen and the sublime in architecture, are often deemed dispensable by the profit-hungry client, or viewed as luxuries by confused contractors. Voids are seen as empty, non-lettable space, rather than elements with the capacity to admit wonder and awe.

— *Wonder and awe in architecture*

You present a quality, architectural, no purpose. Just a recognition of something which you can't define, but must be built ... It isn't made out of a handbook. It doesn't start from practical issues. It starts from a kind of feeling that there must be a world within a world. The world where man's mind somehow becomes sharp.[18]
Louis I. Kahn, ETH Lecture, 1969

The provision of wonder and awe is the single most important aspect of architectural design. Societies and their requirements change, technical needs and possibilities change, but the capacity for awe is eternal. Numinous architecture transcends all questions of functionality, programme and style. It is created by the warp and weft of the rational and the irrational; the interweaving of sublime form, varied scale and attention to detail with the harnessing and manipulation of light, provision of silence and appreciation of the contrast between solid and void.

The components of numinous architecture are forever at risk from budgetary, programmatic or technical concerns – and architects must defend them from attack; no one else will. We can create buildings that not only perform well functionally and technically, but provide us with the perfect platform to experience awe and wonder. This is architecture that inspires profound reflection on the world around us, and our place within it. Architecture that, to paraphrase Kahn, sharpens the mind.

ENVIRONMENT

Architecture d'origine contrôlée

environment, *noun*
From French – *environs* (surroundings)
1. (Nature) The natural world as a whole; the air, water and land in which people, animals and plants live.
2. (Surroundings) The immediate external conditions or surroundings in which one operates; the settings or conditions which influence activity and behaviour.

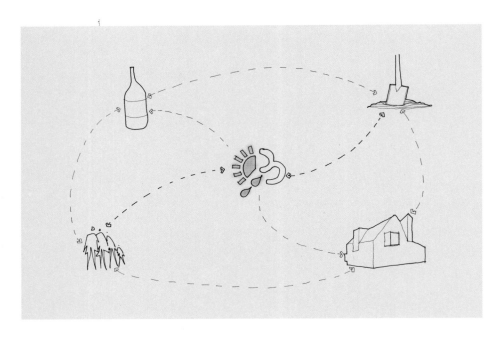

GOÛT DE TERROIR
Architecture – wine (climate, geology, production methods)

In winemaking, the concept of *terroir* refers to the characteristics of a particular place, which combine to produce a wine intrinsically linked to the land it came from. It is this interaction between the vine and its environment that distinguishes the wine from others of the same region (or further afield). There are three basic aspects of *terroir*:
— *Climate* – This includes precipitation (rain), sunlight, slope (orientation/elevation), and wind (coastal/non-coastal).
— *Geology* – Different vines prefer different soils. The water level in the soil is also critical to the success of the crop.
— *Production methods* – There is a process of fine-tuning based on the above climatic and geological factors, allied with generations of winemaking experience; this is the final aspect of *terroir*.

1 — Assess

If all these aspects are considered, a wine of sufficient quality to possess a *goût de terroir* – a taste unique to that region – can be achieved. In the French system such a wine is labelled *appellation d'origine contrôlée*, or 'controlled designation of origin', indicating a wine of unique quality from a particular region.

We can relate these concepts to architecture. Architecture too should have an inherent *goût de terroir* – based on the specific characteristics of a site and its inhabitants, and subject to the same governing factors as a fine wine.

Climate

As in winemaking, the greatest impact on the *terroir* of a building is the climate. Following are some suggestions for how to deal with aspects of climate in architecture:

— *Precipitation:* In a wet climate, embrace the rain rather than trying to ignore it:
  — Include canopies or sheltering elements
  — Provide a rainwater collection pool
  — Use tapered, pitched roof forms, which are best for shedding water

— *Sunlight:* Ensure that the building location maximizes exposure to sunlight:
  — Orient key rooms to achieve the best lighting conditions
  — Provide shading or screening to south-facing elements to protect them from glare
  — Manipulate roof forms to allow daylight to penetrate deep spaces

— *Slope:* Ensure that the building works with the land, not against it:
  — On a steep slope, you can embed the building into the landscape or elevate it on stilts
  — Think of the impact on the ground in either case
  — Ensure that the internal layout maximizes views

— *Wind:* Don't expose the building to prevailing winds:
  — Create tapered, sleek roof forms that don't fight the wind
  — In a warm, windy climate use wind-catchers to provide natural ventilation
  — In coastal regions choose materials suited to a harsh marine environment

Geology

If we think of a building as the wine and the raw building materials as the grapes, then the soil is as important for the building as for the vine. Just like winemakers, architects must understand how various soils behave. Natural soils are a blend of sand and clay, and their behaviour depends on the precise composition.[1] In soils comprising too much sand, rainwater washes nutrients away from the grape vines. Meanwhile, too much clay and the water will move too slowly to transport the minerals the plants need to grow. Similarly in construction, changing water content in expansive soils (clay or silt) can cause shrinkage and swelling, damaging the sub- and superstructure of a building.[2]

Just as with grapes, different building solutions are required for different soil types, and this relates primarily to water content. On an impervious rocky slope, you can embed the building in a durable and stable landscape; on sandy soil with solid ground beneath, piling will be required to achieve a stable base; on silty, coastal land you can

CLIMATE – GOÛT DE TERROIR EXAMPLES

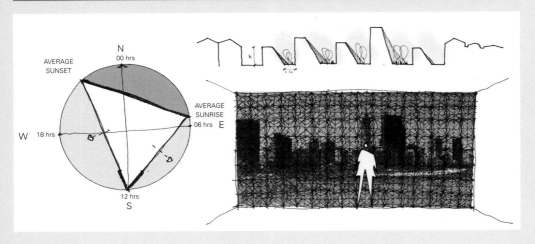

SUN
Height-to-width ratio of solid to void provides light and shade in equal measure; building oriented to maximize sunlight hours; extreme sunlight filtered with screens to manage glare and temperature

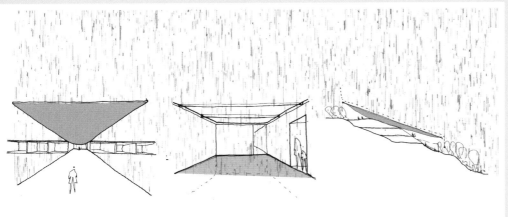

RAIN
Exaggerated canopies provide shelter and refuge from the elements; rain collection can be used as a feature or to collect water for use throughout the building; roof forms accentuated and sloped to provide maximum water run-off

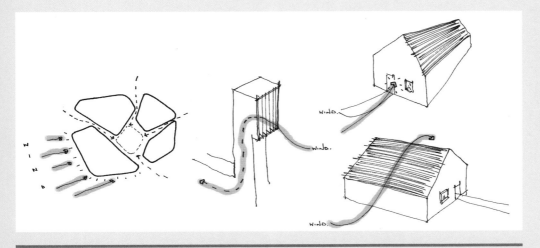

WIND
Collections of buildings can be clustered to provide sheltered space from prevailing winds; wind-catchers can be used to capitalize on strong breezes and transfer their cooling and energy-generating properties through the building; roof forms tailored to respond to and not fight against prevailing wind

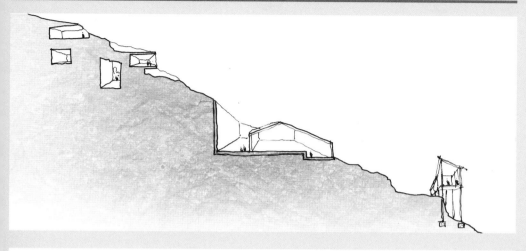

SLOPE

Carved approach in hot, dry areas requiring cooling and shade; retained approach for windy, exposed sites where protection from wind is required; building on stilts to limit frost in freezing, alpine environments

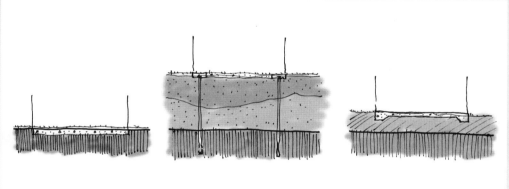

FOUNDATIONS

Building directly on to rock where exposed at surface; piled foundations on chalky, clayey soil where rock is far below ground level; raft foundations to spread the building load on unstable ground conditions such as peat or sand

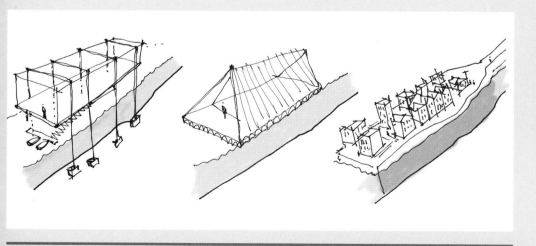

WATER

Stilts or pads used where building is to appear floating and ground conditions allow; floating raft buildings where there is sandy ground and mobility and movement are desired; infilled 'island' approach for larger developments where sea bed is unstable

OF THE LAND

The landscape and the buildings that populate it combine as one – hillside towns or cities hewn from the same rock on which they lie; clay or mud sculpted and shaped to provide dwellings from the earth; slender timber-clad huts echoing the form of and made from the trees of the surrounding forest

 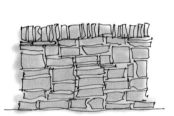 

TECHNIQUE

Traditional wood jointing techniques; stone wall construction; brick bonding – all can be reinterpreted for a contemporary take on ancient techniques using local materials and labour

FINISHING

Weatherproof coatings such as black-painted timber in exposed maritime climates; galvanized steel for environments with salty air; back-painted or fritted glazing contained within a double-glazed unit for areas of strong sunlight and heat

architecture d'origine contrôlée

AoC

FRANCE

elevate the building on stilts. The technical solutions used to support the building will in turn influence the appearance and functionality of the architecture, just as the *terroir* of a wine affects its taste and nose.

Production methods

The first aspect of *terroir* in relation to production methods is the use of local materials, which have three advantages:

— they are generally abundant and don't require overseas transportation
— local craftsmen will have experience of working with them
— they possess an inherent sense of place, allowing the building to 'grow' from the landscape.

Aberdeen in Scotland is known as the Granite City, its centre almost exclusively fashioned from the dense, silvery rock surrounding it; another example is a typical Scandinavian town populated with timber-framed buildings clad in larch or pine from the surrounding woodland; or the terracotta-red mud huts of African villages, clearly from the earth.

Second, post-harvest decisions by the winemaker such as the use of oak, length of maceration and time the wine has in contact with the lees, and temperature during fermentation, among others, can either reduce or emphasize some aspect of the wine derived from the *terroir*.[3]

Similarly, an architect must decide on the appropriate construction methods to bring out the natural characteristics of the *terroir*, and here human experience and skill align with study of the climate and geology. Will overhanging eaves protect against the sun and ventilate the roof space? Might additional waterproofing be required on a façade to protect it from wind-driven rain? Is the plan form of a building suitable for the cultural behaviours and practices of its occupants?

Architecture d'origine contrôlée

In summary, for architecture to possess a *goût de terroir*, it must:

— work with its host climate, not fight it
— respect and be appropriately designed for the specific soil conditions and topography of an area
— use materials, design features and construction techniques that accentuate the locality of a building both in a practical sense and a symbolic one.

These three factors combine to imbue architecture with a unique sense of place. In addition to this, the value of *goût de terroir* in architecture is that our buildings will work technically, spatially and aesthetically with their host environment.

Just as each vineyard in a particular region will have its own character, so no two buildings should be the same despite similarities across a particular region. The specific climatic and geological conditions of the site should be evident – the architecture should accentuate and complement the minute details of a site to create a bespoke building discernibly different from any other.

Achieving *goût de terroir* in architecture is not about tradition, nor recycling perceived notions of history through blind use of vernacular styles. Instead, the concept is an approach that harnesses the local climate, geology and collective knowledge of its people to produce an architecture distinctly of and for its host region. Only then can we truly label our buildings *architecture d'origine contrôlée*.

DISORDER

Form equals function

disorder, *noun*
From Latin – *ordinare* (to order; i.e.
to disordain, disorder)
1. Lack of order; a state of confusion.
2. An irregularity; a deviation from the
normal system of order.

Constant battle between man vs. nature, order (man) vs. disorder (nature) + mechanisation (organised) vs. natural flow (disorder).

Architecture is obsessed with order. Ordered plans lead to ordered space, ordered movement, ordered functions, ordered people, ordered society; an ordered world. The entire architectural design process – from initial response to construction – is one long process of creating order out of disorder.

Every architectural style throughout the centuries has order at its core, from the five classical orders of antiquity to the rationally ordered forms of Modernism. Even styles such as Baroque, Gothic or Brutalism, which may seem at first disordered, are underpinned by rationality in both their planning and symbolism. That most obsessive of orderers, Le Corbusier, once said: 'An inevitable element of Architecture. The necessity for order. The regulating line is a guarantee against wilfulness.'[1]

This 'necessary' ordering in the built environment is at odds with the chaotic disorder of nature. As architect and artist Peter S. Stevens said, 'Nature does not premeditate, she does not use mathematics, she does not deliberately produce patterns. She lets whole patterns produce themselves. Nature does what nature demands, she is beyond blame and sensibility.'[2] Rivers meander according to the terrain they flow through; birds flock and fish shoal at will, sometimes seemingly at random; surf responds to the force and tempo of the waves; rock formations reflect centuries of seismic and chemical processes. Nature's forms are subject to circumstance, chance and will.

But man = nature.
disorder vs order...
or is order found within + vice versa?

So are people – they avoid convoluted designated paths when a more direct route can be forged; they use a lobby as an exhibition space and an exhibition space as a lobby; they use window sills as benches; they pin pictures on white walls. People use spaces as circumstance, chance and will dictate, and disorder eventually asserts itself.

Chaos in architecture is generated by multiple individual elements of order that combine in a disordered manner; created by functional necessity, not subject to learned aesthetic design sensibilities, fashion or taste. Pipes, ducts and wires weave through buildings in the most efficient way – the architect covers them up with suspended ceilings; timber cladding weathers in a natural but unpredictable manner – the architect tries to delay this process with varnishes and stains; shanty towns develop organically from found materials in a riotous explosion of colour and vibrancy – the planning authorities knock them down; the famous New York skyline is created by a multitude of separate zoning laws – not by a singular, ordered architectural vision. All of these examples are generated by circumstance, chance and will.

The order that architects impose is learned – tainted by indoctrination, cliché, fashion and prejudice. We design based on what we are taught by other architects; what our cultivated aesthetic sensibilities tell us; what we think we should be designing at

DISORDER Services

DISORDER Weathering, Saint Benedict Chapel, Switzerland, Peter Zumthor, 1988

DISORDER Spontaneous urbanism, Favéla do Prazères, Rio de Janeiro

DISORDER Chaotic skyline, Manhattan, New York (from Brooklyn Bridge)

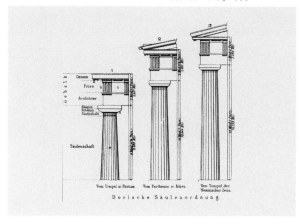

ORDER Ideal Ionic column proportions

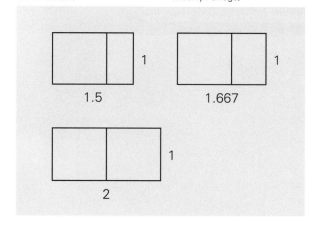

ORDER Ideal ratios

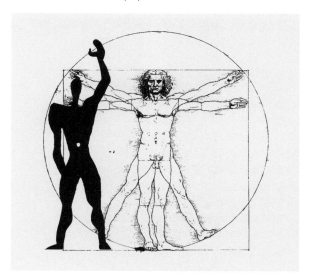

ORDER Le Corbusier's Modulor man (left) and Leonardo da Vinci's Vitruvian Man (right)

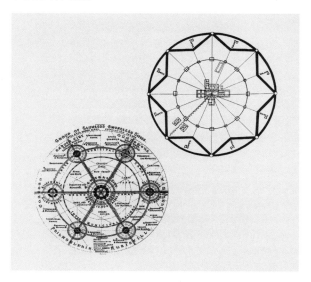

ORDER 15th- and 20th-century ideal cities – Garden City (left) and Sforzinda (right)

COMPLEXITY Oil refinery, Texas, USA

PURITY Wind farm, New South Wales, Australia

a particular point in time – not always with detached objectivity. In short, the order we impose can constrain us, obscuring our view of the real problems at hand.

The great theorists and practitioners of architecture have offered many different prescriptions. Giacomo Barozzi da Vignola taught us that columns should be built in the ratio of 4:12:3 between pediment, column and entablature; Claude Perrault taught us 4.5:14:3.[3] Andrea Palladio said a rectangular room should have a length double that of its width; he later said it could have a length of its width plus a quarter; Vitruvius designed his buildings based on the ideal man who was 4 cubits tall (1.83m or 6ft); Le Corbusier's universal proportional scale was based on the Modulor man at 1.75m (5ft 9in.) tall (later revised to 1.829m or 6ft). Antonio di Pietro Averlino designed his ideal city, Sforzinda, based on an astrological geometry; Ebenezer Howard devised his Garden City concept based on radial geometry. Different orders have been imposed by different minds in different eras.

REPETITION Solar farm, California, USA

Often, though, a lack of order is desirable. Elongated, fattened or proportionally ignorant building components can be intriguing and arresting within a composition; a disproportionate room can add excitement to our experience of an interior. The inhuman scale of certain structures (caves, cathedrals, skyscrapers) is what makes them exhilarating; sometimes the collision of various uses is what makes our cities so vibrant and enticing.

The architect is left with a conundrum; their role as orderer is undermined by the inevitability of disorder, almost impossible to legislate or design for. Perhaps the only building types (with the exception of military buildings) that do not generally require the order imposed by an architect are industrial buildings, designed to contain specific processes and made up of forms based purely on functional requirements – which, as a result, tend to appear visually disordered if not chaotic.

ECONOMY Phone mast, Tokyo, Japan

SCALE Nuclear power station, Torness, UK

Industrial buildings have been fetishized within aesthetic and architectural theory before. The stark documentary photographs of Bernd and Hilla Becher displayed the raw power and sculptural beauty of industrial buildings, while Le Corbusier praised these buildings' use of 'primary elements' in accordance with 'the rules' as the 'magnificent fruits of the new age'.[4] However, the industrial buildings referenced by Le Corbusier in the 1920s and nostalgically documented by the Bechers in the 1960s and 1970s are now outmoded relics: towering grain elevators with conjoined sibling silos; blast furnaces, a tangle of chutes and structure; top-heavy water towers with spindly legs; colliery towers of intricate structural complexity displaying a magnificent disregard for architectural order – and not designed by architects. No abstract 'ideal' proportions are employed, nor pretensions to design to a perfect 'human' scale, or to fit in with the often bleak and uninspiring landscapes in which they are set. While these structures may now have become functionally irrelevant, today's industrial buildings share a similar scale, anonymous authorship and inherent functional disorder.

Think of the complexity of oil refineries rising like lost cities from the future; the purity of wind turbines commanding their rural surroundings; the power of endless repetition found in solar panels, like thousands of carefully oriented interplanetary communication devices; the massive scale of nuclear power stations with utter disregard for their setting; the skeletal economy of telecommunications structures surveying a less ethereal landscape below. These structures, which now dominate our landscapes, have become our own 'magnificent fruits of the new age'.

In their pursuit of functionality above all else, they effortlessly achieve visual disorder in the traditional architectural sense. They are also infinitely adaptable: if a new cooling tower or pipe is needed or an old one rendered obsolete it can be changed with no damage to the overall visual order – there was none to begin with. This combination of visual disorder and adaptability is one aspect that makes these structures so awe-inspiring – their strangeness goes against our learned sensibilities.

Designing with disorder

The le[sson] *[spaces for multiple ecosystems open at different scales.]* buildings in the sense of introducing disorder into o[ur]

— [co]nstrained by abstract and ever-changing [rules] — let the [parame]ters of the project guide the creation of form and [...]

— Process: Let the [pr]ocesses required [to] generate the building form, untroubled by [...] learned sensibilities occlude architectural [responses and solutions.]

— *Scale*: It isn't always essential to design to a 'human scale'. The most exhilarating forms and spaces can be those that evoke our relative nothingness.

— *Context*: Context does not always need to be respected. The power of juxtaposition should not be underestimated, and our buildings don't always need to mimic or fit in with their surroundings. Visual tension is not something to be scared of.

We cannot simply order functions based on our learned assumptions and personal preferences. Instead, we must design our functions in the most essential and economical way possible – and if that leads to disorder, then so be it. At face value the above approach may seem merely a variation on the old Modernist maxim 'form follows function', in which the word *follows* implies that form comes *after* function; they do not evolve together. This approach is instead based on the lessons learned from industrial buildings, and it removes the idea of following, this extra layer of preconceived ideas of architectural order. In this approach, form *equals* function.

MEMORY

Architecture is embedded in memory;
memory is embedded in architecture

memory, *noun*
From Latin – *memor* (mindful, remembering)
1. The capacity of the mind to retain and recall past facts, events, sensations, thoughts, knowledge, experiences, etc.
2. The act of retaining and recalling these past facts, events and sensations.
3. This faculty, possessed by an individual.
4. The period over which retaining and recollection occurs.
5. A specific recollection of an event, thought, experience or person.
6. The act of being remembered; commemoration (esp. after death).
7. The ability of materials and systems to display effects dependent on past influences and treatment.
8. The ability of materials and systems to return to their original state after deformation.

'Like a forgotten fire a childhood can always flare up again within us.'[1]
— Gaston Bachelard

The cupboards we hid in, the paths we cycled along, the stairs we sat on – our early experiences of architectural space have a profound impact on us. We see events, people and objects intertwined with the built environment almost from birth, informing our attitudes to it in adulthood. The buildings and spaces we create are imbued with images, sensations and interests gathered from our childhood onwards, consciously and unconsciously. Memories feed our architecture, and architecture feeds our memories.

Individual memory
Chris Marker's 1962 film *La Jetée* tells the story of a man 'marked by an image from his childhood'.[2] Captured in Paris in the aftermath of a fictional Third World War, the man was sent back in time to save the human race from destruction. Those able to retain strong mental images were selected for the task – only if they could conceive or dream of another time in a concrete manner would they be able to live in it. The man was 'glued

1 — Assess

LA JETÉE (1962)
The pier at Orly airport, where the film's protagonist returns; this non-place becomes memorable because of the events that unfold within it

to an image of his past' and, following days of experimentation, 'images begin to ooze, like confessions'. The strength of his mental imagery was fed by the experience of his physical environment – architecture was embedded in his memory. The denouement focuses on a particular image from the man's past: the pier at Orly airport, *la jetée*, where he witnessed the death of his time-travelling adult self as a child.

Anthropologist Marc Augé categorizes the airport as a non-place ('somewhere that cannot be defined as relational, or historical, or concerned with identity'[3]); however, through the man's memory of the events that unfolded there in *La Jetée*, this 'non-place' becomes distinctive and vivid: the dull concrete grid beneath his feet like a grey chessboard; the cantilevered concrete soffit above seemingly designed to watch over events below; the skeletal masts eerily surveying all; the reflection of the black metal balustrade on flat plate glass. His recollection of the event is forever linked to the space, form and detail of the buildings; conversely, the buildings and spaces forever generate memories of the event. This connection is especially important in *La Jetée* – only through experiencing the physical space of his childhood memories as an adult does he begin to piece together the events that unfolded.

THE CITY OF ZAIRA A city of relationships between the measurements of its space and the events of its past

Collective memory

The correlation between space and memory is taken further, on a more civic and less personal level, by Italo Calvino in his fictional account of Marco Polo regaling Kublai Khan with tales of the great cities of the Mongol Empire. In his book *Invisible Cities*, we see a passage on the city of Zaira: '... I could tell you how many steps make up the streets rising like stairways, and the degree of the arcades' curves, and what kind of zinc scales cover the roofs; but I already know this would be the same as telling you nothing.'[4] Calvino doesn't focus on the steps that make up the streets or the degree of the arcades' curves, or the type of roof tiles, instead focusing on the 'relationships between the measurements of its space and the events of its past'.[5] He describes this as a series of interconnected objects, events and experiences with lucid detail: the height of a lamp post, its distance from an adjacent railing, the angle of a gutter, the proportions of an open window – all become crucial components of the events and stories that have shaped the city. Meanwhile, the city contains its past 'like the lines of a hand, written in the corners of the streets, the gratings of the windows, the banisters of the steps, the antennae of the lightning rods, the poles of the flags, every segment marked in turn with scratches, indentations, scrolls ...'[6]

Calvino highlights the dialogue between events, architecture and the city as an entity, and conversely the idea of the city as a sponge that 'soaks up' memories and expands – the memories feeding it. He tells us that the fabric of any city is inextricably

linked to its past: every door, every window, every paving stone, every grating has sustained and is sustained by the events of a city and the actions of its people. We can imagine memories as the life-blood of the city, a source of growth and expansion.

If we think of Calvino's vivid description of the fabric of the city, its 'indentations and scrolls', we must also deduce that these are vital to the city. Architects must respect every inch of a building or city, appraising what has intrinsic value or a heightened capacity for memory. A design approach should aim to retain the special relationship between spaces and the events of their past.

At the Neues Museum in Berlin, David Chipperfield used the charred semi-ruin of the old museum as a foundation from which to explore and add to the memories of the building. Every available remnant of the existing building (partly destroyed in the Second World War) was retained and elegantly restored, with additional new-build elements to make a museum of past, present and future memories. Even bullet holes were preserved. This is an approach that Calvino would surely approve of, creating an architecture embedded in memory.

The second lesson for architects is the idea of the expanding city, fed by memories. We must acknowledge the importance of this constant flow of memories and events in the life of the city, and our crucial role in designing the containers and spaces that receive and manage this flow. If we design structures and spaces that go against the grain of the existing elements, without due consideration, we risk disconnecting them from the city's collective memory.

NEW CENTRAL ENTRANCE PLINTH Neues Museum, Berlin, David Chipperfield

Street grids, urban blocks, local building typologies and roofscapes should all be thoughtfully analysed and appraised when designing a new building. They contain the memories of a city's past, which we should not eschew in an attempt to create a new, unconnected future (as in many cities across the world, which embraced the future of the motor car at the expense of the urban fabric). Each generation must add their own layer of memory to the city without wilfully erasing memories of generations past.

The house – individual memory

As Bachelard noted, 'Our house is our corner of the world ... it is our first universe.'[7] However, this 'first universe' does not necessarily influence our architecture in a material or symbolic sense. If we lived in a house with a tiled roof, or with timber panelling, this does not necessarily mean our architecture will use these motifs, but instead influences us in an experiential sense – through a combination of architecture and events that formed memories.

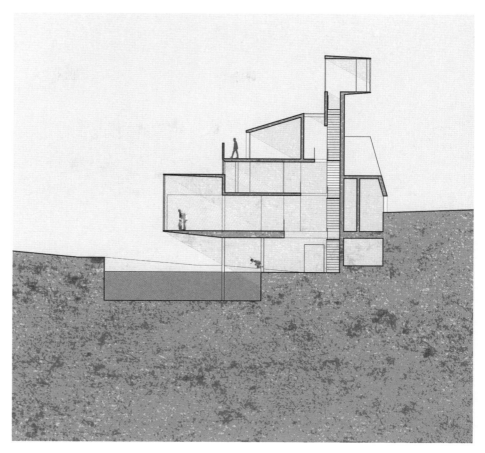

VERTICALITY AND HIERARCHY Cross-section of the Oneiric House – the house rises from its underground 'root' to become a tower reaching for the heavens

Bachelard notes that 'Memories are motionless, and the more securely they are fixed in space, the sounder they are ... If the house is a bit more elaborate, if it has a cellar and a garret, nooks and corridors, our memories have refuges that are all the more clearly delineated.'[8] Essentially this means the more defined, complex and memorable the spaces in a house are, the more the house becomes embedded in our memories, and our memories become embedded in the house. Bachelard links the 'oneiric house', or the house of one's dreams (not in the materialistic, aspirational sense), to the childhood house, which he states has 'engraved within us the hierarchy of the various functions of inhabiting'.[9]

But how do these abstract philosophical concepts translate into real architecture and tangible experiences that will inform our ideas of space as adults? How can the houses we design foster and cement positive and rich experiences of architecture from an early age? Perhaps an ideal, childhood oneiric house would have the following attributes:

DISTINCTIVENESS AND COMPLEXITY Simple yet distinctive forms create a memorable assemblage

— *Verticality and hierarchy*

The oneiric house should have a root as well as strive to reach the heavens. Its vertical hierarchy of spaces accommodate the functions of a home that are engraved on our being. A basement to go down to, an attic to go up to; stairs to ascend and reflect on; compartmentalized spaces for contemplation, boredom, mischief and reflection. The centre of gravity of the house is its kitchen; its living area and its bedrooms are the heart, its comforting and familiar core.

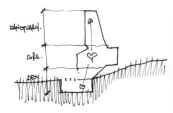

— *Distinctiveness and complexity*

Distinctive, complex spaces more easily forge a link with memory. For a child, this can be manifest in many ways: if a bedroom has a perfectly shaped nook for sulking in; or if a dining room wind̶ deep enough sill on which to hunch, watching the rain trickle down outside; o̶ ̶ ̶ ̶ ̶ ̶ ̶ ̶ ̶ircase taper in a certain way to make space for sitting as well as movi̶ ̶ ̶ ̶ ̶ ̶ ̶ ̶ ̶nished joists of the attic floor are perfectly spaced for a s̶ ̶ ̶ ̶ ̶ ̶ ̶ ̶ ̶ ̶he imagination combine to create memories of i̶ ̶ ̶ ̶ ̶ ̶ ̶ ̶ ̶pletely neutered, by decreasing the complexity of ̶ ̶ ̶ ̶ ̶ ̶ ̶ ̶ ̶ for memory creation.

> *"maternal"
> architecture.
> ≠ ...
> "motherly
> architectural
> space.*

— *Protection*

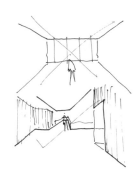

A house best performs its primal function, to provide shelter, when it is under attack from the elements. It is at these times of high winds, heavy rainfall and snow that we feel most at one with the house, when it displays an almost maternal capacity for protection. By connecting with the house in this way, gaining comfort in the enclosure of its walls and roof – we participate in the creation of shared events. We remember how the house whistled in pain during a hurricane; how its gutters spluttered in that freakish downpour. It is these memories we must cultivate as architects when thinking of the solidity and steadfastness of our designed dwellings.

1 — Assess

PROTECTION, CORNERS AND CURVES Solidity of construction and framing of views enhance enclosure; spatial depth provides multiple corner 'nests'

— *Corners*

In the ideal oneiric or childhood home, corners are essential. A corner effortlessly defines space – its limits, extensions, shadows and surprises. The careful manipulation of a building's corners can instruct inhabitants to continue through a space if open, or to rest in a particular spot when closed; provide a viewpoint to the outside world from two aspects rather than one; or allow a living area to receive sunlight at different times of day. Internally, corners can give a feeling of enclosure, with nest-like properties. In particular the curved corner, which Bachelard describes as 'inhabited geometry', welcomes and invites us to remain – as opposed to the harsh, angular corner, which rejects us.[10] By defining and enclosing our spaces, corners also define and enclose the memories created within.

It is these key aspects that will create a house embedded in memories – and, more importantly, memories embedded in the qualities of the house: its hierarchy of space, its distinctiveness, its ability to protect and its capacity to define and enclose. We must take these linked spatial and experiential memories forward into our designs for others.

Play – formative memory

'In this world only the play of artists and children exhibits becoming and passing away, building and destroying, without any moral additive, in forever equal innocence. And as artists and children play, so plays the ever-living fire, builds up and destroys, in innocence. Not hubris but the ever-newly-awakened impulse to play calls new worlds into being.'
— Friedrich Nietzsche

Space of conversation

Play represents our first exploration of physical space. Mats and chalk lines demarcate our limits; steps, huts and slides provide navigable refuges or vantage points; our toys are our first act of creating spaces or objects in space and experiencing their haptic qualities.

STACKED BUILDING BLOCKS Serpentine Pavilion, London, Bjarke Ingels Group, 2016

MECHANICAL KIT OF PARTS Meccano model

MECHANICAL KIT OF PARTS Pompidou Centre, Paris, Richard Rogers and Renzo Piano, 1977

1 — Assess

The quote from Nietzsche, paraphrasing Heraclitus, is critical in illustrating the creative abandon of a child playing. Like the artist, the child creates for creation's sake – ruler of the little kingdoms and universes they create.

This sense of creative abandon is critical to developing our preferences in creating our environments – play is the first step in this process of spatial discovery. It is no coincidence that many architects imbue their buildings and spaces with the qualities of their childhood toys, whether consciously or not. Richard Rogers's Meccano-esque aesthetic of exposed structural skeletons and primary colours; Norman Foster's sleek, space-age Dan Dare constructions; Bjarke Ingels's super-sized algorithmic LEGO towers; and the numerous Japanese architects inspired by the folded creations of the ancient art of origami commonly taught to Japanese children – all of these architects' creations are influenced by the first structures and spaces they created.

For centuries philosophers and educators such as John Locke and Friedrich Froebel have seen construction blocks as a key component of a child's early development.[12] Froebel even designed his own set of toys for children to develop their sense of colour, form and movement, as well as allowing them the freedom to create their own structures and environments – their own sense of order and beauty. Frank Lloyd Wright cited these toy blocks as an inspiration: 'For several years I sat at the little Kindergarten table-top … and played … with the cube, the sphere and the triangle – these smooth wooden maple blocks … All are in my fingers to this day …'[13]

Research into the benefits of playing with construction toys produces an almost endless list of what it develops: concentration; fine motor skills (the link between the brain and movement); awareness of space; a sense of gravity and balance; exploration of shape, weight, texture and size; understanding of the properties of objects; collaboration and sharing. These are also essential qualities for a good architect.

The link between childhood play, the memories it creates and the skills it develops are more closely tied to the role of the architect than in many other professions. It is impossible for a three-year-old child to explore the complexities of surgery; however, that same child has the ability to arrange geometric forms and create spaces. A three-year-old child cannot know exactly how to combine different chemicals to create a compound; but they can develop a response to colour and texture or learn to collaborate with other children on building a structure in their preschool. While there are many constraints in the daily practice of being an architect that a child at play cannot comprehend, the basic outcomes – exploration of space, form, colour, geometry and ultimately the creation of beauty – are the same for the child arranging and stacking shapes on a rug as they are for the architect creating a 1:50 scale model with balsa wood and a scalpel.

The primal response to the materials and parameters provided, and the formation of a structure, a space or a symbol are fundamentally the same. Our childhood responses to spaces, shapes and colours are tied to our creation of architecture in adulthood. Our memories and the skills we learned as children are embedded in our architecture. Through individual experiences, collective events, dwellings and cognitive play, memory has the capacity to influence and be influenced by architecture. It is a reciprocal process of indelible marking and tracing, in which memory and architecture imbue and inform each other.

ONEIRIC HOUSE Hertfordshire, UK, J. Tait, 2014

1 — Assess

Memory

FUNCTION

Same form, different function

function, *noun*
From Latin – *fungi* (to perform)
1. The action or purpose specific to a person, thing or institution; the purpose or role for which something is designed.
2. A factor related to or dependent upon other factors.

Homographs are words that are spelled the same but have multiple meanings: *bow* – to bend, to comply, a weapon, a musical instrument, a curve; *lead* – to show the way, to initiate, to be first, to have a principal role, a connection, a type of metal; and so on. Architecture, too, is full of what I would call 'architectural homographs', which can best be described as buildings with the same form but different functions.

For centuries, a building form communicated its purpose; there was an explicit correspondence between outer form and meaning.[1] A church was recognized as having a cruciform plan, spire, and dome or apse; a typical museum or library used elements from Ancient Greek or Roman architecture (columns, porticoes, pediments) to project a sense of civic grandeur. Such symbols formed the total aesthetic experience of the building,[2] were not typically interchangeable between different building meanings and are still embedded in our psyche. Map symbols generally suggest that churches have a cruciform plan; campsites look like teepees; museums consist of a pediment flanked by two columns; a castle comes complete with moat and ramparts. Buildings are thus reduced to formal, literal symbolism.

However, by the early twentieth century the notion of the building as a symbol was being challenged by architects and philosophers such as Adolf Loos, Walter Benjamin and Ernst Bloch, who favoured abstraction and allegory over literalism and symbolism. As professor of architectural theory Hilde Heynen noted: 'With the allegorical method … there is no intrinsic relation between signifier and signified: in allegory, divergent elements of different origin are related to each other and given a signifying relationship by the allegorist that remains extrinsic to its component parts.'[3]

Yet philosophy was only just catching up with reality. In the early 1900s, the upward expansion of New York created the first skyscrapers, which accommodated many functions within one building envelope. These buildings could no longer be solely a symbol of their meaning, because they had multiple, competing meanings. Instead they became allegorical – a heady mix of European stylistic tropes, Manhattan zoning laws and the attainment of height through repetition. Through the pragmatic reality of New York and the philosophy of Modernist thinkers the infinite possibilities for a building form emerged. As Rem Koolhaas observed: 'In the deliberate discrepancy between container and contained, New York's makers discover an area of unprecedented freedom.'[4]

These developments of theory and practice led to formal licence for Modernist architects that hadn't been seen before. With the form of a building no longer viewed

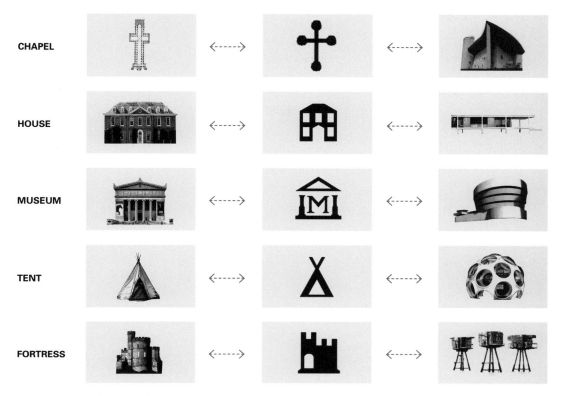

FROM SYMBOL TO ALLEGORY
Built reality of pre-modern form juxtaposed with the Ordnance Survey
map symbol and modern, allegorical form

as a literal communicative device, it could be determined by the arrangement of internal space, its relationship to context and the aesthetic vision of the architect, without having to ascribe to a symbolic code. This allowed radical new forms to emerge: a chapel (Le Corbusier's Notre Dame du Haut) could be a crustacean form responding to the 'visual acoustics' of the surrounding landscape,[5] a house (Mies van der Rohe's Farnsworth House), a floating white pavilion mediating between built form and nature; a museum (the Solomon R. Guggenheim Museum in New York by Frank Lloyd Wright), a spatial helix like a spiralling 'unbroken wave'.[6]

Unencumbered by their individual signifiers, different building types began to share similar or even identical forms. Modernism gave architects the freedom to create whatever form for whatever purpose. However, this ability to repeat design and aesthetic principles across typologies could also be restrictive, leading to a certain sterility and homogeneity. The city was no longer legible as layers of connotative signs.

Homographs in contemporary architecture

The architectural homograph has proliferated since its early days, born of radicalism and progress. Whereas it emerged as a by-product of Modernist architects' belief in the possibilities of technology, form and space, today many architects use homographs liberally and knowingly in three main ways:

ARCHITECTURAL HOMOGRAPHS 1950s–present

MODERNIST		
BUILDING	**SIMILARITIES**	**BUILDING**

Tower block
Base plinth

OFFICE Lever House, New York, 1952

HOTEL SAS, Copenhagen, 1960

Glazed butterfly form
Red brick

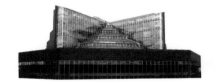

AUDITORIUM TKK Auditorium, Helsinki, 1964

LIBRARY History Faculty, Cambridge, 1968

Glass tower
Dark metal spandrels
Elongated head
Concrete plinth

OFFICE CIS Tower, Manchester, 1962–1964

UNIVERSITY Arts Tower, Sheffield, 1965

REPETITION

BUILDING	SIMILARITIES	BUILDING

Kawneer® AA®
201 unitized
curtain walling

<----------------------->

LIGHTHOUSE Maritime Operations, Aberdeen, 2006

RESIDENTIAL The Quays, Kent, 2009

Trespa® Meteon®
high-pressure laminate
cladding panels

<----------------------->

SHOPPING CENTRE MegaPark, Barakaldo, 2004

UNIVERSITY Architecture Department, Belfast, 2009

Techcrete® acid-etched
precast concrete panels

<----------------------->

COLLEGE Crime Campus, Gartcosh, 2014

OFFICE Scottish Power Building, Glasgow, 2016

	REPRODUCTION	
BUILDING	**SIMILARITIES**	**BUILDING**

Wave/Cloudlike form
Digitally fabricated modules, birch ply

MARKET + PLAZA Metropol Parasol, Sevilla, 2004 (concept)　　　　　　　　**PAVILION** AA Summer Pavilion, London, 2008

Bulbous forms
Metallic disc cladding

DEPARTMENT STORE Selfridges, Birmingham, 2003　　　　　　　　**MUSEUM** Museo Soumaya, Mexico City, 2011

Randomized windows
Chamfered openings
Precast concrete

CONCERT HALL Auditoria, Leon, 2002　　　　　　　　**SCHOOL** Burntwood School, London, 2014

SELF-INDULGENCE

BUILDING	SIMILARITIES	BUILDING

Freeform shapes
Layer upon layer
Titanium cladding

<----------------------------->

MUSEUM Guggenheim, Bilbao, 1997

CONCERT HALL Walt Disney, Los Angeles, 2003

Shard shapes
Angled slashes to façade
Metal cladding

<----------------------------->

MUSEUM Jewish Museum, Berlin, 2001

UNIVERSITY Graduate Centre, London, 2004

Simple dome form
Lightweight skeleton
Lots of glass

<----------------------------->

OBSERVATION PLATFORM Reichstag, Berlin, 1999

GOVERNMENT City Hall, London, 2002

REDECORATE

REINVENT

— *Repetition*

The standardization of the building process has led to the economy of building being paramount, and it is now easy for architects to use components across multiple projects without interrogating their suitability for a building type. Certain trends emerge, encouraged by sales reps who convince architects to use their products on as many projects as possible, with websites containing endless evidence of architectural homography. Meanwhile, the architect, knowing that a particular product was successful on another (perhaps very different) project, designs within their comfort zone and blindly assembles the same components to meet a completely different design problem.

— *Reproduction*

Referring to precedents can often result in architectural copying and pasting. Architects may take their inspiration from a building of a certain typology and apply it to another, creating architectural homographs in the process. For example: the London Architectural Association's 2008 Summer Pavilion was a scaled-down model of Jürgen Mayer's 2005 designed Metropol Parasol in Seville, Spain, home to a museum and market; Fernando Romero's Museo Soumaya in Mexico City, completed in 2011, takes a direct cue from the bulbous form and metallic disc façade of Future Systems' 2003 Selfridges store in Birmingham, UK; AHMM's 2015 Burntwood School in London pays homage to Mansilla and Tuñón's concert hall in León, Spain, completed in 2002.

Of course, these examples could be the product of coincidence, or a hidden memory of a building manifested unwittingly in a design response. However, with the pluralistic nature of current architectural form, and the lack of a unifying architectural style, allied with the instant availability of architectural images – mere coincidence seems less likely.

PUERTA GRANADA

'Following the idea of **metaphor**, we looked into the space sequences of the quintessential monument of Granada, the **Alhambra**, and synthesized spatial **typologies of Islamic influence to which people could easily relate. Geometric pattern ornamentation with variations based on the same mathematical module unfold in a sequence of plazas** that form different skylight prisms, in some cases with honeycomb vaulting, in other cases with stalactite vaulting ... [with] pyramidal kaleidoscopic diaphragms, all of which are intricately detailed in carved whitewashed stucco, along the track mall.' Promotional literature.

PALACE + ABSTRACTED METAPHOR = SHOPPING CENTRE

TROFA RETAIL PARK

'The rich and vivid **community recollections of the mill foster the sublimation of the building in terms of its architecture and local identity.** The proposal preserves the architectural integrity while **graphic elements emphasize the industrial aesthetics of the historical heritage of the place**, both in the rolled-steel façade, the letter-type and colors, as well as in the former water-tank, now reborn as a city icon.' Promotional literature.

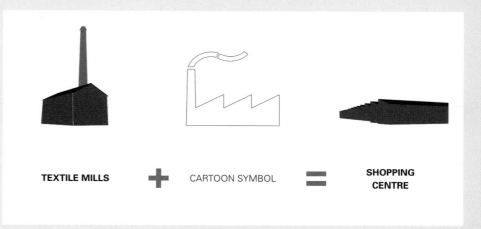

TEXTILE MILLS + CARTOON SYMBOL = SHOPPING CENTRE

CRYSTALS

'Crystals is like its **own metropolitan city ... a day trip on its own ...** Aside from the high-end retail shops, you'll have plenty of photo ops in front of snazzy looking fixtures ... Crystals features a **real aloe tree**, a colorful, living flower "carpet" and even a **tree house** fixture where diners sit and enjoy a meal. Take a peek outside and check out the "pocket **park**" between Crystals and Aria hotel. Enjoy a quiet moment among the **trees** and Henry Moore's "Reclining Connected Forms" **sculpture**. We haven't even touched on shopping yet.'
www.vegas.com

Form of Daniel Libeskind's Denver Art Museum (2006) juxtaposed with his Crystals Shopping Centre (2009)

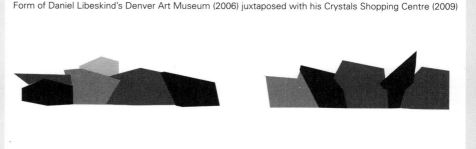

ART MUSEUM
High culture

SHOPPING CENTRE
Low culture

GALERIES LAFAYETTE, PARIS
The function of shopping is accommodated neatly by the Haussmannian block. The building above ground level is almost ambivalent to its function.

GIMBELS, PHILADELPHIA
The building occupies a busy corner on a junction, maximizing its location by curving and opening out to the street along its perimeter, where traditionally the corner would have been orthogonal

— *Self-indulgence*

Once an architect reaches a certain elevated status, they become known for a type or style of architecture – their formal signature. Frank Gehry has freeform metallic layers; Daniel Libeskind angular, metallic shards; Norman Foster has structural skeletons built of simple forms. What is it about the gouges and slashes in a Holocaust museum that translates so easily to a university building? I would argue nothing; it is a stylistic tic applied across multiple projects. By believing their own hype, architects may create forms according not to the buildings' use, context, or purpose but instead to what they think the public and client expects.

There are also many architects who reach such an elevated status but shun the notion of the signature building: SANAA, Herzog & de Meuron and OMA, to name a few. Their buildings instead project an innate sensibility, an approach both to the practice of architecture as a whole, and solutions specific to each individual design challenge.

Exploiting architectural homographs

Homographs are not only used by those who design architecture, but also by those who commission it.

— *Opportunism*

The commissioners of buildings (governments, developers, other private clients), aware that overt symbolism per building typology is no longer required, now build generic office and residential blocks of a unified form derived from economy and rationality. The homograph becomes an architectural safety net to guard against the expense and risk (real or perceived) associated with non-generic construction. These clients know which building forms, materials and construction methods are most time and cost efficient – and apply them across multiple projects.

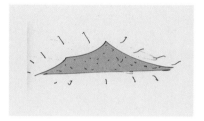

1. ENTRANCE Positioned in relation to undulating topography, with an extended canopy providing shelter that clearly signifies the entrance

2. ARCADE Large glazed openings showcase merchandise, while a sunken walkway gives a sense of enclosure and allows the building to respond to the topography

3. ROOF/SIGNIFIER Freed from obligations at ground level, the roof acts as a symbolic and functional device as a marker and to let light in to the internal atrium; the roof is tapered to suit the surroundings

The use of the architectural homograph is perhaps most opportunistic in the acquisition of one building type, which is then converted to a more profitable building type purely for capital gain. A prison cell becomes a dormitory with a lick of paint and some furniture; a once-thriving factory becomes a trendy Michelin-starred restaurant; an office becomes a shop in the blink of an eye, with no change required to the building form. In each case this is not a testament to the adaptability of the old building, but instead to the power of market forces over architecture. If a retail space is deemed more profitable than an office, that is what the building must be. Architecture is reduced to a cold, hard business transaction.

It is right that old buildings should be reused with new functions, to create layered, varied cities connected to their past. Yet we must also understand the role we play in a building's conversion to an architectural homograph. Do we unthinkingly assist developers in their reduction of architecture to blunt business transaction – or should we instead challenge their motives through design, and awareness of our role?

We can do the latter in two ways: reinvention and layering. Reuse a building, but don't unquestioningly follow its old form to create its new function. Ensure the building is adapted; reinvent the space according to its use. In the case of converting a prison into a student residence, as is being mooted throughout the UK,[7] for example:

— Enlarge the oppressively sized window to create a full-height opening.
— Extend the habitable area of the space by adding a new lightweight balcony accessed from the new full-height window.
— Install a bed that folds into the wall to give more space for activities during the day.

These three simple reinvention strategies would bring in more light and add more space – turning an unacceptable architectural homograph into an acceptable one. Layering is achieved by respecting and retaining important features of the old building but adding new elements to its form that express the new use.

Increasing the window height and adding a balcony are also symbolic, signifying that the building is no longer a prison. Prisoners weren't afforded full-height glazed openings or balconies. The private balcony is an overt symbol of residential architecture employed in multiple domestic building types, from a Parisian apartment block to a Dubai high-rise.

The increased window height and addition of balconies adds another layer to the story of the building. By ensuring that key existing features of the building are retained (brick arches, stone lintels) while adding new elements, a new picture is formed of the building with multiple layers of history through its changes in use, without suffocating its new function.

— *Deception*

The final aspect of architectural homography is deception: deliberately making a building with a certain function appear and feel like another building type to entice its users to spend more time and money there. Architecture as a tool of deception is nothing new – from the *trompe l'œil* of the Parthenon's curved columns to the manipulation of time in 24-hour windowless Las Vegas casinos – but the use of the architectural homograph as a tool of deception is more recent.

In 2002, Koolhaas described how shopping had invaded all building typologies. The museum, the airport, the train station, the university and even the hospital were found to give significant floor space and design importance to retail.[8] Now the opposite has happened, too: all building typologies have invaded the shopping centre, which is made to appear as something else. This 'new type' of shopping centre is created for customers (never people or citizens) who are 'now seeking authenticity and a deeper sense of connection to their community, culture, climate and daily lives'.[9] Capitalism evolves to maintain the flow of money by different means.

A shopping centre in Granada, Spain, becomes a version of the Alhambra palace by virtue of possessing 'a façade which uses the same geometric patterns'.[10] A shopping centre in Portugal is made to look like an industrial building with reference to the area's history of textile production, adopting the simplistic form of a sawtooth roof clad in metal. Neither this form nor the material is indigenous to the area. Or in Las Vegas, a shopping centre by Studio Libeskind is designed to mimic a whole city with real trees, parks, private plazas and sculptures conceived within an exterior form reminiscent of the architect's previously designed theatres, art galleries and museums – made to 'feel like it's not really a shopping mall at all'.[11]

1 — Assess

The shopping centre is thus designed to appear local and familiar by deception: a facsimile of older, more honest building types and spaces. As Heynen said: 'Capitalism hollows life out, perverting the energy produced by hope into a meaningless pursuit of empty values. This can be seen in the architecture, which is the image of sterility.'[12] In a reversal of Modernism's liberating break with symbolism, these buildings now recreate a false symbol to entice and engage their customers.

Ensuring authenticity

To counter this, how should architects deal with the problem of designing a building like a shopping centre without producing a homograph devoid of authenticity?

— *Celebrate use/purpose*

The great department stores of New York, London and Paris celebrated their function through the use of elements from other building types: the escalator for flowing movement; the atrium for navigation; the rooflight for heightened awareness and perception. At street level key architectural devices were used to signify the building's function – expanses of glass to enable elaborate window displays, extended canopies and awnings to shelter customers and denote the entrance, seamlessly designed advertising adding to the overall effect. Many of these elements endure in today's shopping centres, but are now shrouded in fake symbolism.

— *Respond to context to generate form*

Freed from its obligation to draw in the public, above ground level the department store was a prototypical homograph. Not a homograph designed to deceive, but a homograph that responded to its context, assimilating with the urban fabric by respecting local roof profiles, street grids and façade rhythms.

Instead of using a deceptive metaphor to generate the form of the building, use real physical and social indicators of context: topography, ground conditions, surrounding buildings, sunlight, weather, access, transport and function. By challenging our own design methods and our clients' motives we can change the architectural homograph into something better suited to, and reflective of, its function. We can reject opportunism, sterility and deception to make buildings of purpose, distinctiveness and honesty.

FORM

Same form, different place

form, *noun*
From Latin – *forma* (to mould)
1. The shape or external appearance of something distinguished by its colour, material, texture, configuration, etc.
2. The specific way in which a person or thing manifests itself.
3. A particular sort or type.
4. The way in which a work (literary, musical, artistic, etc.) is arranged and composed; its coordination and structure.

In Greek mythology, Procrustes was a rogue smith and thief who lured strangers travelling from Athens to Eleusis into his home. He would invite his unwitting victims to spend the night, providing them with an iron bed of very particular dimensions, and he would then carry out a sadistic exercise in standardization. If the victim were shorter than the bed, Procrustes would stretch them; if they were longer, he would cut them down to fit. Procrustes did not care for or acknowledge the differences between people and their varying forms, instead forcing them to conform to a strict and ultimately incompatible standard.

The term 'Procrustean', based on this mythical character, means 'tending to produce conformity through violent or arbitrary means'. Many of our cities have been subject to Procrustean development – one-size-fits-all urbanism – by property developers aided and abetted by architects. This has been happening for decades, and the trend shows no sign of abating. This pursuit of conformity manifests itself in standardized building typologies ambivalent to their setting, and the surrounding cultural, geological or climatic conditions. A hypermarket in the USA is indistinguishable from a hypermarket in Malaysia; beachfront apartment blocks in Spain are identical to those in Brazil; a multistorey office block is exactly the same in London as it is in Berlin.

With the advent of the International Style in the 1920s, and the technological advances that accompanied it, the possibilities of a universally standardized global architecture emerged. The International Style established principles of unity and inclusion,[1] of shared problems and values, and proposed architectural solutions that crossed borders. Its influence spread throughout Europe, to the USA, to South America and to Africa, with regional variations. In spite of these variations, the style's universal architectural distinctiveness remained in its use of 'lightweight technique, synthetic modern materials, and standard modular construction so as to facilitate fabrication and erection'.[2]

1 — Assess

STANDARD MODULAR CONSTRUCTION Benidorm, Spain

STANDARD MODULAR CONSTRUCTION Rio de Janeiro, Brazil

SYNTHETIC MATERIALS Ohio, USA

SYNTHETIC MATERIALS Sabah, Malaysia

LIGHTWEIGHT TECHNIQUE London, UK (left); Berlin, Germany (right)

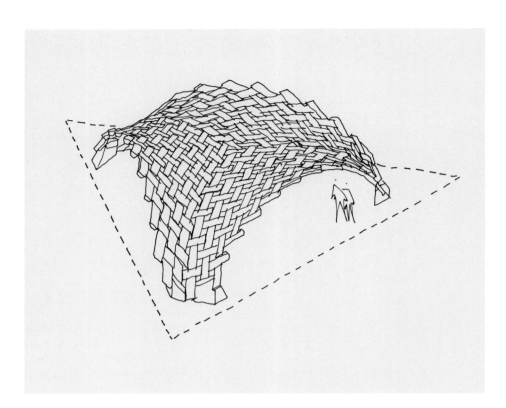

LIGHTWEIGHT TECHNIQUE/MODULAR CONSTRUCTION
AAU Anstas, Stone Matters, Jericho, Palestine, 2017

The architect rescues the local stone from its typical use as thin, applied cladding by resurrecting it as a structural and form-making device through new technology and lightweight technique. Three hundred solid stone pieces are digitally cut to an optimum geodesic surface, allowing the material to connect with the site's history, and with the new technique to connect with its future, simultaneously presenting a global and local architectural language.

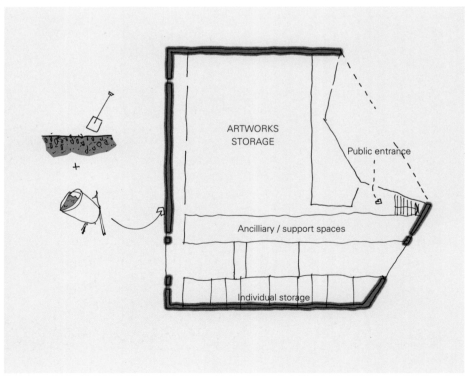

SYNTHETIC MODERN MATERIALS/ MODULAR CONSTRUCTION
Herzog & de Meuron, Schaulager, Basel, 2003

The building acts as a storage warehouse for art, which is also accessible to the public. The brief dictated strict climatic conditions, for which the architect found that an adobe construction (also an important local historical building method) was best. Modern and historical building techniques were combined to create a concrete bound wall containing gravel from the surrounding site, while achieving the same climatic conditions as adobe construction, but constructed in half the time: a combination of specificity and pragmatism.

The attributes of the International Style, intended to create a common architectural language concerned with equality and progress, have now been bastardized by property developers as a facsimile concerned with facility of construction and maximization of profit. These markers of distinctiveness have now been stripped of social and moral obligation.

'Lightweight technique', originally intended as pure honesty of form, now means flimsier materials and the minimum possible surface area. 'Synthetic materials', previously used to create revolutionary new forms, now mean materials that can be fabricated quickly using cheap labour, and shipped worldwide regardless of suitability in their host environments. 'Standard modular construction ... to facilitate fabrication and erection', used by the Modernists to create economical public projects and ensure superior build quality of components produced off site, now means erecting structures as quickly as possible to reduce construction time (the expenditure period) and increase rental or lease time (the profit period).

These tactics are employed across the world in a Procrustean manner, as developers replicate plans regardless of local conditions. They now use the very tools that architects invented in good faith to besmirch the original architectural ideals. Internationalism has been reduced to globalization; progress reduced to profit.

Procrustes finally met his end, killed by Theseus in the same way as his victims. Similarly, architects can only hope to beat property developers at their own game with the very tools used by developers against them. We must reclaim the three properties of the original International Style as tools for architectural and social progress, not simply allow them to be used as a means to build cheaply and quickly. Crucially, we must also prove that we can still make our buildings as economical and pragmatic as those developed in a Procrustean manner. We must prove that locally responsive architecture doesn't mean more expensive buildings; that architecture with deeper resonance and meaning does not cost more. If we can't, Procrustean development will continue, using the justification that any other type of urbanism is too costly.

Achieving lightweight technique

We must develop ways in which to once again combine economy of form with purity and honesty (see Optimize). Optimization should be a generator for the architectural idea and form, adapted to different locations, rather than a value-engineering exercise carried out as an afterthought that leads to a generic solution. Yes, use a lightweight steel frame for a project in the Netherlands and a project in Dubai – but use them in different ways specific to the forms generated by the site response.

— *Using digital tools to minimize waste*
Use digital technologies to ensure that new and radical forms are as economical as possible, minimize the use of on-site labour, and are fully quantifiable at every step of the design process.

— *Using traditional symbolism*
Combine traditional symbolism with a modern, lightweight structural approach; create new interpretations that combine tradition and economy, specificity and standardization.

MODULAR CONSTRUCTION/
LIGHTWEIGHT TECHNIQUE
OFIS Arhitekti, Living Unit, Anywhere, 2017

A flexible and adaptable module of
lightweight timber frame, plywood-lined
construction that can be combined in
different configurations, to create holiday
homes, tree houses, research cabins
or simple shelters. The modules can be
stacked vertically or horizontally to suit
a variety of environments and weather
conditions. Crucially, the units can be used
for different purposes, on different sites
and in different contexts by being clad or
finished in suitable materials.

Using synthetic materials

Synthetic materials will almost always be more economical than traditional, natural materials such as masonry, timber, thatch or mud. Our use of synthetic materials – laminated board, powder-coated metal, synthetic render, aluminium rainscreen – is therefore dictated by market forces. Rather than embrace them unquestioningly (if we must use them), we should learn to use them in a creative and site-specific manner within the confines of the budget.

What clues does the site give about which synthetic materials would enhance its characteristics? Do the site's light qualities demand a reflective or absorbent surface? Does the aesthetic quality of the site dictate that the building should be clad to blend in, or stand out? The site will answer all these questions if we listen.

The second strategy for intelligent use of synthetic materials is to pick up clues from the manmade environment. You might be surrounded by seventeenth-century stone buildings, and pressured by the local planning authorities to use modern, uneconomical facsimiles of these materials. Try to think laterally about material references within the site. Build a case for the use of appropriate materials based on investigation of the full spectrum of materials found nearby, not just the neighbouring buildings. Overhead railway cables are as valid as outdated marble façades; a corrugated metal fence is equal to slates on a roof; the utilitarian brick of a nearby industrial building is as important as the bluff sandstone of residences. By taking this approach a wider range of site-specific synthetic materials can be employed.

Using standard modular construction

Standardized construction methods are possibly the most formidable obstacle to countering Procrustean development. They are beneficial to the developer because they reduce the construction period, providing greater control in terms of quality, contractual warranties and guarantees. Modular construction is therefore here to stay. The challenge for architects is to find site-specific solutions using standardized building components.

One approach is to reference traditional building techniques using modern standardized construction methods. For example, if a site suggests an adobe-type construction, which would typically take half the time to construct using concrete[3] – it would be naive to insist that adobe be used. In Herzog & de Meuron's Schaulager museum in Basel, gravel from the site was added to the concrete mix – effectively blending specificity and standardization, tradition and modernity.

Furthermore, standard components do not need to mean standardization of form and site response. With some thought and ingenuity, they can be as site-specific as non-standardized components.

Combined with careful financial monitoring at all stages of the design and construction process, the above architectural strategies can be employed to reverse the tendency towards globalized Procrustean development. Every architectural project, regardless of market forces, should interact with and accentuate the particular characteristics of a site to create buildings of depth and resonance.

IRONY

A seven-storey Ionic column is not the answer

irony, *noun*
From Ancient Greek – *eirôn* (a stock character
in Greek comedy, characterized by self-
deprecation)
1. The humorous or sarcastic use of words
to convey a meaning opposite to the literal
meaning.
2. A technique (literary) of giving expression
to contradictory or incongruous attitudes,
events or feelings.
3. A situation or outcome opposite to
that which is expected.

'If you are both respectful, loving and critical of our age, these things can be melded through irony.'[1]
— Denise Scott Brown

In my view, overt displays of irony in building must be rejected – to create comic structures is to devalue the design process and the client's needs for your own intellectual gratification. By pursuing a sense of irony in our buildings, the question shifts from 'How do I make this building work with the site?', 'How do I meet the space requirements?', 'How do I juggle the budget?' or 'How do I create a beautiful addition to a city or landscape?' to 'How do I make an ironic gesture?' The real issues get sidelined.

However, irony in architectural discourse and theory is vital, as a means of accurately reflecting on the profession and the buildings it creates. This can be achieved by using irony as a device to criticize how we function as a profession, and by using it to analyse the qualities and failings of our built environment.

Critical irony enables us to learn valuable lessons. For example, Cedric Price's subversion of the traditional role of the architect and use of sarcasm conveyed extreme but viable concepts used as withering ironic devices to critique the architect's role in society. Projects such as his 'Fun Palace' project illustrate this: it proposed an enormous scaffold-like framework within which any activity or function could occur owing to the 'building's' variably prefabricated walls, platforms, gantries and ceiling modules. Or his 'Potteries Thinkbelt', where a series of adaptable temporary structures were proposed to reinvent an area of the industrial north of England into a science and technology hub. Both were serious, revolutionary proposals, which had irony at their core. Here was an architect who believed that permanent buildings were too static to keep up with the constant flux of society, instead proposing an almost non-architecture of movable capsules, adaptable gantries and changeable walls. By creating two projects that challenged the role of the traditional architect – crafting space and forms from solid, permanent materials – he set the agenda for the architecture of the future, influencing everyone from Richard Rogers to Rem Koolhaas. Koolhaas describes this approach: '[Price's] most radical and innovative contribution was his relentless and

1 — Assess

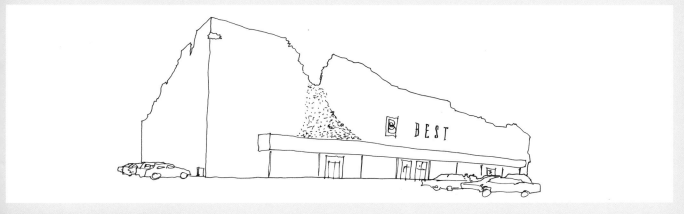

ARCHITECTURE AS IRONIC FAILURE
BEST store, Houston, USA: an otherwise unimaginative response to a dull typology, the building is reduced to a joke that it is crumbling

ARCHITECTURE AS IRONIC SYMBOLISM
M2 Building, Kengo Kuma, Tokyo: a seven-storey Ionic column dominates a chaotic Postmodernist façade

ARCHITECTURE AS IRONIC ONE-LINE 'LIVE–WORK' JOKE
Blue House, FAT, London: a cartoon-like billboard that bluntly communicates its function as a home and office

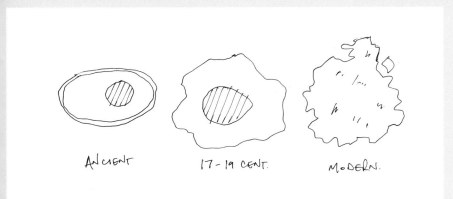

'CITY AS AN EGG' – CEDRIC PRICE
Deft summary of architectural history combining with critique on contemporary practice

'PROJECTS AS MONSTERS' – REM KOOLHAAS
Self-critical critique of past 'unbuilt' projects

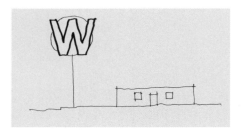

BIG SIGN – LITTLE BUILDING

BUILDING IS SIGN

LEARNING FROM EVERYTHING
Robert Venturi, Denise Scott Brown,
Steven Izenour – sketch; lessons from the
nondescript shed with large communicative
sign analysed to suggest a more symbolic,
descriptive architecture

endless questioning of the claims and pretensions of architecture and architects. He was a sceptic torturing a conservative discipline.'[2] This approach can be summed up in Price's 'City as an Egg' sketches, which succinctly describe centuries of urban planning as it changed from the ordered and planned to the chaotic.

This satirical style is also evident in the works of Rem Koolhaas and his practice OMA. Irony was the central theme of his seminal debut text *Delirious New York*, which told the story of the development of New York with references to seemingly banal or even comical events that would lead to massive shifts in our approach to architecture. This strain of irony was carried through in Koolhaas's built work, as described by architectural scholar Anthony Vidler: 'The irony no longer resides in the shock of representation, nor in the juxtaposition of text and image; it is in a real sense embodied in the formal structure of the works themselves.'[3] Most of OMA's early projects question the function and programme of a building to an extent that borders on the absurd. For instance, at the Zeebrugge Sea Terminal, which becomes a destination and attraction itself, at once mechanical, industrial, utilitarian, abstract, poetic and surreal;[4] or the proposal for the Irish Prime Minister's residence, in which Koolhaas saw two opposing requirements, of private and public space, thus creating a 'composition of two intersecting curves'.[5] Rather than merge these opposing demands into one holistic container as architects have done for centuries, Koolhaas instead generates the building form from its diagrammatic tension. Both question the brief and preconceived notions of building typology through an ironic detachment that goes on to inform the architecture.

This approach is also typified more recently with cartoons of some of Koolhaas's most famous 'unbuilt' buildings, such as the New Whitney in New York or the Astor Place collaboration with Herzog & de Meuron, appearing almost as monsters or mutants. It's as if these unbuilt projects didn't want to be buildings at all. This detached resignation in the face of factors beyond the architect's control displays an ironic self-awareness all the more striking for coming from one of the profession's most powerful and influential practitioners.

Through critical irony of forms and structures we may not love, we can nevertheless appreciate the good qualities (hidden or revealed) of these buildings: why they are designed and built the way they are; the lessons that can be learned from them and incorporated into our designs. Another approach is through critical irony of forms and structures we may not love. We can appreciate the good qualities (hidden or revealed) of these buildings: why they are designed and built the way they are; the lessons that can be learned from them and incorporated into our designs. Most importantly, what is it that the public like about these buildings? Only by understanding these things can we beat

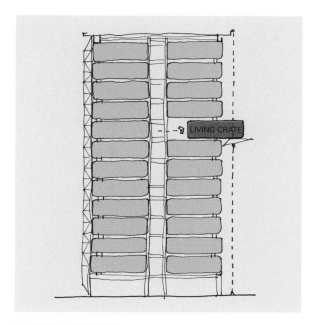

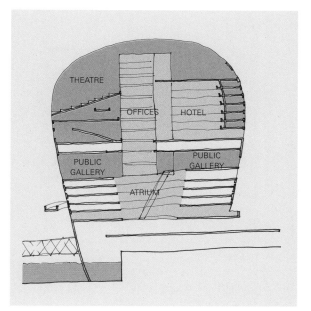

POTTERIES THINKBELT
Cedric Price, Crate Housing, 1963–1967

CRITICAL IRONY OF THE PROFESSION
Cedric Price takes a standard and fashionable system of building housing – the tower block – and subverts it by making the units removable and disposable. Through irony he was creating an anti-architecture, the opposite of the timelessness and solidity his Modernist peers sought. The ultimate irony was this 'crate' housing would set the agenda for the architecture of the future.

ZEEBRUGGE SEA TERMINAL
OMA, 1988

CRITICAL IRONY OF A BUILDING TYPOLOGY
Rem Koolhaas takes a banal and perfunctory building type – the ferry terminal – and ironically creates a 'destination' of a building usually used only as a means to get to other more desirable locations. Through irony, Koolhaas predicted the future trend for transport hubs becoming destinations in themselves, stuffed with restaurants, hotels, offices, beauty parlours and bars.

the developers at their own game – enabling us to provide high-quality architecture that incorporates the best parts of the buildings we don't love (shopping malls, suburbia, retail parks and so on). To simply disregard them is snobbish and myopic.

As Robert Venturi and Denise Scott Brown remark in *Learning from Las Vegas*: 'Architects are out of the habit of looking nonjudgmentally at the environment, because orthodox Modern architecture is progressive, if not revolutionary, utopian, and puristic; it is dissatisfied with existing conditions ... Architects have preferred to change the existing environment rather than enhance what is there.'[6] The book goes on to prove this theory correct through analysing the Las Vegas Strip (a place abhorrent to most Modern architects at the time), and teasing out its symbolic, organizational and transitory qualities as lessons for a less puritanical, more objective architecture of the future. Through the lens of irony the qualities of these under-appreciated structures are extrapolated as a way to inform future designs and proposals; a way to 'learn from everything'.

In summary, irony should be used to evaluate our role as architects within society – to satirize methods of working, interrogate responses to our environment and learn from the successes and failures around us. Irony should *not* be used as the response – a one-line joke façade is not the answer, and neither is a seven-storey Ionic column.

POLITICS

Architecture isn't everything

politics, *noun*
From Ancient Greek – *polis* (city)
1. The art and science of government.
2. The system of relationships involving authority, power and people in society.
3. Political activities or affairs.
4. The business of conducting political affairs.
5. The methods involved in conducting political affairs.
6. The ideological principles driving the conducting of political affairs.
7. Manoeuvres or modes of working to gain power or control any activity concerned with the acquisition of power.
8. Opinions, allegiances and beliefs in relation to politics.

Tuesday 18 March, 2003
Year 1, Design Unit D had an interim design crit, and the United Kingdom had just declared war on Iraq. Drawing tube around my neck and card model in my hands, I passed wild-eyed protesters with whistles and placards. I arrived at the studio as my design tutor was opening the door to leave. 'What are you doing here?' she said. 'You should be out protesting!' Bemused, thinking about the long hours preparing for the crit, I stared back in awkward silence. As usual, the design studio was a hive of activity, with hurriedly pinned-up drawings and hastily arranged models. All the tutors' seats were occupied, except one. The crit carried on regardless with no mention of the war, the protests outside our window or the lone politically minded rebel who had left. Instead, we obsessed over line weights, roof detailing or the height of a room relative to its width. We were content in our architectural bubble; oblivious. Given the global chaos precipitated by this war,[1] I now have a mixture of admiration for my old tutor and regret that I was too wrapped up in a hypothetical building design to care. Architecture consumed me.

Architecture isn't everything. There are many more important things in life, and politics is one of them. In my experience, architects are a generally apolitical group, more concerned about masterplans, building organization or detailing than about how society is governed and how equality, justice and liberty are administered. Architects tend to be liberal and progressive in outlook, yet are often reticent when required to promote or defend these values. The practice of architecture can leave little time or energy to engage in much else, and many architects calmly absolve themselves of any political agency, instead focusing on the technological and aesthetic function of their architecture.[2] However, this political apathy can seem odd, considering that politics affects architecture on every level.

1 — Assess

ECONOMY	WAR	LEFT/RIGHT

ECONOMIC RUINS
Packard Factory, Detroit, USA

ARCHITECTURE OBLITERATED
Civil War, Azaz, Syria

PRIVATELY OWNED PUBLIC SPACE (RIGHT)
Ziccotti Park, New York

RISK-AVERSE ARCHITECTURE
Queen Elizabeth University Hospital, Glasgow, UK

DESTROYED
Temple Bel, Palmyra, Syria

SOCIAL HOUSING (LEFT)
Karl Marx Hof, Vienna

UNEMPLOYMENT
Chicago, Great Depression, 1930s

DEFINED BY BOLLARDS
Terminal, Aberdeen, UK

CULTURE AS CULTURE, NOT A BY-PRODUCT (LEFT)
Louvre Pyramid, Paris

LENINISM = CONSTRUCTIVISM
Tatlin Tower (unbuilt – superimposed on St Petersburg, Russia), 1920

KENNEDYISM = SPACE-AGE MODERNISM
Los Angeles Airport, USA, 1961

STALINISM = SOCIALIST CLASSICISM
Moscow University, 1953

REAGANISM = GATED COMMUNITYISM
Gated community, San Jose, USA, 1985

WELFARISM = SOCIAL MODERNISM
Royal Festival Hall, London, 1951

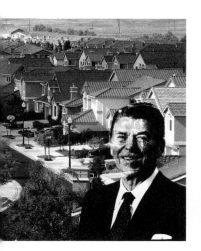

BLAIRISM = CORPORATE MODERNISM
Millennium Dome, London, 1999

Architecture and the economy

Whether interventionist or passive, economic decisions can lead to the boom or bust of certain geographical areas, which has a huge impact on architecture.

— *Dictating volume, location and function*

The success or failure of an area ultimately dictates the location, volume and typology of buildings required there. For example, the rise of the tech industry in San Francisco, aided by government tax breaks,[3] has led to the prevalence of high-rise apartments, office blocks and leisure buildings at the expense of affordable housing or community projects. Meanwhile, in Detroit, the decline of the city's automotive industry, in part due to poor government decisions,[4] has meant that the creation of new buildings has almost ceased, and those left behind crumble into ruin.

— *Putting the quality and longevity of buildings at risk*

Government building procurement routes, such as public–private partnerships, which originated in the United Kingdom but are now used in many countries throughout the world in various guises, allow private firms to finance public projects upfront, then rent the building back to the public for long-term financial gain. This has led to the privatization of once-public buildings (schools, hospitals, train stations), and many of these buildings are hampered by a disconnect between the architect and client, the stifling of innovation through risk aversion, inflexible and unsustainable buildings, and compromise in terms of quality.[5]

— *Putting jobs at risk*

In a recessive economy, the construction industry is often first hit. Work for architects dries up as clients and developers wait until the market picks up and land values increase.[6] This can put individual jobs and often whole architectural practices' futures at risk.[7]

Architecture and war

War is always a political decision, and it can have a severe effect on architecture in a region over a long period of time.

— *Obliterating architecture*

War can decimate the built fabric of a city, destroying buildings and communities. Architecture is erased in seconds, while the urgent demand for new buildings remains unfulfilled until the war ends. War and terrorism also put ancient monuments at risk, as they become targets. This obliterates our connection to the built environment of ancient civilizations.

— *Changing the appearance of buildings and the message they convey*

Over time, wars make our buildings more defensive. New buildings need to have any possible terrorist threat 'designed out'. For example, in London architects are encouraged to minimize the use of glazing, employ bollards and planters around building perimeters to block vehicles, and separate ventilation systems to combat the effects of a poison gas attack.[8]

01 FORM
A sculptural approach creates arches that animate the form and create reveals at ground level for varying depth

02 USE
The pool is simple yet effective, bringing the occupants together into one space while providing relief from the intense climate

03 DETAIL
Oversized openings incorporate a spandrel up to waist level; the openings appear more generous than their function requires them to be

04 MATERIAL
No deviation in material approach; glass and concrete are used just as in all of Niemeyer's buildings

CENTROS INTEGRADOS DE EDUCAÇAO PUBLICA Oscar Niemeyer, Nova Iguaçu, Brazil, 1984

FATA OFFICE BUILDING Oscar Niemeyer, Turin, Italy, 1977

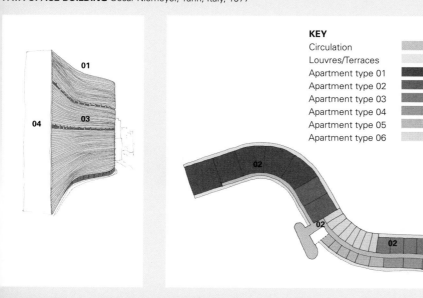

KEY
Circulation
Louvres/Terraces
Apartment type 01
Apartment type 02
Apartment type 03
Apartment type 04
Apartment type 05
Apartment type 06

01 FORM
The sinuous plan is defined by curves that unify the building form such that no hierarchy between internal uses is visible

02 USE
The building plan is egalitarian, with a range of apartments on each floor allowing for a varied social mix at each level, while circulation is staggered to ensure the majority of apartments have terrace access

03 DETAIL
The use of deep brise-soleils performs a functional task of providing shade, while their horizontality reinforces the curves of the building form

04 MATERIAL
The use of one material, concrete, for the skin of the building reinforces the overall unifying concept

EDIFÍCIO COPAN Oscar Niemeyer, São Paulo, Brazil, 1966

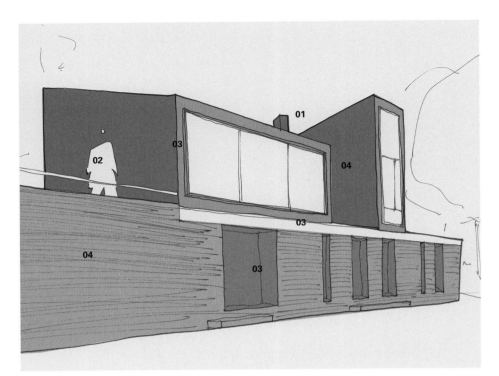

PIRIHUEICO HOUSE Elemental, Pirihueico Lake, Chile 2004

01 FORM
The roof form and base are separated in a playful game; the rectilinear base is a counterpoint to the sculpted roof forms, oriented towards sun and views

02 USE
The varied roof form is used to create a rooftop terrace space for views out across the landscape

03 DETAIL
Deep window reveals, separating trabeation via a concrete lintel between base and roof, and framing of the roof windows in different materials illustrate a considered approach to detailing

04 MATERIAL
A rich palette of materials – dark stone, naturally stained wood, frameless glass, precast concrete – is expertly handled to convey a sense of luxury

SOCIAL HOUSING Elemental, Valparaíso, Chile, 2010

01 FORM
Roof and façade are differentiated only by slight differences in material, not inventiveness of form; no specific account taken of sunlight and views

02 USE
This minimal approach means no space is created for a roof terrace as a result to take advantage of the hilltop location

03 DETAIL
The approach to detailing is to treat different elements with different colours; along with the flush windows and exposed services, a lack of depth and craft is conveyed

04 MATERIAL
Rudimentary materials – reinforced concrete, painted wood, corrugated metal – are handled in a rudimentary manner, giving the impression of social housing

1 — Assess

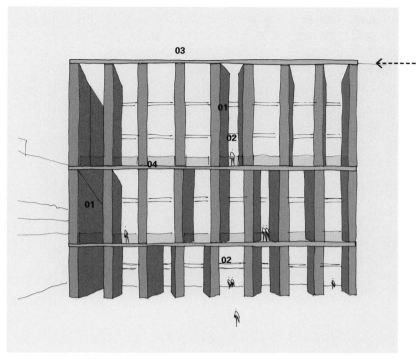

UC MEDICAL SCHOOL Elemental, Santiago, Chile, 2004

01 FORM
At UC, the brick column profile is chamfered and tapered to create variation on the façade as well as in the terrace spaces; in the community centre, columns are simply extruded in one plane throughout repetitively

02 USE
Repetition of form limits function, below, as the façade is purely a colonnade, a shelter from the weather; at UC, terraces become mini double-height atria and intimate social spaces as well as providing shelter

03 DETAIL
The horizontal lines of the façade are picked out in a concrete lintel, while the junction between brick, glass and concrete is seamless; below, there is no hierarchy of detailing to pick out the strong horizontal lintel, while exposed steel bolts become the fixing method

MATERIAL
04 At UC, a rich palette of materials – red brick, precast concrete, frameless glass, timber – is used to convey a sense of permanence; below, the dominant material is crudely painted timber, which has a more temporary feel

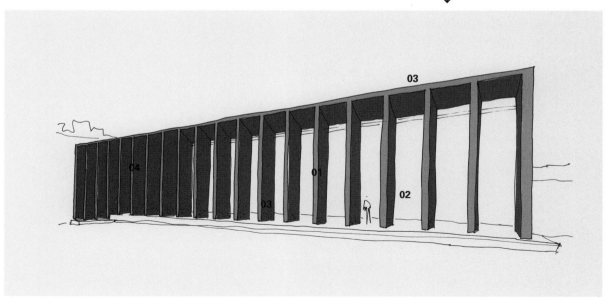

COMMUNITY CENTRE Elemental, Constitución, Chile, 2010

Architecture and left vs right

Left-leaning governments place higher value on public space, promoting its use by all. Meanwhile, right-leaning governments see space as a commodity to be used by those who have paid for it.[9]

— *Making public spaces disappear*

There is a trend towards privatization of public space in cities across the globe, where private space is created for new developments, or existing public space is bought and made to appear like a public space, but without the freedom of expression once allowed there.

— *Affecting building types*

Socialist governments invest heavily in public infrastructure and high-profile public buildings with money raised from taxes, such as the Grands Projets of Mitterrand-era Paris at the end of the twentieth century, when museums, opera houses, libraries and so on were built across the city to promote culture and progress. By contrast, conservative governments allow private enterprise to regenerate our cities through sponsorship and investment, promoting culture as a by-product of profit.[10]

— *Dictating the building of social or private housing*

Leftist governments place importance on the provision of affordable housing; rightist governments leave housing up to the private market. The availability and type of that most basic of architectural needs, the house, is therefore in the hands of politicians.

Architecture and style

Architecture is often the physical expression of the dominant ideology of the time. A building reflects a government's values and goals through its form, material choice and symbolism.

— *Russia*

In the spirit of Russia's social revolution of 1917 led by Vladimir Lenin, an architectural revolution in form and technique emerged. Rejection of the past, oblique dynamic lines, the use of red, and fetishization of industry and technology were all physical manifestations of the revolutionary government. As successive leaders followed, from Alexei Rykov to Joseph Stalin, the revolutionary spirit dissipated, and the architecture became more classicist and rigid in appearance. The past was celebrated through super-sized concrete blocks embellished with motifs from classical and Gothic architecture.

— *USA*

JFK (US president from 1961–1963) was a modernizer, obsessed with the Space Race[11] – and under him architecture too was obsessed with modernity. Forms emerged that seemed the stuff of science fiction, characterized by sweeping roofs like the wings of a space shuttle; 360-degree bevelled glass bands like a lunar lookout station; aerodynamic curves and neon signs. This carefree architecture was in stark contrast to that of the Reagan era (1981–1989). The rise of insular, conservatively styled gated communities in 1980s America[12] mirrored government policies that promoted privatization and individualism.

The social welfare system introduced by Clement Attlee (prime minister of the UK from 1945–1951) led to large-scale construction of public buildings (schools, hospitals, leisure centres) and state-owned housing, creating an architectural style of modern rectilinear forms hewn in concrete, brick and glass. By the early 1980s prime minister Margaret Thatcher had halted this notion of the government as provider of welfare, allowing private enterprise to proliferate and conservatism and individualism to become the governing ideologies. This is manifest in the architecture of the period, increasingly insular and historicist. Meanwhile, the architecture of the late 1990s onwards (under prime minister Tony Blair) was an uneasy mixture of high-profile public projects propped up by private money, visually expressed as an identity crisis between progress and privatization: glass, steel, CCTV cameras, cheap materials and sponsorship banners.

These examples show how politics affects every aspect of architectural production. Architects must be politically involved to fully understand and respond to the factors that influence their work.

Architecture can engage with politics

It is a commonly held view that architecture can't change society (see Rem Koolhaas, Robert Adam, Patrik Schumacher) – it simply mirrors the political forces surrounding it. There is truth in this – architecture can only do so much before being overpowered by external influences. Yet there are many architects who, through their understanding of the political climate in which they operate, find ways to rebel against it.

— *Oscar Niemeyer*

Brazilian Oscar Niemeyer (1907–2012) created his architecture for the people and the landscape[13] – the two basic elements that all architecture should address. Niemeyer did not dissociate his personal views from his architecture: his buildings were 'his weapons', receptacles of his contempt for and protest at the world around him.[14] Yet Niemeyer shunned the architecture of social welfare, describing it as paternalistic and demagogic, and the approach of designing simpler and more rudimentary buildings for the working class as 'unacceptable discrimination'.[15]

Instead he created daring, soaring architecture that transcended building type and social conditions, subversively bringing the architecture he created for the rich and powerful to the oppressed and the poor. This is evident in the comparison between his 1977 FATA headquarters office building in Turin, Italy, and his later CIEP (Integrated Centres of Public Education) project in Nova Iguaçu, commissioned to engage disadvantaged street children in the public school system. The buildings share the same sculptural façade, a cantilever to add depth, common materials of concrete and glass, and even a pool. Disadvantaged school children were treated the same as corporate bosses.

In his Edifício Copan building, a housing project in São Paulo, the wealthy and working class could live side by side. Rather than physically differentiate between rich and poor by placing the more expensive apartments on the upper floors, Niemeyer instead devised a floor plan containing a full range of apartment types on one floor, from small to large. Rich and poor would therefore mingle as well as share the same access to views, sunlight and terraces: the plan was an expression of his personal beliefs in microcosm. A unified, sinuous form also meant there was no visual distinction on the outside of the building.

RIVER DWELLINGS Bristol, UK, J. Tait, 2016

— *Alejandro Aravena*

Chilean Alejandro Aravena, founder of Elemental, poses two questions in his design process: Does a building do what a client wants? Do I understand the human condition better from this building?[16] Aesthetic and technological questions are secondary to the needs of the people who will use his buildings, and humanity in general.

This is evident in his 'incremental' housing projects, which provide residents with a 'half house' (a two-storey, two-bedroom home, with roof, kitchen and bathroom, with an equivalent empty space next to it). Residents complete the second half, if and when they can.[17] Aravena's approach accepts reality – that state provision of social housing is deteriorating, and that the people who would have been provided for by the state cannot afford to own their own homes – but finds new ways to ameliorate this situation through architecture.

Despite his thoughtful approach, it is clear which of Aravena's projects are for social welfare purposes, and which aren't. Different materials, different forms and different architectural approaches are employed depending on the budget and goals of his client. Perhaps this reflects a world where social provision is now less ingrained in society and the architect wields less power than in Niemeyer's day – or it may simply be that Aravena is less utopian in his approach. This is no less admirable, however, given the impact his politically engaged architecture has had in his homeland.

1 — Assess

The future of socially aware architecture

There is a new breed of politically aware architects emerging, who seek to address social, economic and environmental issues. This is to be celebrated, yet often their proposals fall into the trap of paternalism that Niemeyer identified.[18] Rather than subvert or change injustices and inequalities of society, many projects merely mirror the problems they set out to solve.

Why do we propose solid, permanent dwellings for the poor and oppressed in Western Europe, for example, and ad-hoc, temporary solutions for the poor and oppressed in Syria? (See Nicolás García Mayor's Cmax shelters, described as a cross between a tent and a trailer.) Why do we propose the typology of the military bunker for housing in Africa (see Nader Khalili's SuperAdobes made from sandbags), when we propose the typology of the house for housing in the West? Why do we use brick, stone and metal for social housing in the Western world but propose paper, straw, fabric and even waste materials (see DARE's plastic bottle houses) for social housing in the developing world? Surely, if we believe in fairness and equality, our architecture should reflect that?

— *Architecture isn't everything*

We mustn't always see politics through the lens of architecture: this will breed paternalistic and reactive projects, rather than architecture born of our understanding of politics and our social awareness. Not every political or social situation can be solved by design, but every design should show an understanding of the world that shaped it.

Perhaps rather than proposing flat-pack shelters, wearable dwellings, inflatable homes and floating platforms after the destruction has happened, we should be trying to stop the wars and political decisions that cause the need for such things in the first place. We must engage with politics and try to challenge inequalities and injustices as citizens, not as architects. We should ask: Why is Africa continually oppressed and manipulated[19] by Western governments such that it needs temporary shelters and rudimentary abodes? What were the Western foreign policy decisions that led to the mass exodus of refugees from the Middle East, now languishing in inhumane European refugee camps? These global issues are not simplistic design problems to be solved by eager architects. If we are entirely wrapped up in architecture, we remain oblivious to larger events, attempting to solve problems through design once it is too late. Architecture isn't everything.

0 20 40 60 80 100 (m)

N

GREENBELT STRATEGY 1: DISUSED FARMLAND

Hidden Courtyard Houses, Essex, UK, site plan, J. Tait. Seven residential clusters comprising of a total of 210 homes are arranged on flat, disused farmland on a site where the urban fringes meet agricultural land. Dwellings are gathered around communal 'sunken' courtyards and private gardens (both shown in the dark hatch). The apparently random matrix of dwelling and courtyard is in fact generated to provide the optimum number of dwellings in relation to open space, minimizing over-shading, ensuring privacy and that each room is dual aspect. The form of each dwelling is created by a precast, waterproof insulated concrete structure exposed internally and externally. Local clay is used to create terracotta louvres for privacy and shading, and to provide an element of site specificity.

ANALYSE

WALK
Cities of substance

walk, *verb*
Germanic – *walchan* (to wander)
1. (intransitive) To move or travel
on foot at a moderate pace, by advancing
one's feet alternately such that one foot
remains on the ground (bipedal motion).
2. (intransitive) To advance or travel in the
above motion for exercise or pleasure.
3. (intransitive) To be suggestive of
movement in the manner of walking.
4. (intransitive) To follow a certain path
or way of life.
5. (transitive) To proceed through, on or
upon a certain area.
6. (transitive) To give cause; to move
along in a walking motion.

As for your cities, Babels of monuments.
Where all the events clamour at once,
How substantial are they? Arches, Towers, Pyramids –
I would not be surprised if in its humid incandescence,
The dawn one morning suddenly dissolved them ...
— Victor Hugo, *La Fin de Satan et Dieu*, 1854–1862[1]

What is the substance of a city?
Ancient monuments and their modern-day equivalent – iconic buildings – are the
emblems of a city. They project a familiar image, acting as comforting landmarks in the
inherent unfamiliarity and chaos. 'Did you go up the Empire State Building?' 'Did you
sit on the steps of the Opera House?' Answer no to these questions on your return from
New York or Sydney and you will be met with bemusement. Why go to a city if you won't
consume its icons? But, as Victor Hugo asked over 150 years ago – how substantial are
they? What value do they have for the inhabitants of the city? What experiences of place
do they offer that the rest of the city doesn't? They are not the substance of a city – its
people and their interplay with space and time are. Architects need to recognize this.

Iconic buildings
Monuments have always defined our cities, as physical signifiers of the belief systems
of rulers and creators of the city through the ages. Religious signifiers in the form of
cathedrals, mosques, temples; monarchical signifiers manifest in castles, palaces and
ramparts; piazzas, statues and fountains as symbols of citizenship; cultural symbols
in the shape of theatres, museums and concert halls. In the past century or so, belief

2 — Analyse

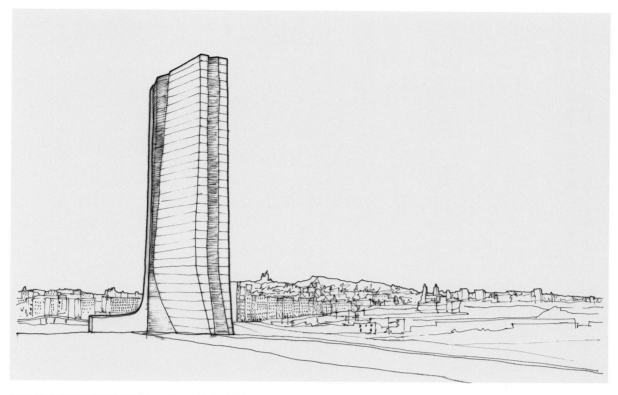

CMA CGM HEADQUARTERS, MARSEILLE, ZAHA HADID An iconic mast rises above the organic chaos of the city beyond; a corporate symbol that proclaims to interact with Marseille's other landmarks – though how the building achieves this is not clear. A striking, svelte form that could have been designed for Munich, Milan or Moscow, that happens to be in Marseille.

systems have generally declined (at least in the Western world), usurped by a more pluralistic society with a predominantly capitalist point of view.[2]

This societal shift has brought about a new type of monument, devoid of meta-narrative (religion, monarchy, enlightenment, progress): the iconic building. With no overarching belief system or iconography guiding their form and function, these buildings now compete to be novel in their own meaningless ways – a phenomenon that architectural theorist Charles Jencks describes as 'generic individualism'.[3] Such buildings strive to be individual, but instead become generic through their ubiquitousness. Rather than monuments of symbolic meaning commissioned by monarchs, religious figures, philanthropists and progressives, these new monuments – commissioned by global corporations, emergent nations and mayors of cities to project an image of modernity and power – have a sense of forced uniqueness.

For examples of corporate icons, see Coop Himmelb(l)au's BMW Museum in Munich – an 'identity-forming architectural ensemble',[4] or Zaha Hadid's CMA CGM Headquarters in Marseille – 'an iconic vertical element that interacts with Marseille's other significant landmarks';[5] for national icons of emergent nations asserting themselves see Abu Dhabi's Capital Gate building by RMJM – a self-proclaimed 'iconic development …

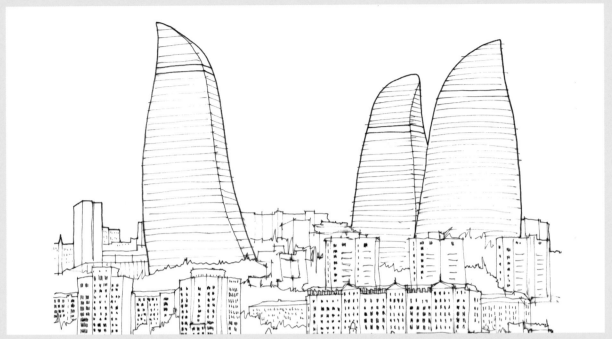

BAKU FLAME TOWERS, BAKU, HOK A metaphor writ large. Inspired by the ancient and extinct practice of fire worshipping in Baku, this collection of flame towers dominates the city's varied skyline, making a cartoonish image. These buildings are silhouettes, filled with the holy trinity of corporate programming (luxury residential, five-star hotel and Class A office space), ambivalent to the geographical, social or programmatic needs of the site and city.

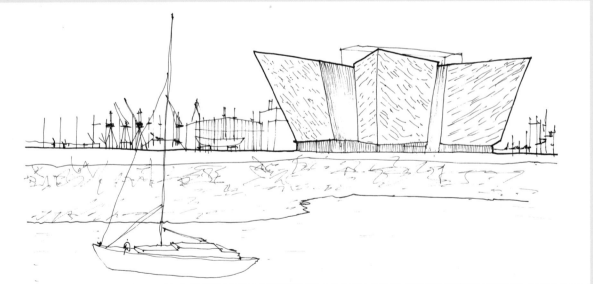

TITANIC QUARTER, BELFAST, ERIC KUHNE AND TODD ARCHITECTS The cultural centrepiece of the redevelopment of Belfast's waterfront is the Titanic Centre. However, rather than focusing on the city's future, the development looks to an event in the city's past – the building of the world's most famous shipwreck, the *Titanic*. The building itself has a mass of 'maritime metaphors'. Its projecting segments evoke the hull of a ship, the wavy anodized aluminium cladding references waves, and the central atrium is deliberately designed with jagged angles to be reminiscent of the forms of a shipyard. A chronic case of mixed metaphors driving the design solution.

KNICK-KNACK	CLOTHING	SYMBOL	BADGE	LOGO

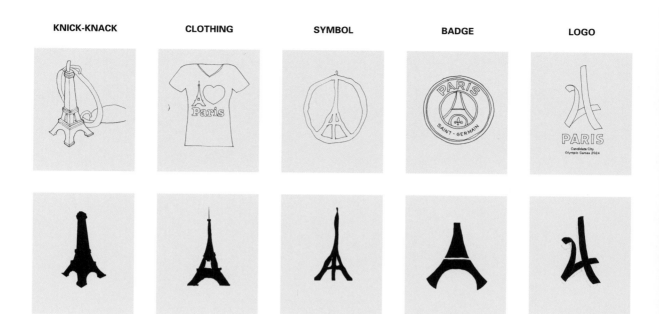

FIVE STAGES OF ABSTRACTION From a miniature replica to a city logo, the Eiffel Tower undergoes a process of abstraction from three-dimensional 'knick-knack' to modified two-dimensional city branding. Architecture as a symbol, where symbol becomes a commodity.

distinguished by a dramatic steel and glass façade with a striking organic form',[6] or HOK's Flame Towers in Baku – 'an iconic trio of buildings that transforms the city's skyline'.[7] City-sponsored icons are usually the physical expression of a superior culture or arts programme, as in Eric Kuhne and Todd Architects' Titanic Quarter in Belfast – 'a dynamic leisure destination of international significance',[8] or Santiago Calatrava's Opera House in Valencia – 'a dynamic urban landmark'.[9]

These ready-made landmarks and destinations are often justified by an 'enigmatic signifier'[10] – an allegory that justifies the 'unique' form of the building. Hadid's Marseille tower is a 'mast' that evokes the city's port; HOK in Baku were inspired by the historic 'fire worship' of its citizens; the Titanic Quarter in Belfast was generated by 'a mass of maritime metaphors'.

What these icons have in common is the need to be different and to innovate, to symbolize the economic and cultural dominance of competing corporations, nations and city-states. They can be marketed as new symbols of the city – and we are told that they define it. This is architecture as tourism, architecture as a product of mass consumption, architecture as a global branding exercise. Tourists duly flock to these structures to consume them like urban knick-knacks, driven by the fear of missing out. However, I propose that the exact opposite is true: these structures are a distraction from the unique experience of a city. To truly understand the substance of the city we must look to the quintessential iconic city: Paris.

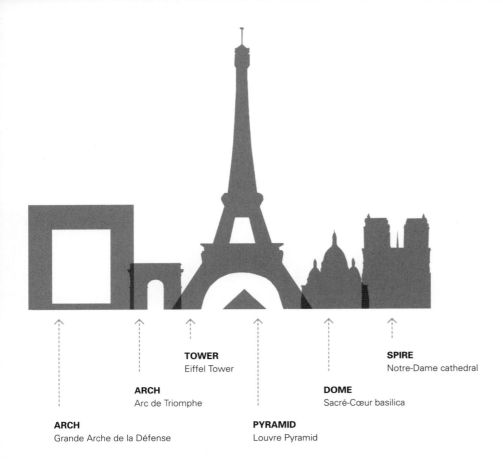

TOWER
Eiffel Tower

ARCH
Arc de Triomphe

SPIRE
Notre-Dame cathedral

DOME
Sacré-Cœur basilica

ARCH
Grande Arche de la Défense

PYRAMID
Louvre Pyramid

Paris – city of icons

Paris is home to what might be the original iconic structure, the Eiffel Tower. Opened in 1889 as the centrepiece of the Exposition Universelle held in Paris that year, the structure was known as 'the highest edifice ever raised by man'.[11] The tower had no functional use; it was created purely as a display of engineering ingenuity, allied with capitalist might. It wasn't until some ten years later that it began to be used as an aerial, and 84 years later it housed its first permanent restaurant – a case of function belatedly following form. In the face of criticism, Gustav Eiffel retorted: '... there's an attraction in things colossal, a special charm to which theories of ordinary art are hardly applicable. The Tower will be the highest edifice ever raised by man – will it not therefore be grandiose as well, in its way? Why would what is admirable in Egypt become hideous and ridiculous in Paris? I've sought an answer, and must confess have found none.'[12]

The Eiffel Tower represented a shift in the monument's status from product of meta-narrative symbolism to pure spectacle, funded by an increasingly competitive industrialist society, as referenced by Eiffel's own comparison with the ancient Egyptian Pyramids, and his critics who claimed that 'the useless and monstrous Eiffel Tower ... overwhelms Notre-Dame, the Sainte-Chapelle, Tower of St Jacques. All of our monuments are debased, our architecture diminished.'[13]

Paris is a city defined by its architectural icons[14] – the Eiffel Tower, the Arc de Triomphe, Notre-Dame cathedral, the Sacré-Cœur basilica, the Grande Arche de la

Défense, and the Louvre Pyramid. These forms entice visitors with their simplicity and familiarity; they are easily digested and universally recognized; they comfort visitors by providing them with the physical proof of the Paris they expected to see. Meanwhile, the city in-between is often left unexplored by visitors, as they travel between sights by Métro or tourist bus. There is an alternative Paris, as there is any big city, not composed of icons but the interplay between people and space, events and buildings, the everyday and the extraordinary.

Paris – in pursuit of the non-iconic

Poet and essayist Charles Baudelaire was among the first to capture the tumultuous hidden beauty in the industrializing metropolis of the mid-nineteenth century. He shone a unique light on Paris, imbuing its burgeoning modernity with a sense of eternity yet intimacy. He focused not on the symbols or monuments of the city, but instead captured its ephemerality through detailed analysis of the everyday.

— *Flânerie and architecture*

Baudelaire's poems captured the city's bustling nature, as well as violently enacted changes in the form of the city following the sweeping reconstruction of Paris by Baron Georges-Eugène Haussmann. He dealt with the 'ravishing monotony'[15] of the Paris of his dreams – always through the lens of human interaction with this urban environment. To capture these unique perspectives of city life Baudelaire wandered the streets of Paris, embodying the concept of *flânerie*, or strolling, to become the archetypal *flâneur*, an urban detective making studies of city life by wandering its streets. *Flânerie* had the ability to 'transform Paris into one great interior', a city 'without thresholds';[16] the *flâneur* 'intoxicated' by their long walks through the streets: 'With each step, the walk takes on a greater momentum.'[17] The *flâneur* places the street as 'dwelling place of the collective'[18] who animate the space between buildings as an individual would within the 'privacy of their own four walls'.[19]

Relating *flânerie* to the practice of the architect, the *flâneur* performs the first essential act that an architect must undertake when designing for the city – to study the interaction between people and place; between city form and human function. Baudelaire's poetry focuses on the everyday and the collective; the anti-iconic. The lesson for architects is not to focus on the monuments of a city, but the spaces and life between them.

— *Expressing city life*

The Parisian fascination with the everyday life of the city continued through the mid-twentieth century in the photography of Robert Doisneau. Doisneau revelled in the 'moment' – capturing an instant expression of city life – of 'ordinary gestures of ordinary people in ordinary situations'. Doisneau and his contemporary Henri Cartier-Bresson pioneered a style of street photography, of 'unmanipulated scenes, with usually unaware subjects'.[20]

Doisneau described his approach as 'guzzling' in the people and the scenery by wandering the streets. He saw the background buildings, cobbles, steps, lamp posts and blank walls as being as important as the people; he strolled the forgotten streets of Paris and its suburbs, where everyday architecture and its inhabitants were stars. Doisneau placed such importance on the qualities of architecture that when asked why he didn't photograph his home suburb of Montrouge in later years, he said: 'Cement has replaced

LES FRÈRES Robert Doisneau, Rue du Docteur-Lecène, Paris, 1934

2 — Analyse

LA MEUTE Robert Doisneau, Place de la Concorde, Paris, 1969

Walk

CANAL DE L'OURCQ
Industrial canal optimistically appropriated as a fishing venue

PARC DE LA VILLETTE
Pavilion as an impromptu meeting place for two children

AVENUE DE FLANDRE
Secret door

AVENUE DE FLANDRE
Courtyard behind the secret door

PLACE DU COLONEL FABIEN
Marketplace as focal point for incensed protesters

RUE DES ROSIERS
Exuberant chaos of big-city life in small medieval streets

the plaster tiles and wooden hutments ... There's nothing to catch the light'.[21] This was seen as an indictment of the material illiteracy of much modern architecture.

Doisneau's work reflected the change and turmoil that shaped Paris from the 1930s to the 1990s. From the innocence of pre-war Paris, to the chaos that gripped the city during the Second World War, to the uneasy juxtaposition of modernity and eternity, Doisneau captured moments of interaction between people and their urban environment, which still stand today as salient lessons for architects. For example, 'Les Frères' (1934) highlights the importance of designing environments that allow children to explore and appropriate their surroundings free from traffic and adult supervision; 'L'asphalte déroulée' (1944) reflects the futility of architecture in the face of extreme events, such as war; while 'La Meute' (1969) is an incisive indictment of a mid-twentieth century urban design which placed the needs of the driver above those of the pedestrian.

— *The spectacle*

Henri Lefebvre was a philosopher and urban theorist who focused mainly on his adopted city, Paris. By the time of his most prolific period, from the 1960s to the mid-1970s, Modernity had asserted itself in Paris and Lefebvre was its chief analyst and critic. In the face of increasing privatization and commodification of city space, Lefebvre promoted the everyday, the non-iconic and the human aspects of city life above all else. He spent his career trying 'to shed light on the complexities and richness of urban life ... the breadth of the everyday richness of the city'.[22]

2 — Analyse

Lefebvre observed the patterns and rhythms of everyday city life. In 'Seen from the window', a chapter in *Rhythmanalysis*,[23] Lefebvre analyses an intersection in Paris, moving from fascinated observer to analyst and critic of the interaction between space and people he saw unfolding before him. In keeping with the increasingly frenetic, congested and homogenized nature of city life Lefebvre focused not on the individual, as Baudelaire and Doisneau had, but on the crowd. He framed his analysis in the context of a new type of urban experience – architecture and urban design as objects of mass consumption – describing a society increasingly disengaged with its urban environment. The individual becomes the 'incongruous crowd' walking around 'metallic knick-knacks'.[24]

Lefebvre framed an urban environment that no longer provided a backdrop for the movements of everyday life; now architecture, and more specifically the financial management of space, dictated the actions of the crowds. What Lefebvre chronicled was how 'the spectacle', and specifically the iconic building, had aided the commercialization of the city, disregarding the intricacies of everyday city life. He raised the same question as Victor Hugo over 100 years previously: how substantial are our cities, really?

Insubstantial icons

Lefebvre brings the story of the icon and its antithesis – the everyday – full circle. He predicted the growing role that 'non meta-narrative icons' would play in the experience of the city and how the city as spectacle, of simulation, would usurp the real experience of the city. Instead, he promoted the architect not as a conveyor of iconic messages but as 'practitioner of space'.[25] Baudelaire, Doisneau and Lefebvre all celebrated the everyday above the emblematic; they found its latent beauty. Rather than relying on iconic messages and illusionism, their message was to focus on a city's people and their interplay with space and time. Above all, to use architecture to create spaces to reflect and enhance the richness of urban life.

The answer: walk more

How can we help to achieve this aim? The answer lies with Baudelaire, Doisneau and Lefebvre – we need to walk more. Baudelaire used walking to explore his muse – the city. Doisneau advocated the 'luck of the stroll', enabling him to capture unexpected moments in the city by chance. Meanwhile, Lefebvre documented the effect that walking, particularly of the crowd, had on the rhythm of the city.

Walking is a unifying act. We all share the same pavement, we all breathe the same air – we don't need to be able to afford a monthly train pass, or payments on the latest car. Walking is how we engage with the space between buildings; as environmental and political writer Rebecca Solnit has said, walking maintains the 'publicness and viability of public space'.[26] Despite recent moves to privatize public space and walkways within cities,[27] walking remains the most democratic and inclusive form of transport. The speed of walking, too, is perfect for thought, reflection and observation. Cycling past a building or event makes it difficult to discern the detail of the subject; travelling by car is a solitary act that leads to disengagement from others around you, while speed obscures your peripheral view. Move past by train and people, spaces and buildings become one long multi-coloured blur. Walking is the only mode of travel that truly allows for immersion in the urban environment and reflection on one's experiences of

GLASGOW Corner detail as macabre humour and storyteller

LONDON Traditional brick detail represents variety and economy in equal measure

BUDAPEST Roof ventilation as architectural roof detail – an ancient example of form and function

GLASGOW Layers of history exposed in the process of demolition

LONDON An incredible display of shocking urban planning – transient car usurps permanent community

BUDAPEST Bullet holes as a reminder of past turmoil

the city. Again, as Solnit said, walking is the 'mind at three miles an hour'.[28]

As a visitor going from monument to iconic emblem, or as an inhabitant going from residence to workplace, walking fills in the gaps of our city experience. We see the city between its brand images, or between our habitual domains and the events, people and time that unfold within these spaces. Walking affords multiple opportunities for us to engage with how people use spaces and buildings in different spontaneous ways. It will surprise us if we let it.

Building cities of substance

Inspired by Baudelaire, Doisneau and Lefebvre, architects can help reverse the trend of city as marketing exercise; of architecture as iconic branding; of buildings as carriers of increasingly vacuous messages. We can do this by becoming urban detectives, observers and analysts:

— Allow ourselves to be surprised and inspired by our urban environments through exploration – not accepting the image of the city we are fed. Instead we should form our own images of the everyday life of the city to allow it to inform our responses to the spaces and buildings we create.

GLASGOW Unique weather conditions create an atmospheric impression of the city

LONDON An unorthodox elevated bridge between buildings surprises

BUDAPEST Look closely and see modern detailing within ancient city walls

GLASGOW A stepped building entrance becomes an elevated platform for speakers and protestors

LONDON Temporary fairground illuminates a grey day in Covent Garden

BUDAPEST A side-street becomes a hive of activity with the help of furniture and lighting

— Walking offers a unique view of how people – individuals and crowds – actually use space, allowing us to reflect on the problems created and opportunities afforded by the buildings and spaces we create.

— Walking allows us to peel back the layers of history in a city through wandering, noting forgotten or neglected spaces, buildings or traces of history that can influence the historical and social context in which we place our designs.

— Learn from the hidden detail of buildings – how a particular brick bond is formed, how a roof vent blends seamlessly into the overall roof form, how a corner can become a humorous device. Walking enables us to observe and then analyse these details.

— By wandering the spaces between iconic areas or buildings we can assess why these areas are less visited. What is it, specifically, about these places that makes them unvisited? How can we improve them?

In this way we can learn to become practitioners of space, rather than practitioners of the image, of illusion. We can create cities of substance, not cities of icons and monuments.

INFLUENCE

Local versus global

influence, *verb*
From Latin – *fluere* (to flow)
1. To induce or effect.
2. To persuade or impel (a person)
to a particular action.

As our relationship with the Internet deepens, until it is almost an extension of us, so too does our relationship with the thousands of images we snap, share and upload. An average American adult spends over eleven hours a day looking at a screen of some kind. Such visual saturation desensitizes us to individual images, and can even lead to anxiety and memory impairment.[1]

Image overload

The process of designing buildings has also become overwhelmed by digital imagery – available at a click for architects to gawp at, covet and ultimately plunder for their own projects. We use the Internet to absent-mindedly mine images to appropriate in our designs, in a cyclical process. This is design by the referencing of titillating images, which will later be referenced by others.

Many of these images are abstracted, picking out particular parts of the architecture. They are often devoid of people or explicit depictions of the building in use; services, shoddy workmanship or clunky design details can all be Photoshopped away. These fleeting, filtered and false images are nevertheless taken as an accurate representation of a work of architecture across a range of platforms.

'Precedent' – image as design method

Architecture students are commonly encouraged to have 'precedent' images pinned up beside their embryonic designs. These are images intended to communicate the intentions and aspirations of a project: the intended use of the spaces being created, the materials to be used, the shapes the buildings will make, and so on. Rather than interrogate designs through modelling and analysis, the precedent images become a crutch on which to rely as a design generator. Few students question this process.

Fast-forward ten years to a design crit in practice as a qualified architect. New office, first chance to impress; I pinned up some initial sketches along with a collection of precedents, or inspirational images. As I presented the project to the directors, one of them tore the images off the wall and tossed them in the bin. Nothing was said about their disposal, but the message was clear: don't refer to other people's images to generate your own design responses to the brief, the site, and the physical and social context.

An alternative design method

Images have always been part of the architectural design process, used as a reference tool by architects to enable them to envisage a place or building without actually going there. Such images are often supplemented by study trips, large-scale model-making

2 — Analyse

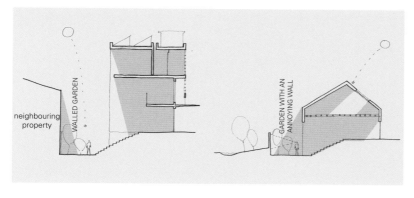

SECTIONS Walled Garden House, inner-city São Paulo (left); useless wall at the end of a garden blocking views, rural Scotland (right)

CORTEN CONCRETE DETAIL Spain

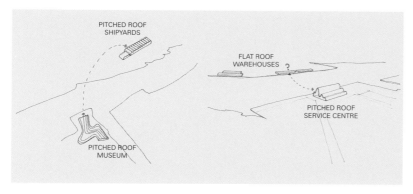
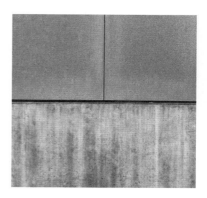

ROOFS Transport Museum, Glasgow, UK, Zaha Hadid (2004–2011); Port Service Center, Kaohsiung, Taiwan, Kubota & Bachmann (designed 2010)

CORTEN CONCRETE DETAIL
London rains, Corten stains!

and study of the cultural context of the architecture. A modern equivalent is to use Google Earth and Street View, which offer us countless detailed images of places across the globe. However, these are blunt reference tools that can encourage us to judge by first appearances rather than rigorous interrogation of symbolic, aesthetic, climatic or technical aspects of a place or building.

Alexander 'Greek' Thomson

One man who understood how to harness his influences was the mid-nineteenth-century Scottish architect Alexander 'Greek' Thomson. Thomson wove the unfamiliar, the foreign and the strange into the fabric of his home city, Glasgow, to create locally responsive yet ground-breaking architecture. Perhaps most heartening for architects of today, 'his knowledge of antiquity and of contemporary architecture seems to have been derived from a magnificent library and from the building journals'.[2]

Thomson had neither the means nor the time to embark on extended architectural study trips – his first foreign trip was in the year of his death, in 1875. However, study enabled him to marshal multiple influences – from the rustic Romanesque, to the pomp of Neoclassicism, ancient Egyptian motifs and decoration, and the new American

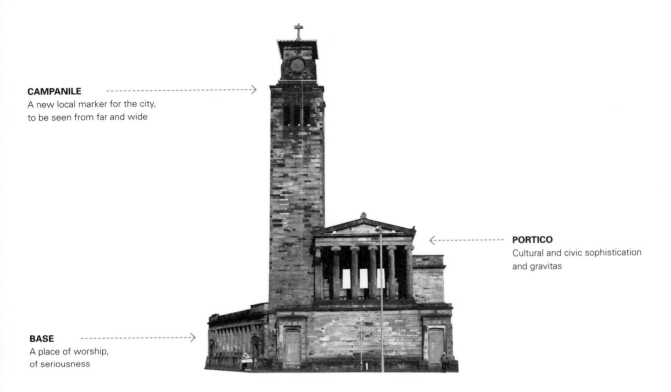

CAMPANILE
A new local marker for the city,
to be seen from far and wide

PORTICO
Cultural and civic sophistication
and gravitas

BASE
A place of worship,
of seriousness

industrial materials – into considered, eclectic compositions ahead of their time. These compositions made the unfamiliar – porticoes, campaniles, Ionic colonnades, Eurasian palmettes – familiar by capitalizing on their universal symbolism, using these elements to reinvent local building typologies, using local materials. Thomson may have been inspired by the images in his library and journals, but he transcended them, as shown in the three examples of his work that follow.

Caledonia Road Church

Completed in 1856, Caledonia Road Church was built in an industrial area of Glasgow to the south of the River Clyde. The prevailing style of ecclesiastical architecture at the time was neo-Gothic, as Scottish architects looked to England and France for inspiration. Thomson instead looked much further back in time and further afield.

By the time the church was on the drawing board, Glasgow had become a major railway city. The site of the church was at the intersection of the main railway lines from the south. Thomson knew his design would become one of the 'markers' of the city, a symbolic gateway for rail passengers arriving from as far away as London. The building therefore had to project the importance of this increasingly global city to visitors, and to achieve this Thomson composed various elements of antiquity as universal symbols of power.

2 — Analyse

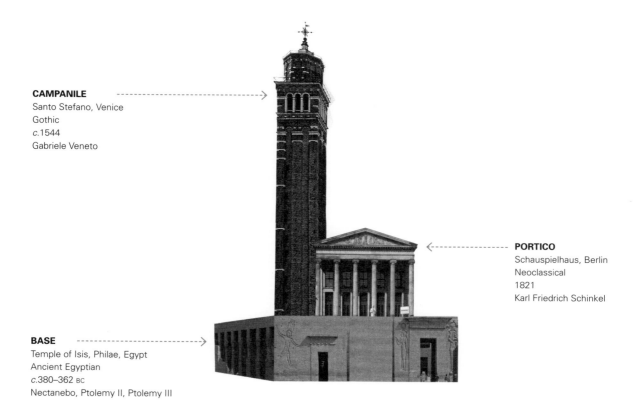

CAMPANILE
Santo Stefano, Venice
Gothic
*c.*1544
Gabriele Veneto

PORTICO
Schauspielhaus, Berlin
Neoclassical
1821
Karl Friedrich Schinkel

BASE
Temple of Isis, Philae, Egypt
Ancient Egyptian
*c.*380–362 BC
Nectanebo, Ptolemy II, Ptolemy III

— *Campanile*

The church's Romanesque campanile (bell tower), crowned by a lantern and cross, is a pared-down take on a typical Italian campanile. With its solid appearance and sheer column of stonework, the tower embodied the fortress-like nature of Romanesque architecture,[3] while also providing a new local marker to enable the city to be seen from far and wide.

— *Portico*

The second of Thomson's influences in seen in the Ancient Greek portico. With an Ionic Hexastyle formation, the portico makes a light, open counterpoint to the solid tower and heavy base. Inspired by Schinkel's 1821 Schauspielhaus (theatre) in Berlin, itself a likely derivate of the Erechtheum in the Acropolis of Athens, Thomson sought to imbue his own building, and the city, with the civic sophistication and gravitas that Ancient Greek architecture projected.

— *Base*

The austere base provides openings to the front only at the main entrance, and the narrow windows to the sides. The overall impression is one of solidity, solemnity and darkness, shared with ancient Egyptian temples such as those at Edfu and Philae. Thomson was making it clear that this was a place of worship, of seriousness.

GLASGOW TENEMENT **REGENCY TOWNHOUSE** **WALMER CRESCENT**

Walmer Crescent

Another building that displays Thomson's ability to harness a variety of influences in a cohesive whole is the block of tenements he designed in 1862, in Walmer Crescent.

The Glasgow tenement is a ubiquitous building type in the city that follows some basic rules: it is between three and five storeys high; it has regular portrait windows with projecting bay windows for living rooms; apartments are separated by a central common 'close' or hallway; it is always built of sandstone and crowned with a slate roof. This adaptable building type had the capacity to house the vast majority of the city's population, and still does – be they tenant or owner; poor or privileged. In more affluent areas, you will see more elaborate decorations and detailing; in less affluent areas close to the city's many industrial and shipbuilding sites, domes and turrets are generally absent, bay windows less frequent and curved corners are faceted.

At Walmer Crescent, Thomson was the first, and arguably the only architect since, to have significantly and successfully played with the rules of the Glasgow tenement. As at Caledonia Road, he did so by harnessing a variety of influences, tailoring them to the specific context and brief of the project.

— *Bay windows*

The bay windows of typical tenements project only slightly from the main façade, providing little more than a better view to the ends of the street and a little more light. At Walmer Crescent, Thomson instead used this feature to define the visual rhythm of the overall composition, and to provide additional internal space. Rather than the meek protrusions of individual windows, Thomson extended and twinned the bays of neighbouring apartments, forming the defining formal feature of the terrace.

— *Roof*

Typically, tenement roofs were gabled or hipped with a central ridge protruding – its steep pitch making the slate roof visible from the street. Instead, Thomson created an extended stone parapet wall and altered the roof line to form two smaller duo-pitched

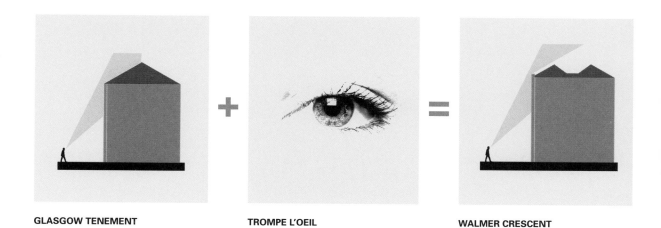

GLASGOW TENEMENT + TROMPE L'OEIL = WALMER CRESCENT

roofs, with a central lead gutter – the roof's reduced overall height ensuring that it would never be seen from street level. This trickery allowed Thomson's tenement to break away from the ubiquitous heavy slate roof, which crowned all of Glasgow's domestic architecture. Presenting only articulated stone gave the building a solid, unified presence and an air of 'rugged grandeur',[4] which was decidedly undomestic in character.

— Banded rustication
Glasgow tenements are built of sandstone Ashlar blocks, large regular blocks with squared edges[5] that give the façades a monolithic quality interrupted only by apertures and cornicing. Thomson again eschewed local tradition in favour of Renaissance and Baroque detailing by using banded rustication (a method of accentuating the horizontal masonry joints and minimizing the vertical ones). In keeping with the techniques employed by the architects of sixteenth- and seventeenth-century Rome, the rustication is graduated such that the ground floor level is heavily banded, with the upper floors increasingly less so. Through this treatment, Thomson gave this domestic, ordinary building typology a grand, civic air.

The consistent theme in Thomson's reinvention of the building typology was grandeur. Thomson was likely playing to his audience, and no doubt impressed his client and future rich apartment owners with his unique iteration of the Glasgow tenement. Crucially, he incorporated global influences by adapting local building elements, retaining a rugged, uncompromising appearance suited to both the building typology and the city.

Buck's Head Building
The Buck's Head Building in Glasgow city centre was completed in 1863 and further extended in 1864. Taking an opposite approach from that used at Walmer Crescent, where an existing building typology was updated and reinvented, here Thomson took a new, foreign building typology – the warehouse – and assimilated it into the fabric of the city on a central, historic site.

BUCK'S HEAD BUILDING Glasgow, 1863

2 — Analyse

GARDNER'S WAREHOUSE John Baird (Primus), Glasgow, 1856

By the 1860s Glasgow had asserted itself as a global city of industry and commerce. Its expansion required a new building typology to store and display the goods that passed through its docks: the warehouse. Thomson designed warehouses before and after the Buck's Head Building, but it was here that he truly embraced the possibilities of this new typology in the materials used, the external colour, and large expanses of glazing.

— *Cast iron*
At first the slim, delicate nature of cast iron when compared with stone does not appear to lend itself to the solidity of Thomson's style. Thomson had used cast iron before, but only internally, as a means of minimizing internal structural elements. This was his first use of cast iron on the exterior of a building. Following the innovations at Joseph Paxton's Crystal Palace in London (1851) and John Baird's Gardner's Warehouse in Glasgow (1856), Thomson experimented with two-storey high, elegantly tapered and exotically detailed cast-iron columns, which provided a counterpoint to the solidity of the stone upper floor and dormers above. Through such prominent use of cast iron, Thomson was making a clear contribution to a modern city of invention and progress.

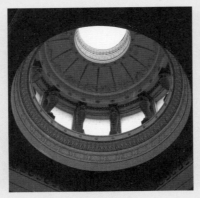

POLYCHROMATIC EXTERIOR
Buck's Head Building

POLYCHROMATIC INTERIOR
Holmwood House

POLYCHROMATIC INTERIOR
Holmwood House

BUCK'S HEAD BUILDING Glasgow, 1863

HORTA HOUSE Victor Horta, Brussels, 1901

— *Colour*

The use of cast iron on the exterior of the building gave Thomson another opportunity inspired by his beloved Ancient Greeks – the use of polychromatic colour schemes. He had become renowned for his daring polychromatic interiors – particularly at Holmwood House, where the interior was fashioned in a palette of muted reds, greens and blues, and in the timber doors of his churches – but with cast iron he had the opportunity to bring colour to the façade of his building. Unlike the sandstone used in his other buildings, cast iron had to be painted to protect it from corrosion.[6] Thomson therefore took this functional requirement and imbued it with an exoticism rooted in his influences, colouring the cast iron orange, blue, ivory and purple. This bold use of colour against the backdrop of local sandstone embodies the harmony between global and local, ancient and modern in Thomson's work.

— Windows

Another innovation by Thomson in the Buck's Head Building was the increased ratio of void to solid, or glass to stone, in his façade. Typically, the openings in Thomson's works are deep reveals carved from monolithic stone with elaborate detailing. At Buck's Head the central section of the façade almost appears like curtain walling – with the stone piers between the large plate-glass windows hidden behind the delicate cast-iron columns. Perhaps liberated by the earlier innovations of Paxton and Baird, Thomson used this structural economy to great aesthetic and functional effect. The warehouses would let in more light for customers to adequately view the goods on display, while the windows were treated with an almost Art Nouveau (a style that would not surface until twenty or so years later) flair, not seen before in his work.

Fittingly, Thomson made this new building typology for the burgeoning city modern and daring. The Buck's Head Building was almost an anomaly in the overall canon of his works, as he embraced and integrated the latest advances in technology with his Antiquarian influences – a watershed moment in structural logic.[7]

Harnessing influences

Thomson's work can teach the image-overloaded architects of today some valuable lessons in harnessing tastes and influences to create exotic yet local, modern yet timeless architecture:

— Influences should always be filtered and analysed, not blindly copied.
— Fully study and interrogate your influences or precedents to appreciate the complexities of applying them to your own designs.
— The use of influences in a design should be driven by what they will achieve, not simply using them because you like them.
— Use influences in a way that will add symbolic or functional gravitas to the building, the aims of its client and its context.
— Don't be afraid to mix your influences – use civic buildings as references for designing a domestic building – or vice versa.
— Remember that all buildings have applicable qualities, regardless of typology.
— Embrace new technology, but do so in a fashion that is timeless and rooted in more ancient ideals. If not, your building will date as quickly as the technology.
— Use global influences in tandem with local conditions and traditions to create a universal yet particular response.

If, like Thomson, we can do all of the above, then we can achieve an architecture borne of the careful selection and study of our influences, at once global and local, radical and timeless.

RECLAIM

reclaim, *verb*
From Latin – *reclāmāre* (to protest, to shout out)
1. (transitive) To claim back; to re-assert one's right to a particular title, possession, role, etc.
2. (intransitive) To protest; to object.

Architects are the compères of the construction industry – no longer the star acts, but the hosts. They host the client's money and aspirations; the authorities' rules and regulations; the engineers' constraints and limitations; the contractors' programme and budget. Architects bring these acts together into a smooth-running, presentable package to be marketed and sold, with the odd punchline or song of their own to sing if they're lucky.

Is that enough, though? How can we reclaim our status as creators and performers, rather than mere presenters surrounded by more influential figures?

Learn to be chief builders
When approached by builders puzzled by a tricky construction detail on the Duomo in Florence, Filippo Brunelleschi would make a wax or clay model or carve up a turnip to illustrate what he wanted.[1] His acute understanding of the technical aspects of building allowed him to communicate his vision in such a natural and intuitive manner. Like Brunelleschi, we need to learn how our designs are actually built, not simply design them halfway and expect the builder to work out the rest. The concept depends on attention to detail to be fully realized. If that means architects learning how to build as students, making 1:1 scale models of details or living on site – then so be it. Without this, the client will ultimately lose trust in the architect's ability to deliver anything better than a half-baked idea.

Develop our own projects
One of the most depressing things I have heard in my career is a former boss worrying about future work and proclaiming 'All I need is to meet a rich man'. He relied entirely on richer, more powerful clients, making all sorts of compromises and concessions along the way.

Let us not simply follow the clients' agendas. Much like a film director who breaks free from the commercial demands of the studios, or the musician who starts their own record label, as architects we need to get to a point where we are designing the buildings and projects we want and need to, not whatever the client or developer tells us to. Why not buy land and do what you want with it, to contribute to society and progress architecture, rather than assisting developers in using land as a commodity? Why not devise a concept and use innovative means of funding to get it off the ground rather than waiting around for the dream job, which may never come? That is not to say that meaningful, beautiful projects cannot be created out of clients' constraints and

　　　　　　　　　　　　　　　　　　　2 — Analyse

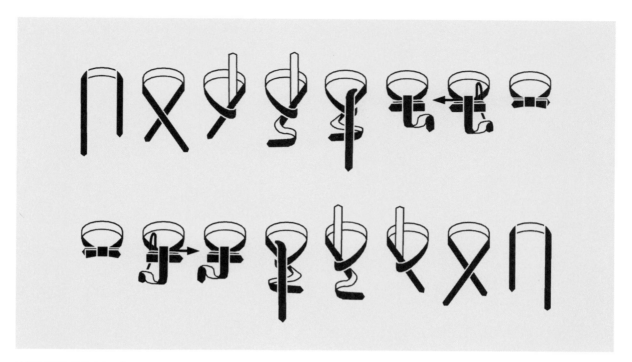

LET'S TAKE OUR COMPÈRE'S BOW TIE OFF ...

desires. However, too often this dynamic can stifle creativity and limit opportunities for social benefit. Only when we redress this imbalance will we be true creators – not simply facilitating someone else's ideas or commercial goals.

Be truthful with our clients

Architects have the gift and the curse of a generally utopian outlook – which can make us visionary and ambitious, but also over-confident and oblivious to potential defects in our designs. We must never lose our utopian spirit; it is what defines us. However, we must prove that our ideas work in reality – and be honest about how they will work and their impact. We need to be more like scientists, quantifying predicted change by gathering evidence. Will the design qualities of a project actually add value to a house or area? Find out how much. What will the psychological impact of a space be on its users? Employ virtual reality technology and a psychologist to predict it. Only by using empirical evidence will we achieve leaner, more productive designs closer to our lofty ideals.

By taking control of our technical role, creating our own projects and proving that our ideas work, we can therefore reclaim our role as creators.

SEAWEED FARM PROPOSAL
Arisaig, UK, J. Tait, 2008

RESPECT

Politicians, ugly buildings and whores

respect, *verb*
From Latin – *respicere* (to look back at, regard)
1. (transitive) To hold in high regard or esteem.
2. (transitive) To show appropriate attention to.
3. (transitive) To take into account, show consideration of.

'Course I'm respectable, I'm old. Politicians, ugly buildings, whores all get respectable if they last long enough.'
— Noah Cross, *Chinatown*, 1974

In Roman Polanski's 1974 film *Chinatown*, the industrialist villain Noah Cross includes 'ugly' buildings in his statement of his own respectability. The implication is that if you are around for long enough to bear the scars of successive events, you start to gain respectability despite earlier actions.

Let's assume there are always buildings deemed ugly by certain groups of people at a particular moment in time. This could be due to a number of factors – perhaps they are formally shocking or bold, maybe they do not adhere to a perceived norm, or they might be juxtaposed with their immediate context in a way that offends – functionally or socially they represent something displeasing to the mainstream. However, these 'ugly' buildings naturally become assimilated into the urban landscape, gathering grime, sustaining knocks, being used daily, and eventually receding into the background as their newness fades. Buildings once perceived as radical or controversial become less so over time. The public become anaesthetized to whatever it was that appalled them in the first place – and there are always new things to be appalled by.

But how can we speed up this process of acceptance, without diluting the ambition and radicalness of our architecture? Here are some strategies:

Do not demolish an old, treasured structure to make a new building
Demolishing an old and loved structure as part of a new development is problematic for two reasons. First, the architect is asserting that their architecture is more worthwhile than whatever preceded it. Second, the architect is at risk of removing something that may have emotional value to the inhabitants of the local or even national area.

That is not to say that everything old is immune to demolition. If the existing structure doesn't work or is in irretrievable disrepair, this can be an option. First, though, you should appraise the case for keeping existing structures and incorporating them into the new proposals. Even if your new building is better than what was there previously, if all traces of the past are obliterated it may take the public a long time to accept this.

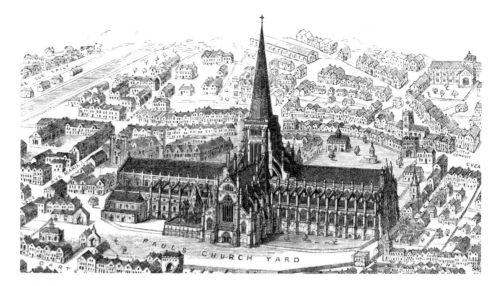

OLD ST PAUL'S Gothic spire

NEW ST PAUL'S Renaissance dome

Sir Christopher Wren devised a creative solution to this conundrum in his original design for St Paul's Cathedral in London. Tasked in 1660 with assessing the structure of Old St Paul's, built in the eleventh century, Wren concluded that the spire and tower would need to be demolished. Wren knew this would not be welcomed – particularly as his proposal was for a new Italianate dome – a decidedly untraditional and un-English symbol. Wren therefore proposed to construct the new dome around the existing spire; only when the dome was built and the spire was hidden from view would it be demolished.[1] Wren's logic was that only when the public saw the 'majesty' of the new dome would they accept the demolition of the old spire.[2] Wren's plan was unnecessary, however, as in 1666 the Great Fire of London did the job of demolition for him.

THE SHARD Under construction with St Paul's Cathedral beneath; view from Hampstead Heath, London, 2011

Do not spoil the view of an old and loved structure

In a circular tale of acceptance, let's fast-forward nearly 350 years from the completion of Wren's dome to Renzo Piano's Shard, also in London. The building was the subject of outcry by various historic and public bodies because of its relative proximity to the dome of St Paul's – the primary focus of eight out of thirteen 'protected city views' in London at the time.

Eventually the Shard, or London Bridge Tower as it is formally known, rose above these concerns – but it was not a straightforward birth. Had it been sited on any number of other prominent riverside London locations, away from the protected views of St Paul's, or had it responded to its location in terms of height or form, it might not have had such a difficult infancy. Then again, it wouldn't be the Shard – an easily recognizable symbol; a bombastic landmark at the very heart of the city. It remains to be seen if the Shard will attain the same level of respectability as St Paul's in 300 years' time.

If proposing something radical, cultivate a nickname

Nicknames are a sign of acceptance. Think of children: a new kid joins a group, and after a while he or she is given a nickname. The nickname is only given on two conditions: the child proves that they are worthy of receiving this token of acceptance; and henceforth they wear their new name with pride.

2 — Analyse

122 LEADENHALL STREET The 'Cheesegrater' (Rogers, Stirk, Harbour + Partners, 2014) and 30 St Mary Axe, aka the 'Gherkin' (Foster + Partners, 2004)

Similar conditions apply to buildings and their nicknames. A nickname reflects a clarity of form and symbolism in the design of a building that makes it instantly familiar. If the nickname sticks, it can help the building become a local or global marker, even an icon. Some examples include London's 'Cheesegrater' (the Leadenhall Building), Glasgow's Armadillo (the Clyde Auditorium) and the 'Beehive' in Wellington (the Executive Wing of the New Zealand Parliament Buildings). Perhaps the most famous building nickname of recent times is Foster + Partners' 'Gherkin' (30 St Mary Axe). Its simple, iconic shape is now an integral component of the modern London skyline – something it achieved within a few years of opening.

It would be impossible and ill-advised to try to design a building with a nickname in mind, but what most buildings with nicknames share is a distinctiveness, sometimes even a radicalness (see Herzog & de Meuron's Bird's Nest Olympic stadium, or OMA's Big Pants tower, both in Beijing) that sets them apart from other buildings of their time and typology. Other less distinctive and ambitious skyscrapers built around the same time as the Gherkin and in the same city include 8 Canada Square, 1 Churchill Place, 25 Bank Street and 40 Bank Street. All are still named by their original address-based names.

Possessing – or not possessing – a nickname is not a marker of quality. However, it can help to fast-track acceptance by those who live with and inhabit your building.

Spend taxpayers' money wisely (preferably not at all)

One of the most effective ways to lose respect, before a crane is even swung, is to be seen to waste public money. If a project is privately financed the general attitude will be more lenient. But spend taxpayers' money and the response is usually very different.

When building with public money, the location of your building project is the first hurdle. If it is in a large metropolis, those outside the metropolis will complain that public money is only ever spent on the big cities. Meanwhile, build in rural areas or smaller towns, and city dwellers will question why public money has been wasted on a project that hardly anyone will see. Secondly, everyone will have a more worthwhile reason for spending the money spent financing your project. More hospitals, more schools, repairing holes in the road ... anything other than your project.

The Millennium Dome project on London's Greenwich Peninsula faced just such criticisms when it was designed by Richard Rogers in 1999 to celebrate the dawn of the new millennium.

Despite being funded almost exclusively by National Lottery proceeds and private finance, 40% of the public believed that the building was entirely funded by public money, and 90% thought that it was partly funded by their hard-earned taxes. Fuelled by tabloid and opposition party outrage the Dome was labelled 'a national embarrassment', 'a shabby tent' and a 'museum of toxic waste' – in stark contrast to the claim that the dome would be a 'beacon to the world'. Many called for its demolition within a year of its grand opening on the eve of the millennium.

There were a number of potential reasons for the failure of the Dome at the time – including financial mismanagement, political infighting and lack of a worthwhile civic purpose – but the moment the project was perceived as being financed with public money it faced a virtually impossible struggle to gain acceptance. These days, however, the building has been rebranded as a privately owned concert venue – and has lasted long enough to achieve an almost benign respectability.

What can we learn from this? An architect cannot shy away from publicly funded projects – that would be commercial and reputational suicide. And when commissioned for public projects, the architect should not curtail their ambition or integrity, playing it safe just because taxpayers' money is at stake. Perhaps all the architect can do is be truthful from the outset about the real projected costs and timescales; advise on sensible and efficient means of procuring the building; minimize changes to the design, particularly at post-tender stage; and communicate swiftly and effectively with team members, contractors and client. The only building less respectable than a publicly funded building is an over-budget or delayed publicly funded building.

As Noah Cross says, all buildings achieve a level of respectability if they last long enough – but by considering the four strategies outlined here, perhaps we can accelerate the process.

THE MILLENNIUM DOME Some of the headlines it attracted

'NATIONAL EMBARRASSMENT!'

'SHABBY TENT!'

'MUSEUM OF TOXIC WASTE!'

OBSCURE

Parametricism is not an epochal style

obscure, *verb*
From Latin – *obscurus* (dark)
1. To occlude, make unclear,
vague or hidden.
2. To cover from view.
3. To cloud over.

Architecture is increasingly subject to the deliberate use of obscure concepts and impenetrable prose. This obscurantism has two main effects.

First, it gives basic ideas a false sense of intellectual worth, perpetuated by jargon. This affects the architectural profession's ability to communicate – with itself, and the wider world. Concepts and projects should be explained concisely – otherwise interest or confidence in what is being proposed is lost.

Second, a circle of obscurantism between professors and students, and between architects, can create an environment in which projects are judged by descriptions of the work, and not the work itself. Obscurantism is particularly prevalent in the discourse around parametric architecture, or parametricism, and the proclamation that it is 'an epochal style', as important as the Baroque or Modernism.[1]

Organization

Parametricism is about 'the ordering of social processes'.[2] To elaborate: 'architecture's societal function is the innovative ordering and framing of communicative interaction'.[3] This might sound radical, but as an example of architecture's 'innovative ordering and framing of communicative interaction' one of the 'styles' key proponents, Patrik Schumacher, encourages us to 'imagine this city, Boston, being covered in an undifferentiated tarmac surface … all social order and distinctions would collapse'.[4] Therefore, a prime example of this 'new' theory is something that people have been doing for millennia – demarcating and defining routes and passages to order movement.

Architecture can create, influence and assist social processes, without that having to be its essential aim. To insist that architecture must 'order social processes' seems overly didactic. Schumacher also proposes that only his new architectural style is sufficient to order the social processes of today's 'post-Fordist' (industrialized) network. However, look at the magnetism of the Place de la Bastille in Paris – a consistent protest space from the eighteenth century to the present day; the daily ebb and flow of people through Grand Central Station in New York over the past century; or the million visitors a year who still visit Stonehenge in the UK. All are structures or spaces conceived in the past that are still relevant today.

2 — Analyse

OBSOLETE?
Place de la Bastille, Paris, 2015

OBSOLETE?
Grand Central Station, New York, 2013

OBSOLETE?
Stonehenge, Wiltshire, UK, 2010

PARAMETRICISM?
Skara Brae, Orkney, 3100 BC

PARAMETRICISM?
Larabanga, Ghana, 1421

PARAMETRICISM?
Franziskanerkirche, Salzburg, 1635

PARAMETRICISM?
TWA Terminal, New York, 1962

NOT DYNAMIC?
Roland-Garros, Paris

NOT DYNAMIC?
The Arches, Glasgow

NOT DYNAMIC?
Swan Lake, Pula Arena, Croatia

Articulation

For Schumacher, 'Articulation recognizes that cognitive, sentient beings navigate space via perception.'[5] This means that people use their memories and power of perception while experiencing and negotiating space, which has been said before – by J.G. Ballard, Henri Lefebvre or Rem Koolhaas, for example. Ask anyone in the street about how they experience buildings and they will probably relate memories or experiences of the spaces or forms.

This 'great epochal style' is aligned with the Baroque, referencing its asymmetry and amorphousness as factors that create unity.[6] Parametricism is often promoted as the answer to the failures of the perceived over-simplicity and disjointedness of Modernism.[7] But what does parametricism entail? The definition of parametricism is that 'all elements of architecture have become parametrically malleable'.[8]

NOT COMPLEX ENOUGH? Habitat, Montréal, Moshe Safdie, 1967

NOT COMPLEX ENOUGH? Casa da Música, Porto, OMA, 2005

NOT COMPLEX ENOUGH?
Serpentine Pavilion, London, Sou Fujimoto, 2013

This translates as the rejection of straight lines and primitive solids in favour of splines, nurbs and blobs, via computational design; supposedly an ontological shift from the preceding 5,000 years of architecture in which only primitive solids (cylinders, cubes, pyramids, rectangles) were used.[9] However, the existence of contour-hugging Neolithic settlements, hand-sculpted adobe huts; complex Gothic vaults, or the free-flowing Modernism of Niemeyer or Saarinen would seem to suggest otherwise.

Furthermore, I would argue that the space enclosed by a square or rectangle can be freer and more open than a space defined by wilfully twisting curves and the unusable spaces they create. A space doesn't have to look dynamic to be dynamic: think of tennis players on a court, ravers in a basement club, or an orchestra in a recital hall. None of these spaces need to be curved to mirror or order the social processes taking place in them. The straight line can also provide variety and complexity. Look at Moshe Safdie's Habitat 67 building, or Rem Koolhaas's Porto Concert Hall, or Sou Fujimoto's Serpentine Pavilion – all provide complexity and richness of form and function without a spline, nurb or curve in sight.

Signification

Last is signification: 'Sentient, socialized learning bodies navigate and act on the basis of signs.'[10] Parametricism is centred on the belief that people need symbols and signs to recognize the world, and that digitally created patterns therefore fill a perceived void in current architecture.[11]

FUNCTIONAL PATTERN
Rock strata

FUNCTIONAL PATTERN
Peacock feathers

FUNCTIONAL PATTERN
Cobweb

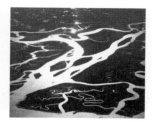

FUNCTIONAL PATTERN
River

DECORATIVE PATTERN
Library and Learning Centre,
Vienna, Zaha Hadid, 2013

DECORATIVE PATTERN
Bridge Pavilion, Zaragoza,
Zaha Hadid, 2008

DECORATIVE PATTERN
Innsbruck Hungerburgbahn,
Vienna, Zaha Hadid, 2007

DECORATIVE PATTERN
Opera House, Guangzhou,
Zaha Hadid, 2010

STRUCTURAL PATTERN
Palazzetto della Sport, Rome,
Pier Luigi Nervi, 1957

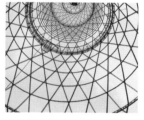

STRUCTURAL PATTERN
Shabolovka Tower, Moscow,
Vladimir Shukhov, 1922

STRUCTURAL PATTERN
Metropol Parasol, Sevilla,
Jürgen Mayer, 2008

STRUCTURAL PATTERN
GC Prostho Research Center,
Kasugai-shi, Kengo Kuma, 2012

Such patterns may be unrecognizable to their inhabitants, however, losing their value; there is also a fundamental problem with creating patterns for patterns' sake. As a counter-example, consider the varied and beautiful patterns in nature: the strata of a rock formation, the feathers of a peacock, the intricate weave of a cobweb, the gentle meander of a river. All of these are driven by necessity; the fact they are beautiful is incidental. To create patterns not born of necessity and function is to risk creating forms devoid of purpose. Again, obscurantism clouds the view.

For examples of honest structures that create functional, beautiful structural patterns born of economy and necessity, look to the ribbed ceilings of Pier Luigi Nervi, the diagrid structures of Vladimir Shukov or the recent interlocking timber structures of Kengo Kuma. Ideas should be progressive, daring and revolutionary, and the language used to describe them should not be constructed purely for effect. Radical ideas and direct words will give clarity to what we are trying to achieve, enabling us to connect with the people who really matter – the users of our buildings.

HEROIZE

Oedipus Rex and the Modernist architect

heroize, *verb*
From Ancient Greek – *heros* (a hero or
warrior)
1. (transitive) To represent as heroic,
or as a hero.

In Ancient Greek tragedies, the plot focuses on a central figure, a hero – defined by Aristotle as one who 'falls into adversity, not through vice or depravity, but because he errs in some way'.[1] In other words, he is the architect of his own downfall. The ideal tragic hero invokes pity, that someone once so great could fall so far – and fear, that this fate could befall any of us. I would argue that the Modernist architect was a tragic hero.

The original tragic hero was Oedipus Rex in Sophocles' eponymous play. Oedipus searches for the truth that will rid the city of a plague brought by the gods to avenge King Laius's unsolved murder. The citizens turn to Oedipus for answers, as the 'king of the land, our greatest power'.[2] Oedipus furiously dismisses advice, believing only he can save the city from destruction. This hubris is his downfall, though, as he discovers the truth: he is the source of the plague, unaware that King Laius was his father, whom he killed in a fight. Distraught, Oedipus blinds himself and cedes the crown to his brother-in-law, his fall from grace complete.

Like Oedipus, the Modernist architect searched for truth. Like Oedipus too, their quest was unflinching and they stopped at nothing to achieve it, as expressed by Le Corbusier: 'A question of morality; lack of truth is intolerable, we perish in untruth.'[3] This search for truth was all-encompassing; all that had gone before was seen as a 'lie'.[4] Modernist architects sought truth in architecture at all scales and in all building typologies:

— *Use* – from strict, rational zoning of ideal cities and masterplans to the reordering of domestic life at the scale of the home.
— *Form* – from pure, white unadorned forms of buildings to the clean lines and uncomplicated perspectives of interiors.
— *Construction* – new methods based on machines and industry were promoted, ushering in universal standardization and repetition.
— *Detail* – the details of a building were seen as an expression of its entire ethos: 'God is in the details' was a common mantra.

Like Oedipus, Modernist architects were men and women of courage and idealism, but also of action – they sought to express the spirit of their epoch in built form. Like the diseased city of Thebes over which Oedipus Rex presided, the war-ravaged cities of Europe in the 1940s provided the perfect setting in which to implement the discovered 'truths'. As Oedipus says of his plague-ridden city, 'After a painful search, I found one cure. I acted at once.'[5]

2 — Analyse

TRAGIC HEROES Oedipus Rex and Le Corbusier

Modernist architects' *tabula rasa* approach to design was heroic in scale, ambition and action. It was also undoubtedly noble in intention. The pretext for much Modernist architecture was to provide environments conducive to rapid social change; to bring architecture in line with technological advances; to provide dwellings that would meet the needs of all social classes; to build with modern, appropriate materials; to provide greater access to greenery and fresh air.

However, like Oedipus, the very traits that made Modernist architects heroes – courage, vision, intelligence, decisiveness – were paired with those that led to their downfall – hubris, overzealousness, ignorance and hastiness. These combined, opposing traits were responsible for the creation of glistening new forms of architecture that embodied purity, clarity and vision, yet which revealed their flaws over time.

Reliance on the car

Modernist city plans were designed around the car at a time (the early 1960s) when only 4% of the world's population owned one.[6] The intention was to allow traffic to flow unimpeded through the city, while pedestrians could enjoy open space and freedom of movement, undisturbed by the noise and pollution of cars. In reality this separation created vast swathes of land not navigable on foot, and necessitated bridges and tunnels that took pedestrians away from street life. As architectural theorist Kenneth Frampton has noted, this concept was flawed from the outset: '... the automobile having effectively destroyed the great city (in the eyes of Le Corbusier) could now be exploited as an instrument for its salvation (also in the eyes of Le Corbusier)'.[7]

INTENTION

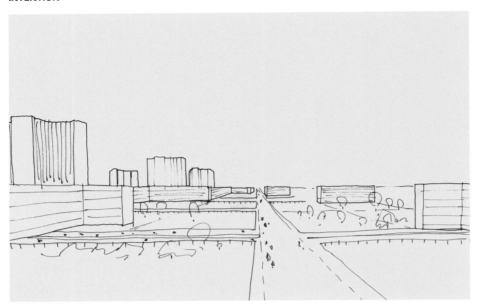

HAMARTIC FLAWS
Was reliance on the car a product of ignorance? Modernist architects had not bothered to imagine what these elevated highways would look like or how they would function at street level. Barriers were created to pedestrian movement, views out from the apartments were blocked, and there was a linear rupture in the continuous urban grain of the pre-Modern city.

REALITY

Reliance on abstracted geometry, order and repetition

In opposition to the organic evolution of the historical city and its layers of activity and function, Modernist architects favoured 'zoning'. They arranged the city as a compartmentalized series of functions according to use: educational, business, cultural, residential and so on. This strict zoning, implemented in cities throughout the world, was intended to rationalize both the movement of people and the appearance of these zones. In reality this approach 'marooned' its inhabitants – for example in strictly residential zones where they were separated from the centres of leisure and production previously on their doorstep, or in business zones that were deserted at night when the workers were at home. Meanwhile, sameness and repetition characterized buildings in these zones. The chaos and confusion that make city life so exhilarating had been designed out.

Reliance on technology

Modernist architecture often used height and verticality, favouring dense 'point' blocks over the mid-rise (three- to five-storey) buildings of the past. This abrupt shift in height was facilitated by technology – specifically the invention of the elevator. Towers were intended to free up green space at ground level, providing inhabitants with enhanced views and sunlight. However, this open space between buildings was often little used and soulless, and people no longer interacted spontaneously in busy streets. The reliance on technology also ignored the possibility of failure of the elevators.

It was in part the implementation of Modernist ideals that sullied the architects' heroic intentions – failure was not purely a result of design. Cost-cutting by developers and local authorities minimized glazed openings and eroded the commitment to high-quality materials of early Modernism, and poor workmanship and build quality often accelerated buildings' deterioration.[8] By the 1970s, new Modernist living environments were turned into scapegoats, erroneously held responsible for a rising crime rate.[9]

When Modernist ideals have been applied more sensitively, the architecture has proved more enduring. At Le Corbusier's Unité d'habitation in Marseille, or Lafayette Park, Detroit, by Mies van der Rohe, or the Southbank Centre in London, incredible forms and structures create enjoyable, timeless places that add immeasurably to their environment and the lives of their users.

What does this all tell us about how architects can avoid becoming tragic heroes or heroines? Various answers emerged from the late 1960s onwards, ranging from the implausibly futuristic to the depressingly retrograde. Think for example of the fantastical creations of Archigram and Superstudio, with their provocative and subversive 'Walking Cities' and various mega-structures, which Frampton deemed 'either truly indeterminate or incapable of being realized and appropriated by society'.[10] Other Modernists defected to Postmodernism, choosing to embrace symbolism and detail,[11] like Philip Johnson and James Stirling, who knew that clients and the public no longer supported Modernist ideals. Meanwhile, Leon Krier led a historicist revivalism, producing versions of buildings from past epochs – and others favoured 'community architecture', claiming to return

INTENTION

HAMARTIC FLAWS

Was reliance on repetition a product of hubris? Modernists believed in the power of their abstract pattern-making – city as repetitive pattern. The danger latent in these theoretical plans was not exposed until they were built, as repetition became dull, stifling and constricting to the surrounding city and its inhabitants.

Was reliance on technology a product of over-zealousness? By swiftly positioning technology at the core of these radical concepts, the ubiquitous tower block was born. The advance of technology eradicated the millennia-old need for streets, as the spaces between the blocks become sterile and bleak – exposed to weather and lacking in surveillance.

REALITY

power to a building's users by engaging them in the design process but relinquishing their design capacities and responsibilities as architects.

Perhaps such approaches lacked the potential for tragedy as they did not possess its prerequisite – heroism. Of course, there was the heroic work of Brutalism – the late work of Le Corbusier, along with Marcel Breuer, Paul Randolph, Alison and Peter Smithson, Erno Goldfinger and Denys Lasdun, for example. The Brutalists expanded the Modernist vocabulary in their own way with the sensuality and freedom that the earlier dogma lacked. However, as a movement Modernism was dying, and by the late 1970s, the raging fire had burnt out.

The answer to achieving the lofty ideals of Modernism, while accounting for the realities of the world around us lies, I think, in the approach of a man who arose from its embers – Rem Koolhaas. Koolhaas had the benefit of hindsight – setting up his practice, OMA, in 1975.[12] In my view, Koolhaas is neither tragic nor heroic. For him, the failure of Modernism had already occurred ('Modernism's alchemistic promise – to transform quantity into quality through abstraction and repetition – has been a failure, a hoax ...'[13]), meaning that his approach was not the heroic Modernist one of bending the world to his will. Instead, he proclaimed that 'Architecture can't do anything that the culture doesn't'.[14]

Koolhaas recognizes that he operates within 'Junkspace' – 'the residue mankind leaves on the planet' – in a world of 'terminal hollowness'.[15] It is an architecture of effect, not substance, characterized by escalators, partitions, mirrors, atria, domes and of myriad different styles and regurgitated histories. Its lack of purity and honesty is the antithesis of Modernism. As he puts it, 'Architects could never explain space; Junkspace is our punishment for their mystifications.'[16]

Koolhaas does not fight this chaotic, untruthful environment, attempting to purge its ills as the tragic hero would. Instead, he reviews that which fascinates and abhors him (shopping, globalization, genericness) – analysing things objectively and then using his findings to inform his architectural approach. He doesn't seek an absolute truth, but instead discovers multiple, conflicting truths. Explaining his seemingly contradictory approach, he says: 'That has been my entire life story. Running against the current and running with the current. Sometimes running with the current is underestimated. The acceptance of certain realities doesn't preclude idealism. It can lead to certain breakthroughs.'[17]

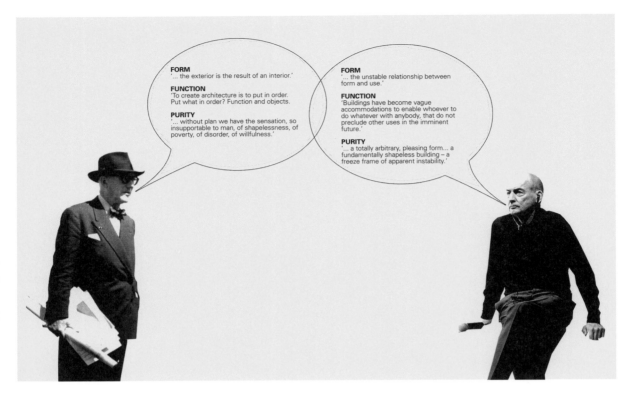

TRAGIC HERO AND PRAGMATIC UTOPIAN Le Corbusier and Rem Koolhaas

The designs of Rem Koolhaas are always:

— *Believable, buildable but daring and new* – Koolhaas is a man of dreams and action – neither a 'paper architect' nor one who builds without ambition or thought.

— *Unconcerned with style* – His designs are embedded in analysis; a unique response to the forces exerted on them rather than influenced by a particular style.

— *Aware, never historicist* – He is acutely aware of the historical context in which his designs are placed. He doesn't dismiss or eradicate, ape or copy. His buildings are of their time and of their future.

— *A product of authorship* – Koolhaas is not 'blinded'[18] by other architecture, or generic architecture for the masses. He recognizes the importance of authorship by studying the conditions of a project and proposing bespoke solutions.

In short, this is the antithesis of the didactic Modernist design approach, as demonstrated in the examples that follow:

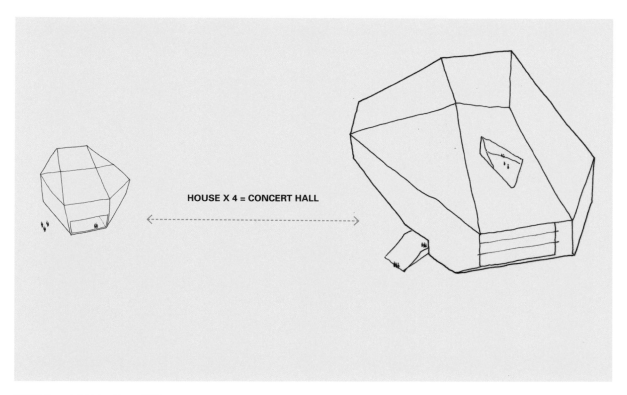

HOUSE X 4 = CONCERT HALL

FORM Casa da Música, Porto, 2005

Form – Casa da Música, Porto (2005)

Arguably Koolhaas's finest realized work,[19] perhaps the true message is in the design process rather than the finished product. Casa da Música began life as a house. The client was never convinced, however, and eventually cancelled the project around the same time as the competition entry for the Porto Concert Hall was due to be submitted. Struggling with that design, Koolhaas saw a glimmer of hope in the discarded house project. By simply scaling the design up, he found the way through his designer's block. The tunnel form of the living room became the perfect shoebox auditorium, while the multiple storage and utility spaces that fed into the original living room became breakout and circulation spaces for the audience when enlarged. Koolhaas had turned the old Modernist maxim that 'form ever follows function' on its head: 'what had been tailored for one very specific condition could be suddenly used for a completely different purpose'.[20] By allowing chance and opportunism into the design process, Koolhaas created one of the finest buildings of his career.

CONTRADICTORY FUNCTIONS + ARBITRARY ENVELOPE = IMPURE RANDOMNESS

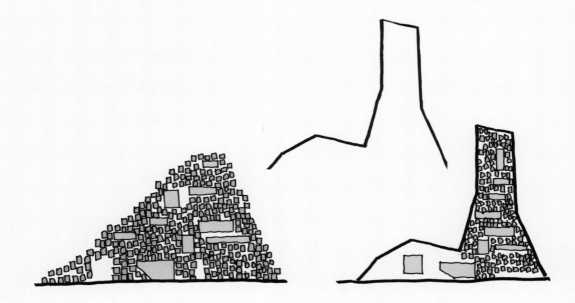

PURITY TVCC Building, Beijing, 2002

SPECIFIC TOWERS + GENERIC FLOORS = ADAPTABLE BUILDING

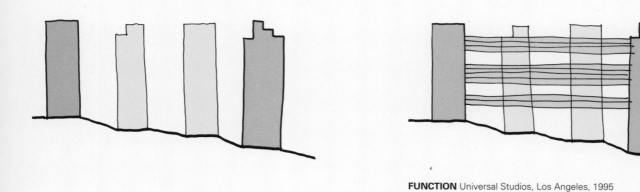

FUNCTION Universal Studios, Los Angeles, 1995

Purity – TVCC Building, Beijing (2002)

The TVCC Building is the lesser-known sibling of the CCTV Headquarters in Beijing. Containing a vast array of functions – including theatre, digital cinemas, recording studios, conference and exhibition spaces, hotel, ballroom and spa – the building posed a challenge: how best to order and arrange these contradictory functions? Koolhaas did not attempt to resolve these contradictions, instead casting them all as separate volumes and arranging them in a 'totally arbitrary, pleasing form.'[23] This created a varied collection of volumes clad in a single skin, which made for an arresting architecture of chance, while creating new relationships between seemingly incompatible functions, and between public and private spaces. By recognizing the contradictions in the brief, Koolhaas did not attempt to resolve them by reduction like a Modernist would; instead he embraced them to create a complex architectural response.

Function – Universal Studios, Los Angeles (1995)

Recognizing the inherent conflict in the fact that a construction project takes around five years from inception to completion, while a large corporate entity is in 'constant flux, if not turmoil',[21] Koolhaas again went against Modernist dogma with this building. Rather than slavishly design the building around functions that might be obsolete in five years' time, Koolhaas instead designed the building to accommodate various unknown future uses. He achieved this by building in both the generic and the unique: no matter how turbulent the composition of the company becomes, the office floors provide the necessary flexibility, while the towers guarantee that a single entity is maintained.[22] By designing in this way, Koolhaas designed for every possible future function. He did not impose an order that might have been out of date before the building was even realized. Rather than Modernist order, hierarchy and functionalism, Koolhaas embraced consolidation, expansion and reconfiguration in the future life of the building.

These three examples show how Koolhaas's work challenges architectural conventions, and in so doing avoids the flawed characteristics of Modernism: hubris (he recognizes that the architect is no longer 'master of all things'), overzealousness (he has no desire to bend society to his will, instead finding ways to achieve his aims by stealth and lateral thinking), ignorance (he is fascinated by the world around him, studying it intensely) and hastiness (his architecture is never absolute, always considered). He shuns over-organization, overstating of influence, over-reliance on function, overestimation of architecture's ability to change society for its own sake. Instead, through acute awareness of the current metropolitan condition and economic climate, he reconciles the loftiest of ideals with the harshest of realities simultaneously in his architectural approach.

IMPROVE

Challenging the brief

improve, *verb*
From Latin – *prodesse* (useful, to do good)
1. (intransitive) To bring about or make
better in quality or condition.
2. (transitive) To render land or buildings
more useful and profitable by betterments.
3. (transitive) To achieve an increase
in quality or standards in comparison
with previous or others.

Altruism and architecture

What is the point of designing and building anything if you don't believe it will improve on existing conditions? Why invest emotions, ink, your time, other peoples' time, building materials and PR if your work does not in some way positively contribute to people's lives? This may seem a naive viewpoint in today's world, dominated by market forces and greed, but I would argue that altruism and the improvement of our world are the essence of the architect's role.

In the design and construction process of a building the architect often stands alone in pursuit of this improvement, sometimes aided by the client. Structural engineers solve abstracted problems; services engineers remedy ventilation and heating problems in the finished space; project managers focus on process, schedule and budget; contractors build to make money; developers hope to convert architecture into profit. All these collaborators contribute immeasurably to the final project, but essentially their roles are limited, restricted to the conception and birth of a building rather than its life. Conversely, everything the architect does should place the eventual life of a building above all other concerns. Will it bring the users joy? Will it bring those who look at it joy? No one cares now that the Sydney Opera House was completed ten years late and fourteen times over budget.[1]

The quest for improvement transcends architectural scales, types and functions: from the adaptation of a small apartment to provide more light and storage for its inhabitants; through creation of a protected outdoor play space in a nursery; to an aesthetic intervention that creates a new marker for an area or city; or the implementation of a masterplan to open up new routes and provide greater permeability through a city.

The challenge for architects

An optimistic viewpoint is more often challenged than accepted in the real world. The challenge becomes more acute for architects, the scope for altruism less clear, with a brief that does not appear to be concerned with the life of the building. Some architects don't accept the challenge: they build to attract clients, to stroke their own egos, to make money. They are facilitators, not creators.

2 — Analyse

DESIGN BY A FACILITATOR

DESIGN BY AN ALTRUISTIC ARCHITECT

STUDENT HOUSING, TYPICAL
Minimum of openings in corridor wall, minimum width, minimum everything – corridor is only a route

STUDENT HOUSING, PARIS, OFIS ARCHITECTS, 2012
Wide corridors, open mesh wall with views and light – turn corridor into a social space

Student housing stacked like rabbit hutches, private gated complexes that shun life outside, or offices defined solely by rentable area are examples of how, in the hands of the architectural facilitators, the client's or developer's will is bluntly translated into built form. Meanwhile, in an altruistic architect's hands the latent possibilities, however small, are made clear through approach, negotiation and delivery.

— *Student housing*
  — Typology characterized by: meanness, economy, repetition
  — Altruistic act: turn circulation into social spaces

OFIS architects proposed 'open-air corridors that run along the rear elevation of the building and are contained behind a tessellated mesh screen' in student accommodation in Paris. Rather than lightless internal corridors, walkways became 'open common space for students',[2] with views out and light brought in. Additionally, common spaces such as entrance areas were widened, with recesses created for built-in furniture. The strict space standards of the individual studios could not be altered, so OFIS focused on the spaces in between, elevating pure circulation to social space.

Improve

COMMUNITY CENTRE
Prague, Czech Republic, J. Tait, 2013

DESIGN BY A FACILITATOR

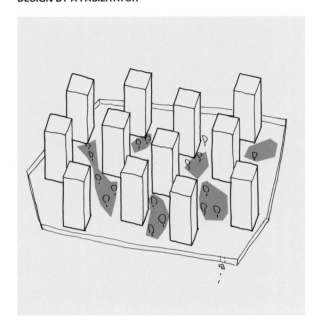

GATED COMMUNITY, TYPICAL
Protected point of entry guards development from outside world;
greenery and open space secondary to built form and private space

DESIGN BY A FACILITATOR

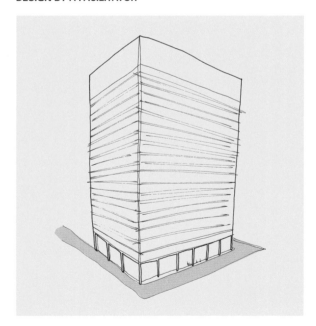

OFFICE BLOCK, TYPICAL
Office block occupies entire site ensuring clear distinction between
public and private, business and society

DESIGN BY AN ALTRUISTIC ARCHITECT

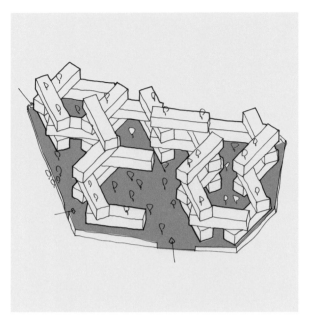

**GATED COMMUNITY, SINGAPORE, BURO OLE SCHEEREN/OMA,
2014** Multiple points of entry increase site permeability; ground and
rooftop public and shared green spaces between informal blocks

DESIGN BY AN ALTRUISTIC ARCHITECT

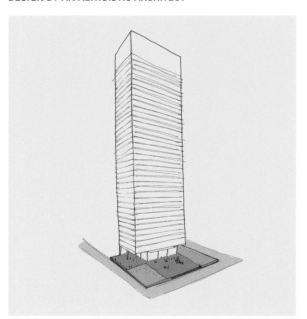

OFFICE BLOCK, NEW YORK, MIES VAN DER ROHE, 1958
Block set back from street to create public plaza; office block tall,
slender and elegant while occupying a smaller base

— *Gated community*

Typology characterized by: defensiveness, enclosure, insularity

Altruistic act: open garden spaces to the public

At the Interlace in Singapore, Ole Scheeren created a gated community that provides public space discreetly and invisibly – flipping the very notion of a gated community on its head. Scheeren created multiple entrances while providing open, green and public space in the form of sky gardens and ground-level plazas where private gardens or cordoned-off spaces would typically be. The informal arrangement of blocks and multiple levels allow the public spaces to recede into the architecture rather than dominate it.

— *Office block*

Typology characterized by: efficiency, rationalization, maximization

Altruistic act: provide public space outside a private building

Mies van der Rohe's Seagram Building in New York responded to a brief to create office accommodation, but also a highly active open plaza, by setting the building back 27 metres (89ft) from the street edge. By raising the plaza above ground level Mies created a threshold space that mediates between office and city, private and public. By using high-quality materials and incorporating seating, water features and sculptures he also ensured its legacy.

In these examples the architects' altruistic instincts compelled them to find ways in which to improve the lives of users and other city dwellers. To paraphrase Oscar Niemeyer: all architecture should be created with an awareness of 'what is important in life ... attempting to make this world a better place in which to live',[3] no matter how challenging that may seem.

IMPROVISE

Calculated spontaneity

improvise, *verb*
From Latin – *improvisus* (unforeseen,
to prepare for a future circumstance)
1. (transitive) To make quickly or compose
without previous preparation.
2. (transitive) To create, arrange or compose
from whatever materials are available to hand.
3. (transitive) To perform on impulse.

To improvise can be described as 'to discern multiple futures, latent inside the constrained present'.[1] Each architectural project presents fleeting opportunities for improvisation. An architect must recognize these and act on them, turning possibility into reality. Here is a short story of architectural improvisation.

The Accidental Heliostat

CLIENT (via text): I'm looking into heliostats for the garden so light can get into the house. Cx

What's a heliostat?! [Quick internet search] ... Hmmm ... OK, basically a big outdoor mirror to reflect sunlight – not quite the minimal aesthetic I was going for. Judging by her furniture, she'll pick the one shaped like a massive mirrored sunflower. And jeez, it costs as much as the rooflight! Surely that will put her off? Need to do something about this ... My fault, though; I told her the north-facing extension will never really get any sunlight – and didn't propose a solution. But hold on, what if the heliostat were integrated into the design? What if it became an extension of the rooflight – a mirrored upstand bouncing south, east and west light back through the glass? She was talking about a roof terrace too, but I dismissed it as too clunky for the scale of the building. Well, the new upstand could form the balustrade for the terrace, giving it more coherence and unity. So let's solve the north-facing problem by bouncing light back via this integrated heliostat (new word learned!), use it to provide part of a balustrade around the roof terrace, and provide a bit of visual interest, too. Right, back to the client quick, before she buys a mirrored sunflower ...

ARCHITECT (via text): Heliostats can be good, but they are expensive. One of the options I'm looking at would make the roof into a kind of heliostat – we can talk about it more when I see you.

CLIENT: Can't wait! Cx

OK, that seems to have covered it for now. Right, how will this thing actually work?

2 — Analyse

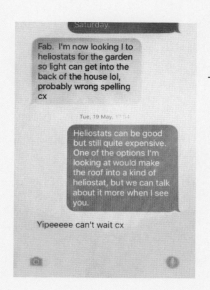

?

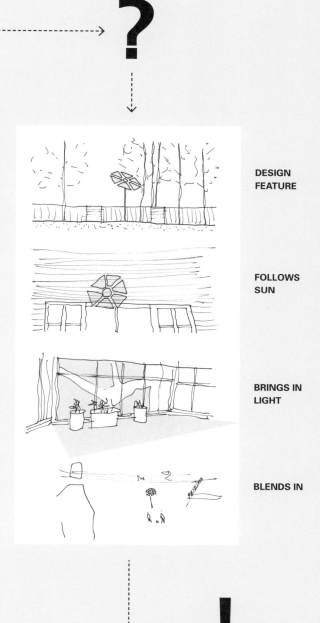

DESIGN
FEATURE

FOLLOWS
SUN

BRINGS IN
LIGHT

BLENDS IN

!

BEFORE HELIOSTAT

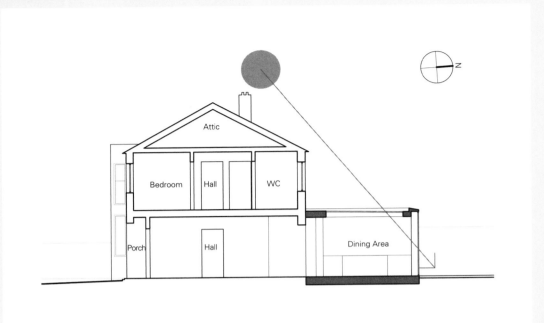

ACCIDENTAL HELIOSTAT

FOLLOWS SUN
All four sides of the upstand are reflective, meaning that east, south and west light can be harnessed and reflected from dawn until dusk

BRINGS IN LIGHT
1m high reflective upstand around rooflight reflects south light into the living area

BEFORE HELIOSTAT

ACCIDENTAL HELIOSTAT

DESIGN FEATURE
The creation of the heliostat unlocked the potential for extending the upstand across the whole area of roof, creating a unified balustraded roof terrace

BLENDS IN
By adapting the roof form the heliostat adds extra visual interest to the previously proposed flat-roofed box – tying in with the roof level of the neighbouring property

EXTENT OF HELIOSTAT

EXTENT OF TERRACE

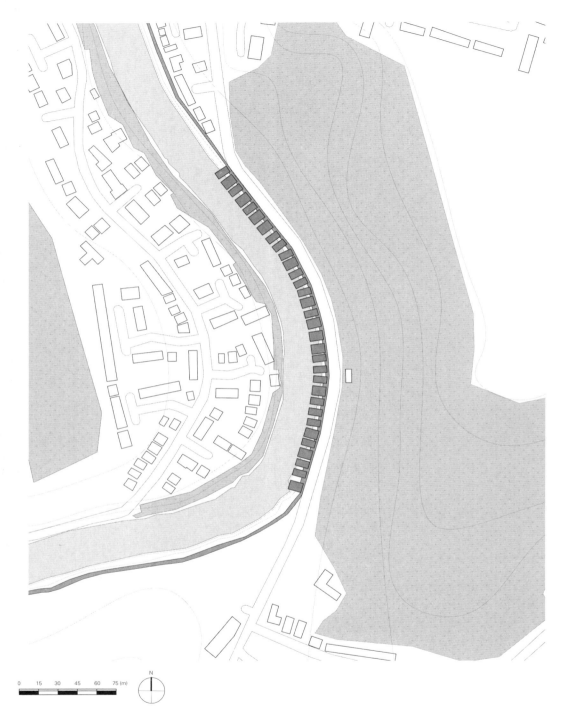

0 15 30 45 60 75 (m)

N

GREENBELT STRATEGY 2: RIVER BANKS

Floating riverside dwellings, Bristol, UK, Site Plan, J. Tait. Architects cannot simply wait around for the UK housing crisis to be solved. Instead, we should reclaim our ability to generate solutions. This lower density example of 33 homes along the banks of the River Avon proposes floating riverside dwellings following the bends of its course. This approach addresses the housing crisis in a discreet manner, while its lightweight concrete base, which allows the dwelling to float when river levels increase, avoids the usual pitfalls of building on a floodplain.

3
ASSEMBLE

FLOOR

Unblocking the tower

floor, *noun*
From Latin – *planus* (level)
1. The lower surface of a room.
2. Rooms or areas on the same level
or storey of a building.
3. The bottom surface of a sea, river,
tunnel or cave.

We need to stop our buildings from snoring. In humans snoring is caused by blockage of the airway, forcing air to vibrate through the nose and mouth and make the characteristic sound. Meanwhile, many of our tower blocks have the same problem – they are snoring too. Standard floor-to-ceiling heights are prevalent throughout the world, meaning these blocks comprise storey after storey of equal-height infilled floors. This does three things:
— causes tall buildings to have a monotonous external appearance
— limits the functionality of the building
— fails to respect the context – each level is exactly the same, no matter how high up the building.

Of course, there are benefits to standardized floor heights – they are cheaper, quicker and more accurate to build. However, they also cause a 'blockage', both visually and functionally. Floors close to the base of a tower do require a regularity that respects their surroundings. Similarly, there is a need to maximize the number of floorplates at the upper levels, where rental yield is highest. That leaves the middle part of the building – which is where we can let it breathe using voids, mini atria, gardens and terraces, breaking the tyranny of the regular floorplate. The middle is where the variety is created.

This flexibility reverses the three problems associated with the 'blocked' building: the building's external appearance will be improved, making it varied but not incongruous; a greater variety of functions and uses can be accommodated, adding value and interest; and it can integrate more intelligently with its neighbours at all heights. Ultimately, the building has added value with the new spaces and visual interest created; the highest floors are most valuable, with better views and light. Let's stop the snoring, and our buildings will become more interesting, more profitable and more functional.

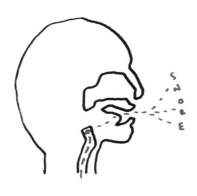

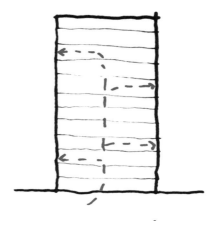

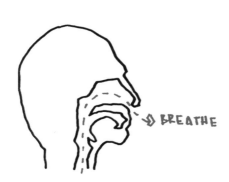

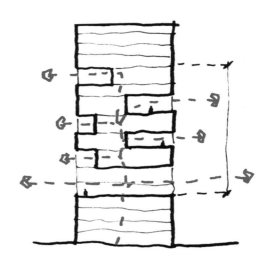

The typical repetitive tower block is constrained, unable to breathe, creating a blockage. The top building is snoring both formally and functionally. However, the tower block above has had its blockages removed creating varied, previously untapped open space within its strict footprint. This building is unblocking its potential.

BLOCKED

UNBLOCKING

UNBLOCKING

UNBLOCKING

UNBLOCKING

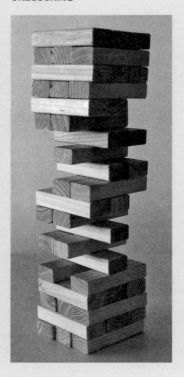

UNBLOCKED

OPPOSITE
By unblocking the central
floors of the tower,
new spaces and forms
appear. Voids, mini atria,
terraces begin to unlock
the potential to enrich the
generic typology of the
tower block by subtraction.

Floor

WALL

The inhabitable void

wall, *noun*
From Latin – *vallum* (palisade)
1. A vertical construction with a length and height greater than its thickness. Used to separate, enclose or divide.
2. A rampart built for defensive purposes.
3. An immaterial boundary possessing wall-like properties.

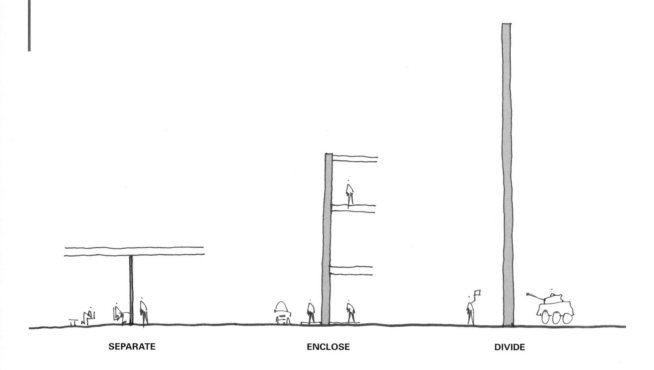

SEPARATE **ENCLOSE** **DIVIDE**

The construction of a wall is both a defensive and an offensive act. Walls define what is 'inside' and 'outside', 'mine' and 'yours' – they are the physical and symbolic embodiment of division. These dividing lines appear in a multitude of scales, materials and strengths according to what needs to be protected, the perceived threat, and the local conditions and resources. Be it the waist-high fence around a garden or the fortifications of a city, building a wall is a deliberate act to demarcate territory.

Walls can be constructed for many purposes and at different scales from a range of materials. They define space and provide shelter and enclosure, as well as being tools of division. There are few more useful, or emotive, architectural elements than a wall.

Walls can also be inhabited. This was a common feature of medieval castles across Europe, which contained habitable space within their thick stone walls. Inhabited walls

3 — Assemble

INHABITABLE WALLS

The original 'walls as space' building typology is the castle, evidenced here at Little Cumbrae, Scotland. The thick, solid walls are hollowed out to become a dual device, offering defence and containing a multitude of spaces and functions.

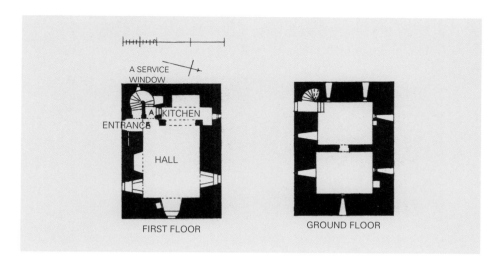

FIRST FLOOR

GROUND FLOOR

A SERVICE WINDOW

ENTRANCE

A KITCHEN

HALL

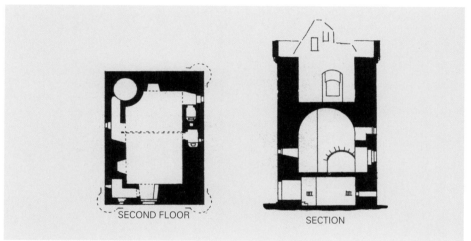

SECOND FLOOR

SECTION

can also be seen in the work of Louis Kahn, particularly at his Kimbell Art Museum in Texas, where internal walls are thickened to contain storage and staircases. This is an oblique nod to a building type he was known to admire, the Scottish castle,[1] but was also a practical way to create concealed space. This device was also used by Alberto Campo Baeza at his Benetton Nursery building in Treviso, Italy, where the entire building perimeter forms a hollowed-out playground contained within the double curved walls. This creates secret courtyard spaces for the children, with the desired level of privacy and shelter.

Let's look at three possible categories of wall: walls used to *separate* (internal spaces and rooms), to *enclose* (the outer 'skin' of a building) or to *divide* (as a defensive device):

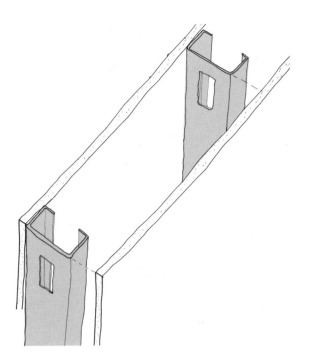

PARTITION
Typical metal-framed partitioning, comprising a floor and head channel with vertical supports at 600mm (23½in.) centres. The frame is made of paper-thin metal, ranging from 0.5mm to 1.0mm (⅟₅₀in.–⅟₂₅in.) thickness.

Walls to separate

Internal walls or partitions are generally lightweight and temporary, and have a lifespan of around 25–30 years, by which time they may have been replaced or reconfigured as a new use or layout is required. This is typical within a commercial office building, for example, where new seating arrangements necessitate regular changes. The partition is therefore somewhere between furniture and architecture. Too lightweight to truly define space, it merely separates it. You might take this one step further and decide that a partition really isn't a wall, and can therefore be furniture.

There are many situations where this would not be appropriate. A Japanese teahouse, for instance, is defined by the translucency of its partitions. But in cases where this lightness of touch is not required, the wall *could* become like the furniture. This would enable the partition to become more integrated into the function of the spaces it separates, while maximizing the use of space with the wall depth containing shelving, desks or seating, for example.

Walls to enclose

The enclosing wall clearly defines inside and outside. However, it is not always so simple. As philosopher Gaston Bachelard noted, 'Outside and Inside … are always ready to be reversed, to exchange their hostility.'[2] The enclosure represents a painful tension between outside – vastness, vagueness and void, and inside – clarity, intimacy, solidity. There have been an increasing number of buildings that exploit this tension. The skin becomes a sacrificial covering over the protective enclosure, leaving a void between the two. As philosopher Slavoj Žižek has noted, this 'parallatic' skin creates an 'incommensurability between outside and inside … the reality we see through a window is always minimally spectral, not as fully real as the closed space where we are'.[3] In cases

3 — Assemble

SEPARATE

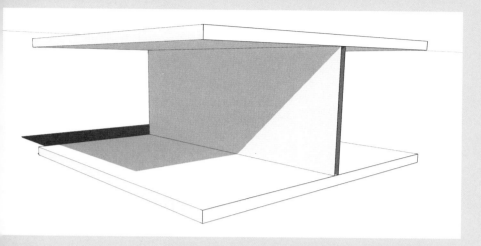

SEPARATE
The partition does one job only –
it separates.

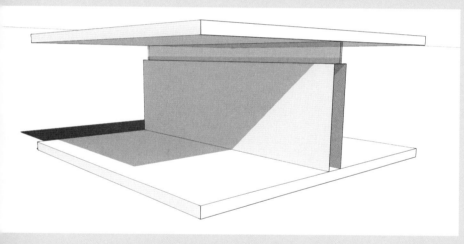

THICKEN
The standard partition thickness is increased
from 100–150mm (4–6in.) to 400–450mm
(15¾–17¾in.). A clerestory band of glazing
to the head provides a connection between
the two separated spaces while introducing
borrowed light.

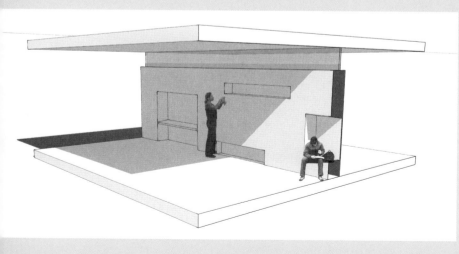

INHABIT
With thickening and the creation of
openings the partition becomes inhabitable
through a series of niches providing storage,
seating and desk space.

COMPARATIVE SECTIONAL DIAGRAMS – ENCLOSURE

Seattle Public Library, OMA

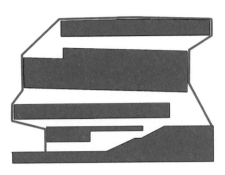

Dalian International Conference Centre, Coop Himme(l)blau

▬▬ Enclosure ☐ Inhabitable void

■ Building ▩ Uninhabitable void

3 — Assemble

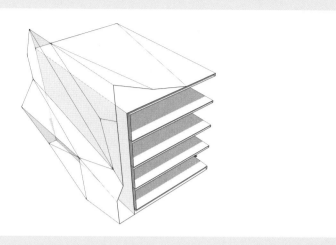

ENCLOSE
A useless void exists between skin and enclosure, created by an uneasy relationship between form and function, outside and inside.

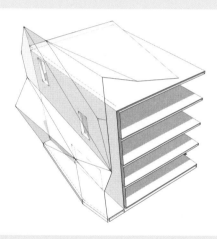

OPEN
Openings are created in the enclosing wall to create a visual connection between enclosure and skin, redressing the blurred boundary between inside and outside.

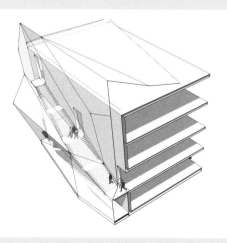

INHABIT
The uneasy gap becomes inhabitable, creating a new circulation space between the enclosure and the skin, which are no longer separate. By containing inhabitable space the void between the two becomes an integral part of the building.

PUBLIC SQUARE
Vigo, Spain, J. Tait, 2016

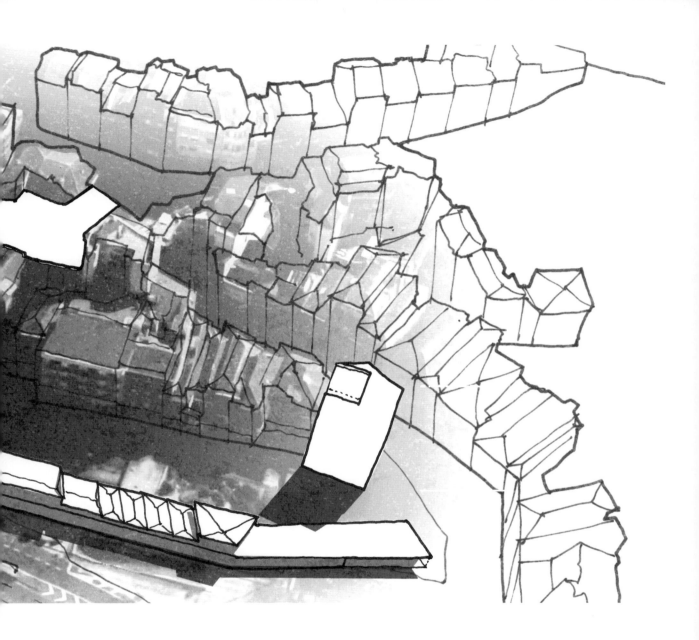

DIVIDE

DIVIDER OF CITIES
Jerusalem, Palestine (above) and
Jerusalem, Israel (below)

DIVIDER OF LAND
Horgoš, Serbia (left) and
Röszke, Hungary (right)

DIVIDER OF SEA
Playas de Tijuana, Mexico (left) and
Border Field State Park, USA (right)

such as OMA's Seattle Central Library, this distance is maximized to create dynamic interstitial spaces between the solid mass and the building skin, which are inhabitable. The interstitial spaces are integral to the building, and therefore successful. Yet in other examples the distance between skin and enclosure is not separated sufficiently and the floorplate does not extend to take advantage of the interstitial space. This creates a void between skin and enclosure, a useless purgatory of inside and outside. Voids can become circulation spaces, freeing up the plan while also ensuring that the function that inhabits the void does not impact negatively on the façade.

Walls to divide

Beyond providing protection and enclosure, walls have the ability to transcend their composition to become emotionally and politically charged devices. This is true of border walls, for example, built to make a physical barrier between opposing nations, ethnicities, religions or political viewpoints. From the rubble and mortar barriers of Hadrian's Wall and the Great Wall of China to the concrete panels of the Berlin Wall or the Israeli West Bank barrier, border walls have long been utilized as tools of protection and imperialism, becoming symbols of oppression and security.

There is a worrying global trend in politics towards protectionism and divisiveness, causing an explosion in demand for border walls. Of the thirty-five border walls that at the time of writing are active or proposed globally, nineteen have been built or are being constructed, since only 2014:[4] from the barbed-wire fences of Eastern Europe, erected to keep refugees from the Middle East out; to the trenches topped with concrete panels built between Pakistan and Afghanistan to combat terrorism; and the 670-mile-long concrete and steel border wall along the Mexican and US border. To take this wall as an example, it was built with the multiple aims of 'apprehending terrorists', 'restricting the smuggling of narcotics', 'preventing violence', 'improving environmental health' and 'restricting potentially harmful diseases'. All these stated aims have failed,[5] yet the administration in 2017 planned to rebuild the wall along the entire 2000-mile border between the two countries.

Architecture, specifically the wall, can become a physical manifestation of the tensions and insecurities of global politics. In each case the wall's effectiveness is debatable, built more for symbolism than purpose. Instead of building walls to keep refugees out, perhaps we should use the money to help the war-torn countries from which they are fleeing; or to combat terrorism through more proven means of information exchange, cutting terrorist groups' cashflow or rehabilitation;[6] or to deal with the social issues on both sides that mean illegal drugs flow into a relatively affluent country from a neighbouring poorer country.

Border walls are as preposterous as they are divisive; as useless as they are costly. What if we imagine these walls taken over by guerrilla tactics to make them not only a much better use of the vast sums of money, but – more importantly – to subvert the concept of a border wall and make it something useful and inclusive? A humane, civilized approach to border architecture could be taken, replacing a wall whose only functions are division and destruction. If we must build border walls, let's make them inhabitable.

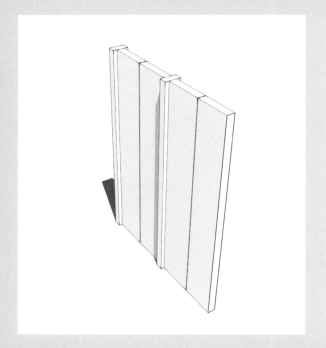

DIVIDER
A series of precast concrete planks, 55m high x 3m wide (180ft x 10ft), with stiffening columns at 6m (20ft) centres

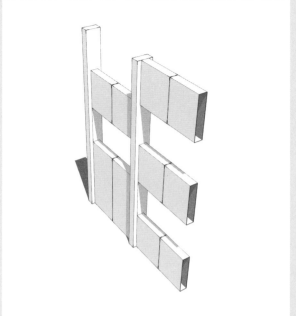

DIVIDER
Cut out sections of the precast panels, but leave enough spare (+50%) so that the columns support the integrity of the overall wall

BORDER WALL

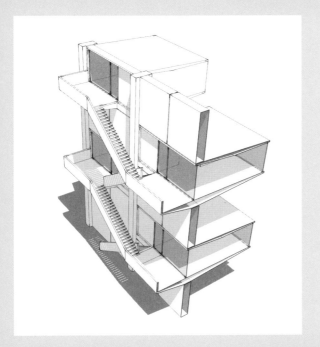

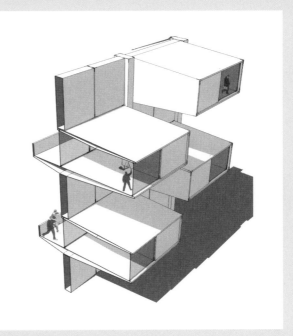

INSERT

Insert prefabricated dwellings (providing a two-person, one-bed apartment of around 42m² / 452ft²) with a south-facing terrace facing towards home

INHABIT

The projecting cantilevered insertions are both symbolic and functional; by entering neighbouring airspace the building becomes an illegal alien, but it only ever touches the ground in its homeland

SUBVERTED WALL

STRUCTURE

Let the supports sing

structure, *noun*
From Latin – *struere* (to build)
1. The arrangement or organization of parts and elements of an entity.
2. A mode of building or constructing.
3. A built construct, e.g. a building.
4. The organization or composition of a work of art.
5. A system considered as a complex, integrated whole rather than individual parts.

'Anyone who hides a column or load-bearing part, whether exterior or interior, is depriving himself of architecture's noblest and most legitimate element, and its finest ornamental feature. Architecture is the art of making supports sing.'[1]
— Auguste Perret

Often the mathematical problem of supporting a building is separated from the task of creating form and space – structure is dissociated from architecture. The engineering is a reaction to the architecture,[2] and vice versa; there is not a symbiotic relationship between the two. This reactive approach creates structures that are developed as rational responses to load paths and stresses created by the architecture – not in response to the overall concept or visual effect sought, the function of the building, or how the building interacts with light, for example. This can result in solutions based on prior calculations, industry norms and standard components: structure created in spite of the architecture, not because of it.

With this approach structure and architecture are ambivalent to one another at best, and incompatible at worst. They progress along separate paths until eventually the gap between them is bridged. The architect might achieve this by *embellishment*, or by *vanishment*.

Embellishment of structure

To bridge the gap between what the architect wants the structure to be and what the structure actually is, it can be added to for the required visual effect. Ironically, the purpose of this exercise is to make the structure appear more honest, though the opposite is the case. Embellishment can be seen as the architect apologizing for any aesthetic deficiency arising from the separation of structure and architecture.

For example, steel columns may be clad in precast concrete, wood veneer, 5mm (⅕in.) plastic, 3mm (⅒in.) brushed aluminium – or whatever else the architect deems more in keeping with the building than the exposed structure. This cloaks the structure

EMBELLISHMENT

■ Structure

COLUMN TORTURE DEVICE
3mm (⅒in.) aluminium cladding fixed with clamps and bolts

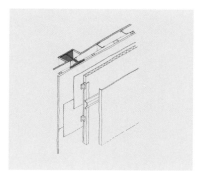

STRUCTURAL APOLOGIST WALL
13mm (½in.) plasterboard traces an outline of the structure

TRYING TO BE SOMETHING YOU'RE NOT
50mm x 35mm (2in. x 1⅓in.) painted timber battens create a new false structure

VANISHMENT

■ Structure

WALL AS LAYER CAKE
Seven layers of construction (brick, fixings, insulation, waterproofing, plywood, insulation again, plasterboard) conspire to hide the structure

PITCHED ROOF? WHAT PITCHED ROOF?
A plasterboard ceiling on hangers hides the form and material of the roof structure

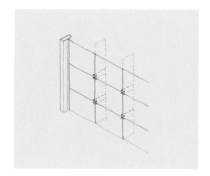

I'M TRYING TO BE INCONSPICUOUS …
Stainless-steel fixings hold the glass together

and architecture together, giving an impression of seamlessness, but neither emerges with its distinctiveness or integrity intact. Walls, once structural mass upon structural mass, are now layers of skin of varying thicknesses, each working in isolation. The structure becomes a collection of standard, ready-made components – lintels, beams and columns – carefully positioned within an allocated wall thickness, giving only the impression of structure.

Roof beams are no longer expressed; instead, they are wrapped in polystyrene or mineral wool insulation then falsely expressed as a facsimile in the form of applied painted timber battens. Perhaps worse, flat concrete roof slabs may have the same timber treatment applied – even though there were never timber roof beams in the first place.

STRUCTURAL MASS
Chichen Itza, Mexico

STRUCTURAL INTRICACY
Yakushi-ji, Japan

STRUCTURAL SYMBOLISM
Temple of Zeus, Greece

STRUCTURAL HONESTY
Ulm Cathedral, Germany

STRUCTURAL AMBITION
St Peter's Basilica, Vatican City

STRUCTURAL ELEGANCE
Bibliothèque Nationale, France

STRUCTURAL SCULPTURE
Palácio do Planalto, Brazil

Vanishment of structure

Vanishment, meanwhile, is the end game of structural embellishment: not so much an apology for structure as a complete denial of it. Structure is hidden, or methods are developed to avoid the expression of it, effectively reducing architecture to an exercise in creation of visual effect, rather than the synthesis of structure, form, light and space.

Vanishment embeds columns in external or internal walls to make them disappear. The organization of the architecture is then driven by the location of the structure. The architect must ensure that the external wall openings that define the façade and the partitions that order the internal space hide it. It is ironic that the thing being hidden becomes the organizing principle of the building.

Roof structures, when there is little budget for high-quality timber or concrete, are hidden from view by flat, suspended plasterboard ceilings. This lowers the ceiling height and reduces the ceiling to a monotonous plane rather than a combined expression of structure, form and material.

STRUCTURAL SCULPTURE
Phaeno Science Centre, Wolfsburg, Germany, Zaha Hadid, 2005

STRUCTURAL MASS
Inverted Portal, Montana, USA, Ensamble Studio, 2016

STRUCTURAL ELEGANCE
Milwaukee Art Museum, USA, Santiago Calatrava, 2001

Vanishment gives rise to new techniques – curtain walling that was once composed of thin, honest mullions becomes butt-jointed 'structural' glass held together by silicone or mastic, with transparent glass fins and stainless-steel clamps, wires and bolts for support, compromising the relationship between structure and skin.

This dual challenge to structural synthesis – embellishment and vanishment – has meant, as Rem Koolhaas has observed, that the art of building has a new vocabulary: clamp, fold, wrap, stick, bond, seal, glue, fuse. It is a vocabulary associated with transient coupling, of isolated negotiation[3] between the components that make up the separate entities of architecture and structure.

Many examples from the timeline of architectural history show that in the past, structure was an integral part of architecture:

— The Maya, Incas and Ancient Egyptians created space by arranging structural mass on top of structural mass, or carved out space as void from solid structural stone mass.

STRUCTURE AND LIGHT
Columns and roof apertures combine to allow the laterally braced supports to bring light into the space as well as perform its functional task of supporting the roof.

— Ancient Chinese and Japanese civilizations employed jointed wood techniques in their structures, which created forms and spaces of elegance and simplicity.
— The basis of Ancient Greek and Roman architecture was the column and lintel (post and beam); simultaneously structure, form and symbolism. (Now columns are merely structure.)
— Vaults, flying buttresses and arches are typical of Gothic architecture: originally developed as structural solutions, they became synonymous with the style of architecture.
— The soaring domes of the Renaissance would have been impossible without the engineering awareness and ability of architects such as Filippo Brunelleschi and Donato Bramante.
— The elegant iron structures of the mid to late 1900s sought to bring purity, refinement and economy through the naked expression of structure.
— The more expressive Modernist architects such as Oscar Niemeyer, Eero Saarinen and Marcel Breuer moulded and shaped structural concrete as a sculptor would clay.

STRUCTURE AND LIGHT
Light enters the building by the removal of solid, standardized elements such as brick. Light exists only where structure, or mass, doesn't.

The reasons for the break with historical precedent might be twofold: regulations and money. Regulations dictate that structural elements in a building be fireproofed to safeguard against the collapse of the building. However, technological advances mean that intumescent (fire retardant) paint can now be applied to steel or timber to provide the necessary fire resistance. Alternatively, concrete is inherently fire resistant. Regulations also specify high thermal values in buildings, meaning they must be insulated. Exposed structure can cause a 'cold bridge', where an un-insulated part of the building envelope causes a cold spot in the building and allows cold air into the interior. Again, this is easily solved by creating a 'thermal break', an element of insulation within the structure or between two elements of it at the point where it passes through from exterior to interior.

Meanwhile, standard components are often favoured for cost-efficiency in construction – but surely by the time we have covered the structure in concrete, wood, aluminium or plastic, the original cost benefits have been negated? It could be better to simply design and fabricate a finished structural and architectural element without the need for additional material or building trades to cover it up. The impending 3D printing boom and mass customization of building elements might help to economize and accelerate this process.

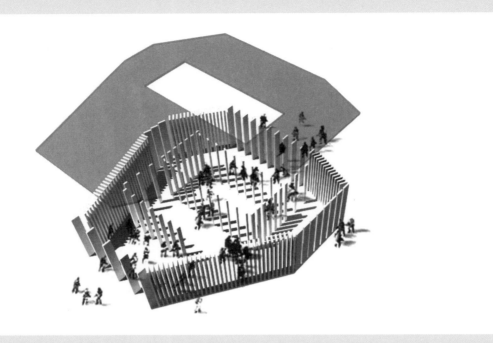

STRUCTURE AND SPACE
The arrangement, dimensions and angles of solid structural columns alone define the space. When spaced apart, columns define an opening; when grouped together they provide privacy. When angled or turned horizontally, they shield against sun.

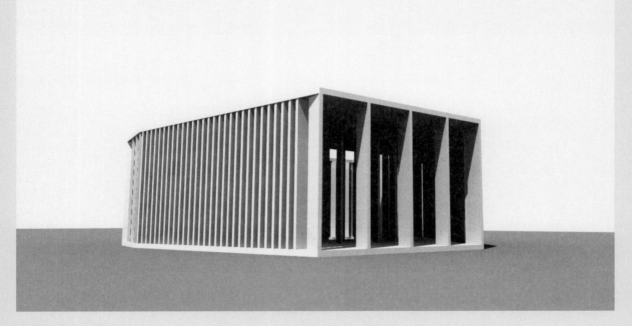

STRUCTURE AND FORM
The form of the building and its structure are one and the same. By arranging structural columns as both functional and form-giving devices the building retains a sense of honesty and purity.

STRUCTURE AND SPACE
The careful arrangement of structure allows for layers of space to emerge – a toplit courtyard,
a private ante-chamber, a colonnaded walkway; all defined purely by structure.

STRUCTURE AND FORM
By exposing the roof structure and allowing light to pass through the structural members, the roof
becomes a form-giving device created by repetition and shadow.

There is also something more fundamental at play, however, perhaps epitomized by a detail that showed a prominent architect compensating for the aesthetic discrepancy between architectural intention and structural reality. At Mies van der Rohe's Seagram Building in Manhattan, the structural steel was required to be fireproofed; encased in concrete. This left Mies with a dilemma, particularly regarding the steel at the corners of the building. How could he express the purity of the structure if it was covered in concrete? His solution was to embellish the now-vanished column with metal cladding to give the impression of structure. If this famously logical and rational purist could do it, then so could his generations of followers, and is now an accepted, if erroneous in my view, approach to dealing with structure in the profession.

Of course, there are engineers and architects who still seek to reconcile structural reality with architectural intent. The collaboration between engineers Adams Kara Taylor and Zaha Hadid Architects has produced structures that skilfully blend wall, roof, floor, space, light, structure and form into one fluid whole, with a notable example being the Phaeno Science Center in Wolfsburg, Germany. Think also of the soaring ribs and masts of Santiago Calatrava's works, which treat structure as an architectural device that defines form and lets in light; or the primitive structural elementalism of Ensamble Studio, who celebrate the strength and purity of structure in their works either through enlargement or the use of solid blocks.

However, these buildings are atypical in terms of budget and ambition. Importantly, they are also designed by atypical, structurally literate architects and architecturally literate engineers. With this in mind, how can we develop strategies to integrate structure and architecture in our own buildings? How can structure combine with light, space and form in all architecture, not just the rarefied exceptions? Following are some suggestions:

Structure and light
— *Column* – Let the openings around column heads bring in light, allowing structure and opening, support and void to combine.
— *Wall* – Rather than create arbitrary openings in walls, allow the modules of the building envelope (bricks, stone, concrete panels, etc.) to define openings. Let in light by removing structural mass.
— *Roof* – Create rooflights between exposed structural elements. The rhythm of light and shadow created will mirror the rhythm of the structural grid.

Structure and space
— *Column* – Don't be scared of columns. Use them to define and articulate space – close together for intimacy and privacy; spaced apart for openness.
— *Wall* – Use the structural grid to create voids, allowing the space to be defined by the structure and the structure to be defined by the space.
— *Roof* – Create soaring, heightened interior space. Push the boundaries of mathematics and exploit the shells, parabolas and catenaries it can create.

Structure and form

— *Column* – Rather than spend money on the materials and labour used to hide a column, sculpt it for structural economy and efficiency, and to suit your architectural needs.
— *Wall* – Reject the notion of the wall as a series of layered components. Use materials that are both structural and form-giving – brick, concrete, steel, stone, timber.
— *Roof* – Express the structure of the roof both inside and out. Allow structural elements to display their form honestly and articulate the spaces above our heads.

If we try to reverse the trend for embellishment and vanishment of structure, perhaps we can achieve a more symbiotic relationship between structure and architecture. Structure need not be a reactive solution, but an integral architectural device.

ROOF

Finding hidden space

roof, *noun*
From Old Norse – *hrof* (boat shed)
1. The external upper layer
covering a building or other structure.
2. The frame or structure
supporting this external layer.
3. The highest point or summit.

I've had enough of buildings that make bold moves and shapes but waste space – prime klatsch space (for informal social gatherings). Let's decide to centre the forms of our buildings around meeting places, gathering points and hidden courtyards. Let's activate leftover, forgotten spaces – and allow them to be coloured with life.

The perfect klatsch space should:
— make usable space out of a forgotten or hidden space
— be generated by the design of the building, not be a generator for it, otherwise it will be a formal rather than an informal space
— be semi-enclosed to provide a sense of privacy and enclosure
— have views out towards the city or landscape, or the rest of building
— be directly accessible from a circulation space to allow for maximum use.

With this in mind, why roof a potential terrace when you could pave, plant and inhabit it? Why not create a larger habitable space between a staircase and a bridge, instead of an awkward passageway? Why not turn a blank wall into a retractable deck? There are pockets of ready-made space everywhere in our buildings; we just need to activate them.

When looking for the perfect klatsch space, roof spaces appear to provide the best opportunities. They are often neglected, used only for maintenance or plant access; they are generally hidden from view from the outside; they will usually provide the best views and sunlight within a building. There are some very good examples of these spaces, both recent and less so. That Modernist classic, Le Corbusier's Unité d'habitation in Marseille, sets the benchmark with its running track, pool and crèche all contained within space usually reserved for ventilation machinery; Herzog & de Meuron's de Young Museum provides a sculpted rooftop courtyard that doubles as intimate garden space and as a reflection point on the circulation route between galleries; OMA's Porto Concert Hall hides a surreal roof terrace that opens out to the city below, despite being hidden from view.

Yet other roof spaces do not capitalize on this opportunity. Some roofs create dramatic sweeping forms whose beauty will never be appreciated up close; or don't take advantage of potential rooftop views at a waterfront location; or generate multiple varied spaces that the addition of a door and some decking would make inhabitable. In the examples where klatsch space has been incorporated, the forms and spaces created by the roofscapes are not only beautiful elements of the overall architecture, but add another functional dimension and enable appreciation of unique spaces. The beauty of the klatsch space is that it does not deliberately impose on the overall design, concept or execution of a building. Instead, by making a few shrewd design decisions we can inhabit and bring purpose to forgotten spaces. Take a nothing space and turn it into a something space: let's klatsch our buildings.

I HEART KLATSCH SPACE

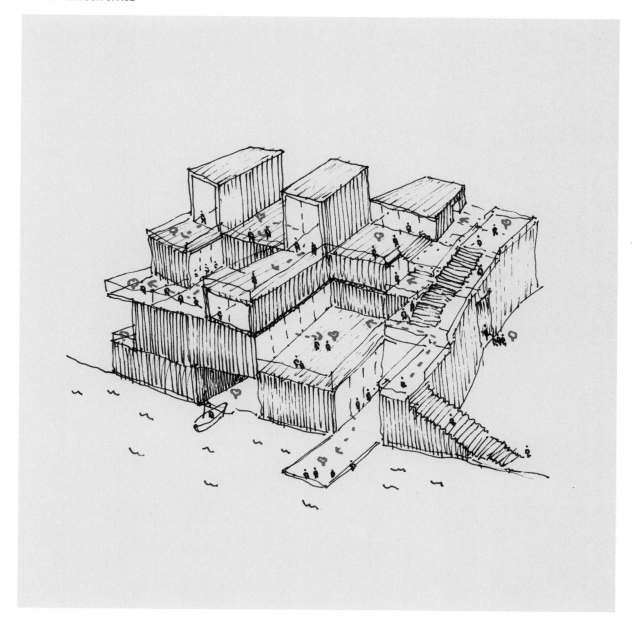

UNITÉ D'HABITATION ROOF

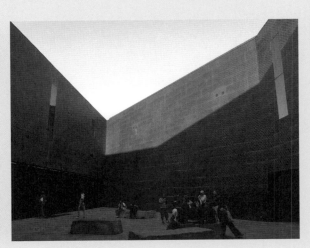

DE YOUNG MUSEUM ROOF

PORTO CONCERT HALL ROOF

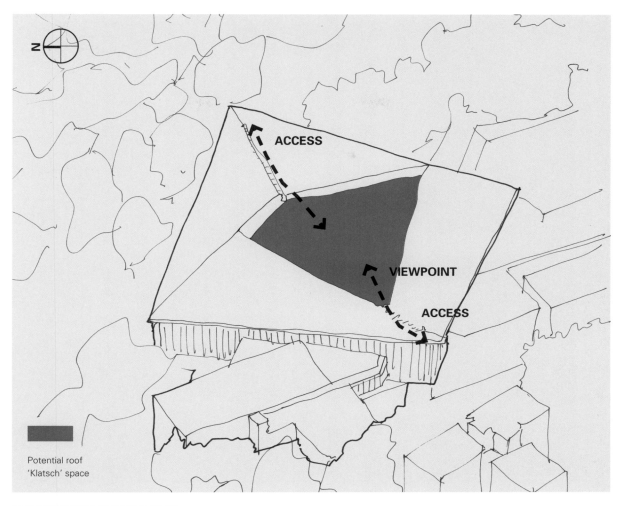

ACCESS

VIEWPOINT

ACCESS

Potential roof
'Klatsch' space

COMMONWEALTH INSTITUTE ROOF

COMMONWEALTH INSTITUTE ROOF Existing

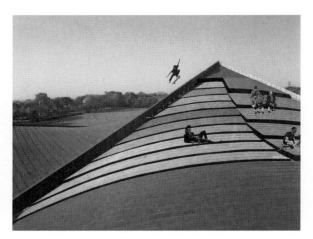

COMMONWEALTH INSTITUTE ROOF Klatsched!

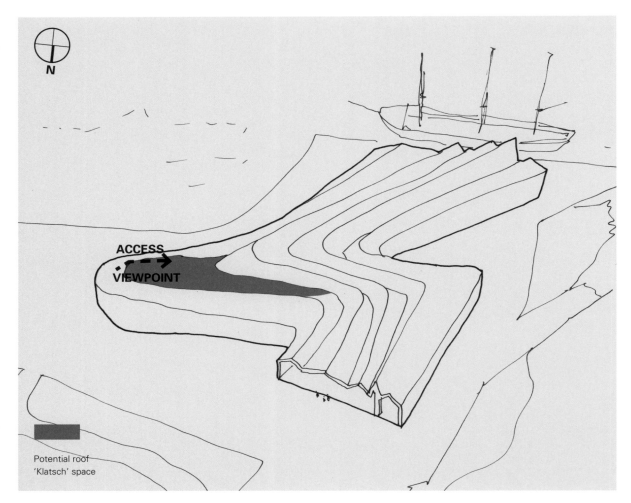

ACCESS

VIEWPOINT

Potential roof
'Klatsch' space

RIVERSIDE MUSEUM ROOF

RIVERSIDE MUSEUM ROOF Existing

RIVERSIDE MUSEUM ROOF Klatsched!

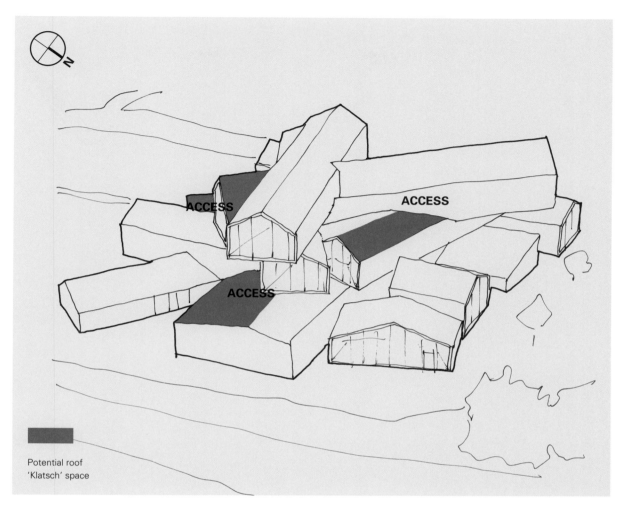

ACCESS

ACCESS

ACCESS

Potential roof
'Klatsch' space

VITRAHAUS ROOF

VITRAHAUS ROOF Existing

VITRAHAUS ROOF Klatsched!

PARK
Miami, USA, J. Tait, 2013

Roof

DOOR

A warm embrace: the importance of the entrance

door, *noun*
From Ancient Greek – *thura* (door)
1. A hinged, sliding or revolving panel to the
entrance of a building, room, vehicle or space.

The entrance of a building is its opening salvo. Salvo derives from the Latin word *salve*, meaning 'be in good health!' – a Roman greeting. Later, important visitors were often greeted with celebratory gunfire, and the term 'salvo' is now applied to any concentrated period of gunfire,[1] but is also used to mean a statement of intent; an indication of things to come.

First impressions are critical: will a building's entrance welcome the user, or shun them? Will it be an integral part of the building, or leave people feeling disoriented and desperate to leave? Will it hint at the delights within, or act like a grumpy bouncer? This is up to us as architects. The key components in a successful opening salvo to a building are as follows:

Threshold
One of the most ancient and important features of the entrance is the arch. The form of the arch signifies an opening in a solid wall, defining a point of entry, while the curved head is derived from its structural function. It is the perfect synthesis of form and function – signifier and supporter. However, doorway arches are now rarely used; steel lintels concealed with brick render the compressive strength of the arch obsolete. The signifier doesn't support, and the support doesn't signify.

Perhaps a solution is to again allow the signifier to be the support. Take the steel lintel outside of the wall, stretch it to the ground, and create an arch out of it. This steel arch could be a standard component, to be adapted as required. The steel creates the arch, defining the threshold – and also supports the wall above, in a modern interpretation of the ancient arch.

SHELTER Entrance, Campion Hall, Oxford, UK, Edwin Lutyens, 1936. Threshold is extended to provide depth, drama and shelter from the elements.

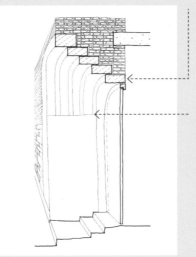

SUPPORT + SIGNIFIER
The arched keystone supports the wall above while signifying a symbolic threshold.

VERTICAL
The entrance is defined both vertically and horizontally. The arched entrance extends to the ground, providing a unified combination of form and function.

NO SHELTER Entrance, Haus Lange, Krefeld, Germany, Mies van der Rohe, 1928. Advances in construction mean walls are thinner; doors are generally placed towards the outer masonry leaf; the lintel is embedded with the brickwork and doesn't extend to the full depth of the wall.

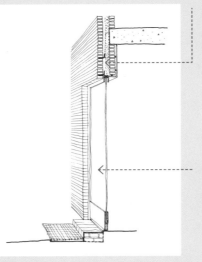

SUPPORT/NO SIGNIFIER
The concealed lintel supports the wall above, but it is hidden within the wall – devoid of symbolism or the ability to express its function.

VERTICAL
The omission of a vertical signifier renders the threshold two-dimensional; not a three-dimensional threshold envelope as in the Lutyens arch.

PROPOSED ENTRANCE
J. Tait

SHELTER

New arch creates threshold to provide depth, drama and shelter from the elements.
A grate at the base provides a graded slope for drainage.

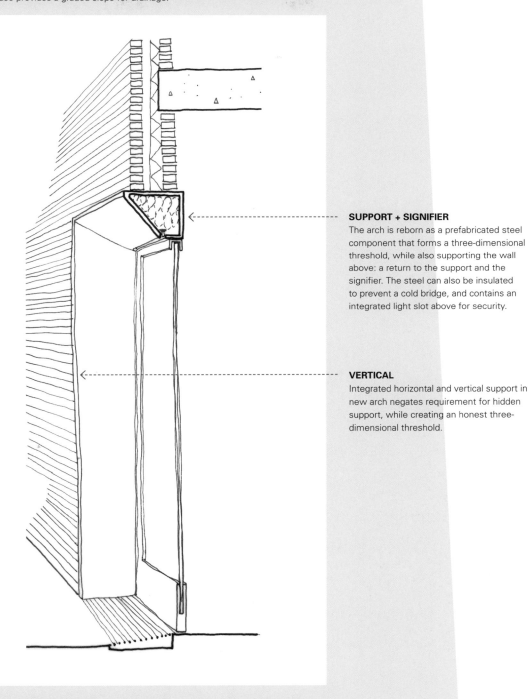

SUPPORT + SIGNIFIER

The arch is reborn as a prefabricated steel component that forms a three-dimensional threshold, while also supporting the wall above: a return to the support and the signifier. The steel can also be insulated to prevent a cold bridge, and contains an integrated light slot above for security.

VERTICAL

Integrated horizontal and vertical support in new arch negates requirement for hidden support, while creating an honest three-dimensional threshold.

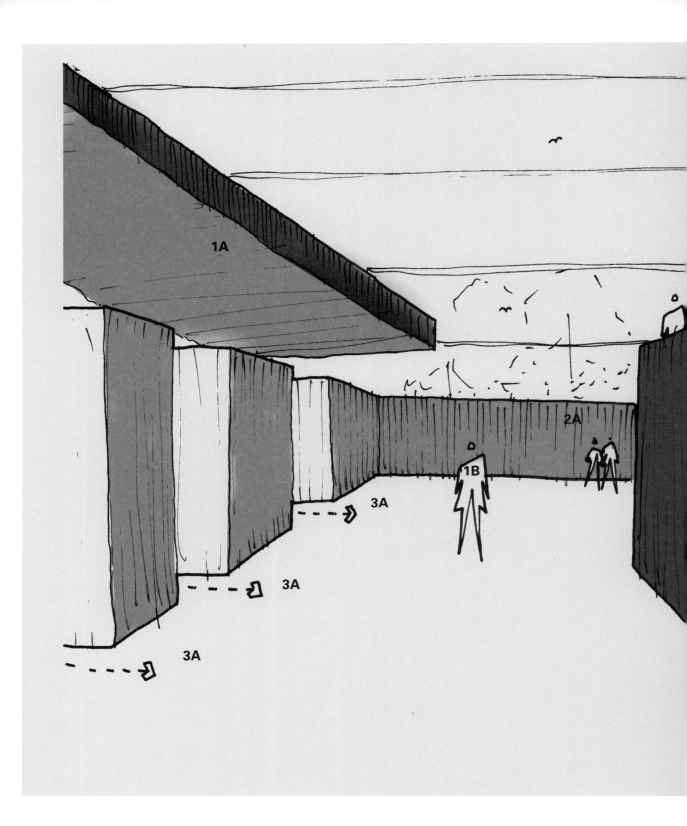

3 — Assemble

ENTRANCE SPACE

1. EMBRACE (Comfort and engage the building audience.)

a. Shelter the user from the elements. Provide canopies that protect from rain and sun but also define the threshold symbolically.
b. Use generous but appropriate proportions. Too narrow and the entrance will appear constrained and claustrophobic; too wide and it will be overly imposing and grand, losing its warmth.
c. Use materiality to accentuate this notion of shelter and embrace. Haptic, textured surfaces provide comfort above smoother, shinier surfaces. Would you rather hug someone wearing a cashmere sweater or a wetsuit?

2. NAVIGATE (Never rely on signage as a navigation device; form and layout should be the building's primary navigation device.)

a. Use solid, tapered walls to signify a route you wish your building user to take.
b. Use the termination of wall edges and perspective to define the entrance and its division with the spaces that flow into it.

3. TEASE (Ensure you use the entrance to help 'unlock' or expose the inner workings of the rest of the building.)

a. Use apertures and openings to provide specific views into other spaces, or outside to bring in light and allow views out.
b. Increase reciprocal connectivity to other spaces within the building with the use of voids, rooflights and mezzanines.

4. INTEGRATE (Ensure that all of these aspects are integrated into the overall building form.)

a. Don't create a flat, nondescript entrance space that provides no threshold or entrance sequence; conversely the entrance should not dominate the overall architectural form.
b. Think of the entrance space as *a* distinctive and integrated feature of the building, but not *the* distinctive feature of the building.

FAÇADE

The arch: hierarchy, adaptability, rhythm

façade, *noun*
From Italian – *faccia* (face)
1. The face or front of a building,
especially a decorative one.
2. A superficial or illusive appearance.

For millennia the arch has dominated architecture, combining structure, symbolism and shelter. From the corbelled stone and sand arches of Mesopotamia, to the Roman refinements in geometry and purity, to the gravity-defying experiments of Gothic parabolas, arches have defined our civilizations in a way unlike any other architectural device. The arch is a universal symbol of form and function, support and signifier.

With the rise of Modernism in the early twentieth century, there was an abrupt halt of the use of the arch as an architectural device. Technical advances in construction techniques and a desire to break with the past meant that arches were eschewed in favour of curtain walling panels, steel lintels and concrete floor slabs. As a structural and symbolic device, the arch was deemed obsolete – thrown on the architectural scrapheap along with the entablature, portico and dome, as standardized components took their place.

However, the power and value of the arch endures. It still has the ability to provide hierarchy and layering in façades with simplicity of structure and purity of form.

Colonnades and loggias

The Doge's Palace in Venice, whose famous Piazzetta façade was completed in 1442,[1] is an exceptional example of how the arch creates a façade that expresses the function of the interior and the building's role within the public space.

The wide-arched colonnade at ground level creates a permeable façade through which the public can stroll in the shade. The ratio of solid to void at this level is 1:4, reflecting the public and open nature of the colonnade.

On the first floor more ornate, narrow arches form a semi-public loggia with a solid-to-void ratio of 1:3. The arches provide views out and let light in, and they also signify a more refined and private function, reflected in their ornate decoration. This is the breakout space for consuls' and advisors' discussions and deliberations.

The third-level arches emphasize the power and nobility of the building's occupants. Large arches into the great private halls allow views out into the city and let light in, but they are separated by expanses of stone, which create a largely impenetrable façade at this level. The arches are big enough to express power, but sporadic enough to provide privacy.

The arch as a device can therefore support a structure, create space, act as an integral structural device, and articulate a façade. However, this systematic structuring and articulation of buildings through a hierarchy of arches has been lost. If we compare the Doge's Palace with a later Italian *palazzo*, the Casa del Fascio in Como, Italy, we see a stark contrast. Commissioned in 1932 by Mussolini's government as the headquarters

PALAZZO DUCALE (DOGE'S PALACE) Venice, Italy, 14th century

CASA DEL FASCIO (FASCIST HOUSE) Como, Italy, Guiseppe Terragni, 1936

of the Fascist Party, and designed with strict rationality, the main façade comprises twenty identical squares distributed over four levels, flanked by a bare concrete wall. As an essay in the aesthetics of Modernist rationalism, it is sublime. However, it lacks the multi-valency and depth of its older Venetian cousin.

Repetition reigns in both the Casa del Fascio and the Doge's Palace. However, where the repetition of the Doge's Palace is countered by an imposed hierarchy, with varying ratios of solid to void, the repetition in the Casa del Fascio creates sameness, almost sterility. The façade is separate from what takes place behind it. In rejecting the malleability and versatility of the repeating arch, the concrete frame – while functional, rational and sometimes beautiful – tends towards monotony.

The entrance at ground level is defined by four steps protruding from the façade; no colonnade is provided for shelter. Here the ratio of solid to void is 1:11. The five concrete-

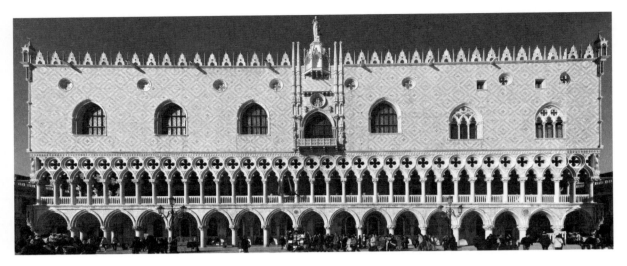

GOTHIC

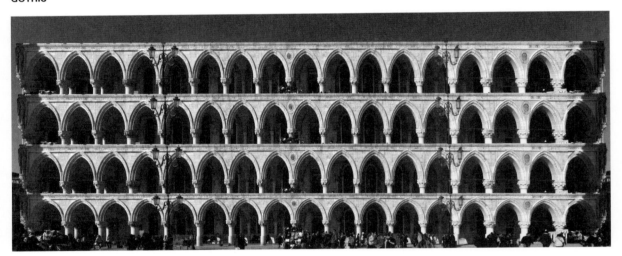

MODERNIST

framed apertures continue upwards to the middle two floors, which are populated with meeting rooms and offices, much like the middle floors of the Doge's Palace. Despite the more private nature of these spaces, again the solid-to-void ratio is 1:11. We see a little of what is going on behind the façade at the top level, where the internal courtyard peeks out through the concrete frame. However, this is a building governed by the rationality of its structural grid.

This is not a criticism of the Casa del Fascio, but is intended to demonstrate how arches can lend a façade variation, shelter, space, decoration, symbolism and, above all, structural support – if you let them. To reject the arch is to reject a device that can imbue our façades with these qualities, in favour of the relentlessness of the structural grid. Sometimes we let the technical solution override layering, hierarchy, decoration and symbolism – but using arches can help us bring them back into the equation.

MODERNIST

GOTHIC

PALAZZO DUCALE AND CASA DEL FASCIO MONTAGE

The Gothic façade of the Palazzo (opposite, top) is re-interpreted as a relentless modernist structural grid (opposite, bottom), eschewing the multi-valency, hierarchy and external expression of internal function present in the original. Repetition is absolute and detached.

Conversely, the Modernist façade of the Casa del Fascio (top) is re-imagined as a Gothic hybrid (bottom). Different internal functions are expressed in the ordering and layering of the façade, providing hierarchy and multi-valency. Repetition is varied and connected.

PLANT

TERRACE

OFFICES

COLONNADE

FAÇADE ARCH BUILDING

The arch allows for equal repetition and variety due to its adaptability and honesty.

- The ground floor consists of large 7.5m x 7.5m (25ft x 25ft) arches with set-back glazing providing a colonnade. The rhythm of the arch is widened to signify the entrance.

- The arch effortlessly conceals the fact that the middle of the building – housing its offices, classrooms and so on – requires lower ceiling heights by spanning two floors, allowing the grander proportions to define the façade without interruption.

- The top floor consists of an inverted arch, which allows for an open roof area while providing depth and variety to the façade.

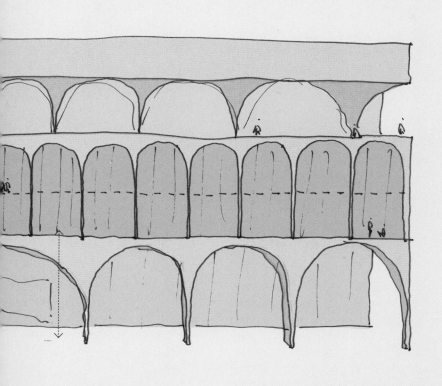
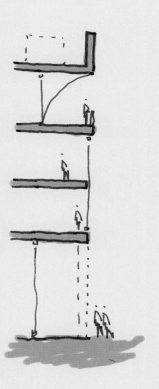

STAIR
Connector of space

stair, *noun*
Germanic, from *steiger* (to climb)
1. One of a flight or series of steps ascending or descending from one level to another.
2. Such steps collectively as one whole.

'So if you find nothing in the corridors open the doors, and if you find nothing behind these doors there are more floors, and if you find nothing up there, don't worry, just leap up another flight of stairs. As long as you don't stop climbing, the stairs won't end, under your climbing feet they will go on growing upwards.'[1]
— Franz Kafka, 'Advocates'

The essence of the stair is its function as a connector of spaces separated from one another vertically. This simple but profound purpose should not be reduced to the stair solely as a means to get from one level to another, though – it can be much more than that. It can be an architectural element that enhances the overall experience of a building through its interaction with space, its manipulation of light and shadow, how the form and function of the stair combine, and its architectural detail.

The stair and space
A stair should be used as a way of experiencing space in transit as well as a device that helps navigation through a building. The building should not be designed around the staircase; rather the staircase should be designed to optimize the experience of space.

— *Approach*
Circulation should be apparent on entering a building, but stairs should leave something to the imagination. They can reveal their first few steps at the end of a corridor, be inserted within the reveal of a wall, or even show their underside as you enter beneath them.

— *Type of stair*
The type of stair employed is critical:
- Using a long, linear Jacob's Ladder-style stair works best in a similarly linear building. When combined they allow for efficiency (they can run along a wall and not cut into a narrow plan), while emphasizing the linearity of the building.
- A building arranged around a central space of assembly (such as an educational building or a workplace) can benefit from an agora-type stair, which allows for variation in riser height to integrate seating, while also forming a social space that links parts of the building.

3 — Assemble

THE STAIR AND SPACE Entrance

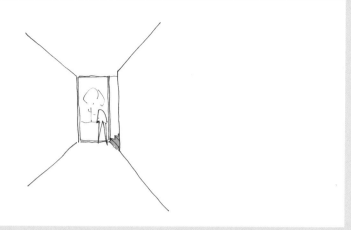

REVEAL
First few steps

REVEAL
Occluded form

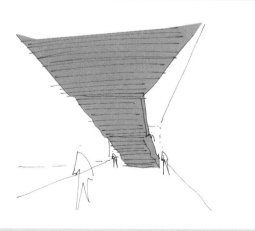

NO EMBELLISHMENT
Reveal underside

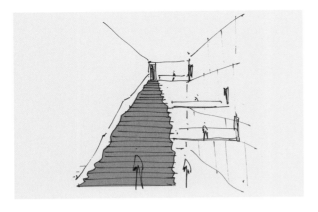

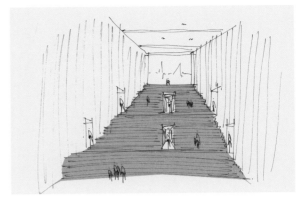

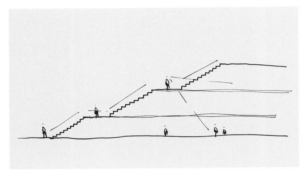

Jacob's Ladder

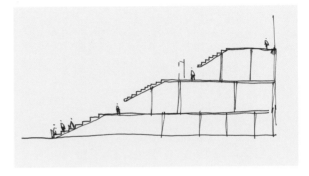

Agora

— A ship's prow staircase can be used as a sculptural navigation device in an open-plan building; its efficient doubling-back form also makes it ideal for a functional escape stair where space is limited.
— A courtyard-type staircase can allow the person climbing to go upwards through a central space, such as a garden or void – allowing them to experience the space in full and gain a different perspective on what is below them.

(I have deliberately discounted spiral stairs; a typical tight winding spiral stair doesn't move through space laterally, becomes an object in itself rather than a connector of spaces, and is often uncomfortable to ascend.)

The stair and light
A stair can be used to harness and manipulate light for a range of purposes.

— *Signage*
The void created for the stair can guide people through the building: natural wayfinding without the use of applied graphics or typefaces. Through subtraction the stair adds light.

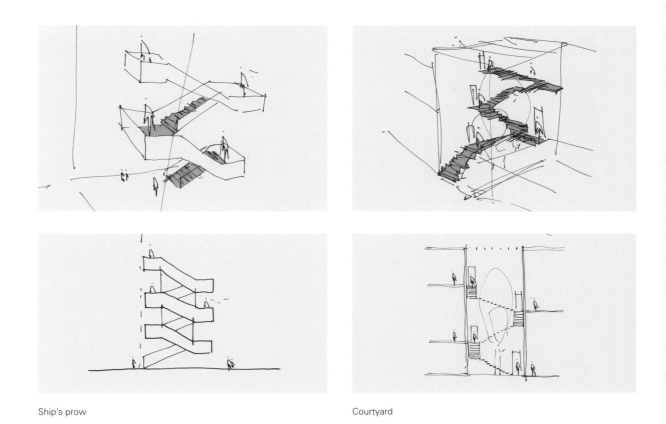

Ship's prow

Courtyard

— Toplighting

The ideal provision for natural lighting is from above with a rooflight, brought deep into the building via the stairwell. This gives the most even light, and also has the minimum impact on the façade or building envelope.

— Windows

If toplighting is not possible, windows can bring light in at the half-landing levels, also providing views out. However, the difference in level between the half-landing and the main floor can cause problems with the façade design as openings become staggered. This can be solved by keeping the windows at the main floor level, allowing users to see out as they descend or ascend, not when stationary.

The stair and form

You can manipulate the form of the stair to achieve various effects.

— Make it recede

The stair form shouldn't dominate the overall building composition; its main job is to connect spaces. Hide a stair between walls if necessary.

THE STAIR AND LIGHT

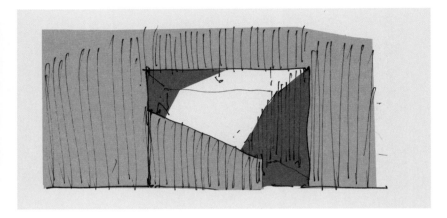

Light as signage

Toplit

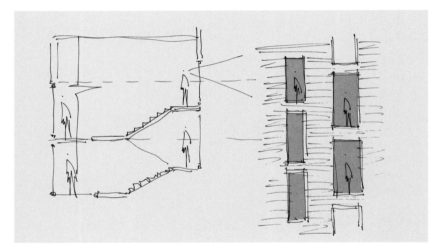

Stop and view

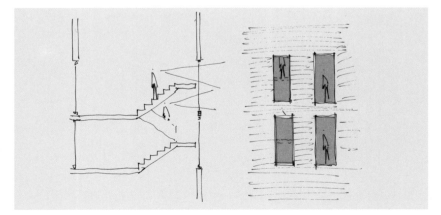

Walk and view

3 — Assemble

— *Increase the landings*

How often have we met someone we want to talk to on our way up or down a staircase? Increase the area of the half-landings to provide an informal meeting space for spontaneous interaction.

— *Taper*

Narrowing the form of the stair as it rises reinforces its verticality and intensity, and could be used to signal ascending to a more private, intimate space. Alternatively, widening out a stair can bring a sense of openness and relief. This works best when the stair opens out to a view or void looking down to another part of the building.

The stair and detail

The detailing of the stair affects it experiential qualities.

— *Solid balustrade*

A solid balustrade is beneficial for four reasons:
- There is greater potential for creating a sculptural staircase form without the need for fussy vertical elements and visible fixings.
- Sweeping continuous lines can be designed unencumbered by a staccato of vertical elements.
- The issue of the newel post and balustrade needing to be at different levels can be subtly resolved by altering the angle of the balustrade to create a continuous form.
- Lighting and other services can be integrated.

— *Treads*

The stair pitch is critical, dictating how you want your building users to ascend. For escape, make stairs as steep as building regulations allow for ease of movement. In a central communal space, or a viewpoint, make them shallower, slowing down movement and increasing the chances of pausing. The final tread might not touch the landing, to give it the appearance of floating, signifying a change in floor level.

THE STAIR AND FORM

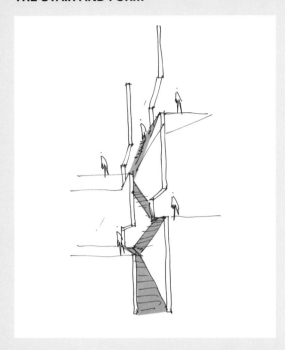

Stair in wall

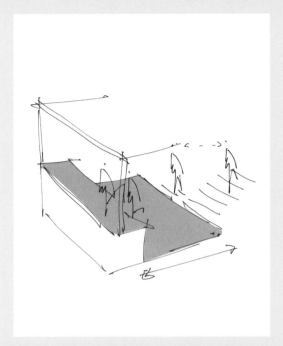

Extended landing as meeting point

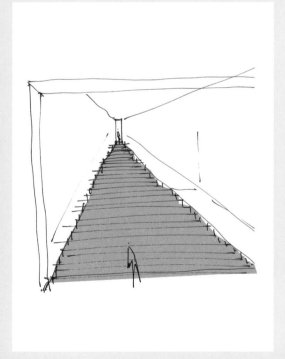

Taper for intensity

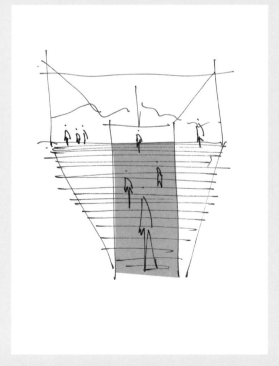

Taper for relief

THE STAIR AND DETAIL

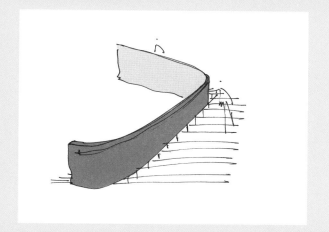

Sculptural form

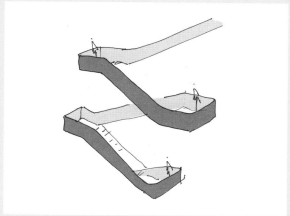

Newel post and balustrade collide

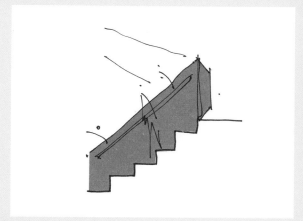

Seamless transition

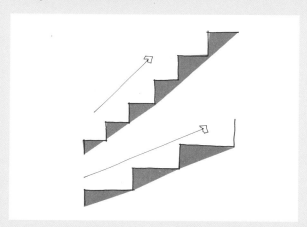

Finding the right speed

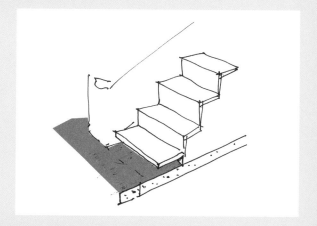

Floating step marks new level

SERVICES

Servant and served

services, *noun*
From Latin – *servus* (slave)
1. An act of help, aid.
2. Work performed for remuneration.
3. The supply or supplying of utilities –
electricity, water, gas, cleansing, etc.,
as required.

In the 1960s, Louis Kahn wrote the following call to arms for architects:

'*Structures should be devised which can harbour the mechanical needs of rooms and spaces ... If we were to train ourselves to draw as we build, from the bottom up, when we do, stopping our pencil to make a mark at the joints of pouring or erecting, ornament would grow out of love for the expression of the method. ... The desire to express how it is done would filter through the entire society of building, to architect, engineer, builder and draughtsman.*'[1]

In my experience, Kahn's challenge is often not taken up by architects, and the quality of interior space is compromised by building services. Accommodating air handling units and ventilation ducts can mean that the ceiling level has to drop to hide plastic aprons and rudimentary fixings; meanwhile, radiators sit proud of clean, crisp walls (or even in front of glazing). Such problems are more severe in projects where the structure is exposed – there are no suspended ceilings or fattened walls in which to hide the services. Waste and water pipes are often left exposed on walls – their plastic flanges or rough metal finish marring the aesthetics of the space (or worse, an apologetic box is built around them). It is an unenviable choice: to accept that the quality of our spaces will be compromised by taking the honest option and letting services show; or to try to cover them up in an act of well-intentioned dishonesty that will also cost more.

When I think of accommodating services, I look with envy at older buildings. What did they do at the Alhambra palace in Granada, Spain, when it got too hot? They took refuge in a courtyard – they didn't have a plastic box pumping recycled air over their heads. How did the Romans heat their spaces in winter? They used a *hypocaust* – a simple underfloor heating system – rather than radiators, grilles and heaters all over the place. How did the Victorians deal with the problem of waste pipes running down solid stone walls? They fabricated them from cast iron with bespoke detailing, rather than a brown plastic pipe running incongruously through the architecture. These approaches to services were in keeping with the buildings that housed them.

Kahn attempted to resolve the dichotomy by designing 'servant' and 'served' spaces. The servant spaces (stairwells, elevators, vents, pipes, ducts) are separated from the served spaces (the spaces building users inhabit – offices, classrooms, laboratories, etc.), and Kahn elevated this practical solution into an architectural feature. His approach aimed to minimize, or in some cases conceal, the routes that the services took, while ensuring that they were expressed in a way befitting the architecture. This is evident in his design for the Trenton Bath House in New Jersey, which employed a grid of enlarged, hollowed-out columns to house services; or in his Salk Institute laboratories in California, where he introduced an interstitial floor to accommodate ducts and pipes, freeing up the soffit below and minimizing obstructions in the space; or perhaps most successfully in the services towers for ventilation at the Richards Medical Research Laboratories in Philadelphia. Kahn's desire to express services was not born out of love for them. As he noted: 'I do not like ducts, I do not like pipes. I hate them really thoroughly, but because I hate them so thoroughly I feel they have to be given their place. If I just hated them and took no care, I think they would invade the building and completely destroy it.'[2]

As our buildings are subject to ever more stringent environmental codes, they risk becoming suffocating boxes stuffed with pipes, ducts and vents to meet multiple conflicting requirements. For example, relying on natural ventilation might mean you fail to meet acoustic requirements. Regulations might demand an HVAC system, with exposed units; meanwhile, the relative economy of using radiators and wall-mounted heaters rather than underfloor heating will mean they will continue to be used in the majority of projects. These environmental and technical concerns are overloading our buildings with services, and dictating their design.

The need for a solution to this problem has never been greater. If we ignore them, services will become the served while space and beauty in architecture becomes the servant. Countering this requires a coordinated process from draughtsman to builder, led by the architect. At present services and architecture progress separately until they meet awkwardly on site. We need to take up the challenge of expressing services honestly but in a manner that is in keeping with the building. We should ensure that architecture remains the served and services the servant. Following are some suggestions to help us achieve this:

Prevent – design for passive natural ventilation, cooling and heating

Designing for passive cooling and heating makes buildings appropriate for their climate and more energy efficient, and will ultimately reduce the number of ducts and pipes required to heat, cool and ventilate the building. For instance, a hot, dry climate would suggest a compact plan with a central courtyard to provide shade from the sun, while a building in the tropics would benefit from a long, thin plan raised on stilts to maximize through ventilation. A tropical climate might also use a roof form separated from the main body of the building to allow hot air to circulate, while a building in a cold, wet climate would have a unified roof form, designed to shed rain and snow. Buildings should always respond to the local climate – this is the first and most crucial step in addressing reliance on mechanical services.

Organize – create space for services and align it with the structural grid

Where ducts, pipes or conduits are required we can plan our buildings according to Kahn's served and servant approach, by consolidating the routes that services are

PASSIVE SERVICES
Building proposals for an arid climate

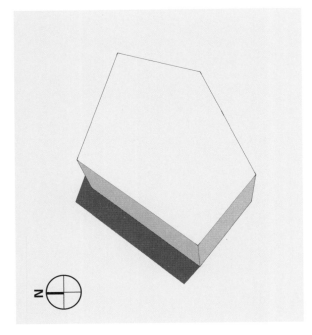

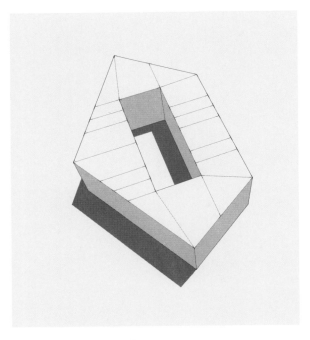

1 ORIENTATION

The plan form is tapered to minimize directly east- or west-facing walls, which receive the highest intensity of solar radiation in summer.

2 CROSS-VENTILATION

A central courtyard is carved out of the building to ensure every room has cross-ventilation and that low-level air coming into the building is naturally cooled. The courtyard also provides a shaded outdoor space for building users to occupy.

required to take. This reduces the amount of ductwork required and also allows us to arrange the services in a coordinated manner. Problems occur with services, especially where the soffit is exposed, when they 'bend' across a plan, particularly where they crash through a wall. The other main problem is that they are usually located randomly in relation to the structural grid, and may clash with it. We can remedy this by creating larger 'servant spaces' rather than multiple individual service risers dotted around the building. You might use the idea of a 'service spine', which contains all services running parallel, not at odds with the structural grid. If you do not consolidate the services, engineers and contractors will tend to install them in the most economical manner, which won't necessarily be in keeping with the architecture.

Remodel – propose new ways to make services

Building services are generally not attractive; they are designed to be hidden, solely a product of economy. Perhaps, though, to paraphrase Kahn, we should retrain ourselves

3 STACKS

Wind towers and solar chimneys are incorporated into the building form, which draw cleaner air from a high level down into the building, funnelling it down to create a breeze through the building. Forms are enlarged to double as building accommodation.

4 MATERIALS/OPENINGS

The building is inward-looking to protect it from harsh winds and strong sunlight. The exterior comprises a series of narrow openings (to north and south façades), with solid walls with minimal openings to the east and west. A fully glazed courtyard provides the required light levels and transparency. Openings to the chimneys to south and west face prevailing winds. Thick walls with a high thermal mass are used throughout.

to draw them. We can accept that radiators, pipes and ceiling-mounted units will pervade our architecture, but suggest new ways to make them more palatable. At present we deal with services either by apologetically covering them up (with plasterboard 'box-outs') or we leave these elements, designed to be concealed, exposed. What if there was a third way that allowed for the services to be expressed (and therefore easily maintained), but remodelled to fit better in our buildings.

By applying the principles outlined here we can try to stop the potential imbalance between architecture and its services; served and servant space. By responding to the specific climatic requirements of our designs; arranging plans in a manner which ensures that the services align with our designs; and remodelling the kit that houses these services we can ensure that architecture – quality of space, clarity of plan and form – remains the primary aim of our buildings.

SERVICES ORGANIZATION

KEY   ☐ Riser   ▨ Ventilation   ▨ Electrical   ▨ Heating

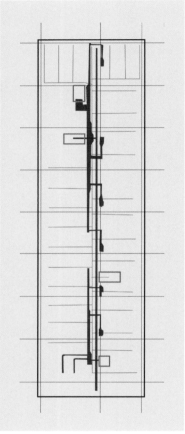

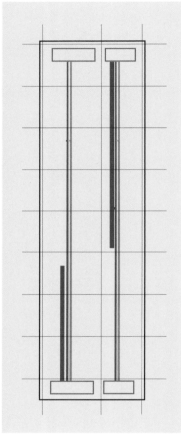

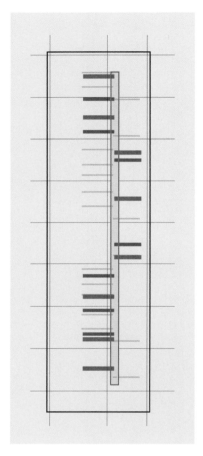

TYPICAL – SEPARATE RISERS

The random nature of separated risers means that different services cross over one another and the structural grid. This will amount to multiple clashes and visual conflicts in the soffit.

PROPOSED – CONSOLIDATED RISERS

Risers are combined and placed at either end of the building, parallel to the horizontal structural grid. This means that the service runs can be combined, allowing for two consistent service 'spines'.

PROPOSED – CONSOLIDATED RISERS

Risers are combined into one along the vertical structural grid. This means that services can be arranged such that they will never clash with the structure or with each other.

SERVICES REMODELLING
Show how it is done

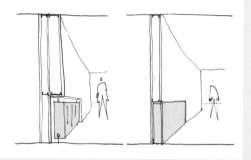

PROBLEM
The radiator protrudes, disrupting visual lines and using additional space.

CURRENT SOLUTION
The radiator is boxed in, requiring additional wall depth and material.

PROPOSED SOLUTION
The radiator becomes flush and integral to the wall or floor to provide support and keep wall depth to a minimum.

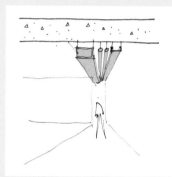
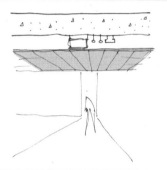
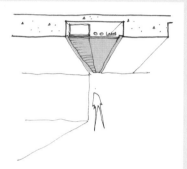

PROBLEM
Services are exposed to the soffit.

CURRENT SOLUTION
Reduce the ceiling height and cover them up.

PROPOSED SOLUTION
Maintain original ceiling height by casting a void into the floor slab to allow for an accessible services tray.

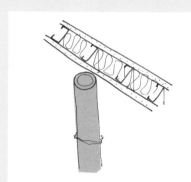
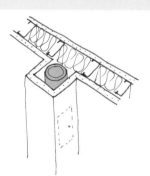
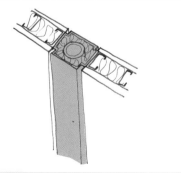

PROBLEM
A pipe is exposed on the wall.

CURRENT SOLUTION
The pipe is boxed in with thin, apologetic lining.

PROPOSED SOLUTION
Create a pipe 'cassette' made of coated metal to express the pipe in an honest yet visually coherent way. The cassette can be easily removed and replaced as required.

0 15 30 45 60 75 (m)

GREENBELT STRATEGY 3: ROOF AND FLOOR

Carved terraced apartments, M62, UK, site plan, J. Tait. Proposed within the hills of North West England, between its many towns and cities, the example above shows a new community of 1,400 homes carved out of the limestone beneath unused moorland. Each is connected by bridges over a light well (shown in the dark hatch), which also acts as vertical circulation to a chain of perimeter amenities. Large interlinked terraces and social spaces between apartments allow the roofs of the dwellings below to become the extended floors of the terraces above, providing a new multi-level manmade topography inserted into and combining the natural one. For more drawings and information, see www.jtait.com

4
AUGMENT

REVIEW

Don't stop, keep going

review, *verb*
From French – *revoir* (see again)
1. (transitive) To go over, examine again.
2. (transitive) To look at again, to reflect.
3. (transitive) To formally or officially inspect.
4. (transitive) To survey a situation mentally.
5. (transitive) To assess (a literary work, work
of art, film, etc.) in a critical manner.

In architecture, we must constantly respond to the changing parameters of a project, while continuing to make progress. The design review, or 'crit', is a mechanism that allows for evaluation to formulate the best response to a brief and the shifting parameters of a project.

Architects first come across the crit, short for critique, in architecture school. The crit is built into architectural pedagogy, and allows more experienced practitioners – tutors and fellow students – to objectively assess the progress of a project, and by extension the student. A crit can range from a friendly peer over the shoulder, to an informal weekly pin-up and discussion, or a full-blown jury focusing on one individual and their work, covering a sliding scale from assistance to judgment, from light tension to high pressure.

It is essential to the development of a design idea, or for that matter the development of an architect, to carry this process out at regular intervals. Through regular and varied design reviews, a dialogue is fostered that can unearth hidden opportunities in a project and correct unwitting errors at an early stage. Most importantly, for the student, the crit allows them to improve their analytical skills when responding to site constraints and the parameters of the brief, in tandem with their social and aesthetic intuition.

In architecture school the crit is intended to simulate an aspect of life in practice as an architect: your boss having a quick look at your computer screen; an informal pin-up among colleagues; to the presentation to the client, pointer in hand and heart in mouth. The crit offers the opportunity for reflection and assessment, helping the architect develop from student to professional. In practice, the purpose of the crit is to interrogate the multiple parameters contained within a project – client, brief, site – in order to create a coherent design. Personal development is not the primary purpose of the design review in practice.

The projects we carry out at architecture school are generally static; concocted and executed in an academic bubble. The brief remains unchanged from start to finish, unencumbered by changing client needs or budget constraints; the site is fixed and clear, free from planning legislation or financial disputes; the project is not intended

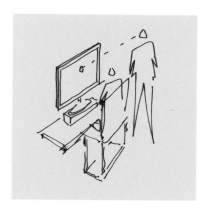

DAILY
Instant/Fortuitous

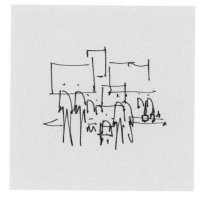

WEEKLY
Informal/Loose

MONTHLY
Formal/Structured

to actually be built, so is detached from the technical and contractual challenges that realizing a building entails. Yet despite an arguably more pressing need for regular design reviews in practice than in academia, in my experience there are fewer of them.

However, I believe that the discipline of the crit is essential in professional practice. Without this pause for review opportunities are missed, problems are not averted, and ideas may not develop fully. We should try to build time into our practice for regular design reviews regardless of office hierarchy and time and budget constraints – the models and sketches we create for this purpose are never in vain, as the following examples show:

Example 1 – retaining public space

A new residential quarter was to be located in the heart of a city, following the demolition of an unloved building that once occupied the site. In an effort to integrate the project with the surrounding community, the proposal included a new cultural and leisure centre funded by local government. The privately funded development would provide local amenity at no additional expense to the private developer, while the local government would be able to create new facilities (including a library, auditorium and swimming pool) without having to pay for land acquisition and services.

As the distinguishing feature and social heart of the project, the public element became the key generator of the design. Plans, sections, models and 3D images were all generated in anticipation of an application for planning permission. However, weeks before the submission date we were informed that the local government could no longer invest in the public facilities at the heart of the project.

The client seemed unfazed by this. It was made clear to us that the planning submission must remain on track, and that loss of time and revenue was not an option. However, the public element was the heart of the proposal. Functionally it would provide much-needed amenity and culture to the local area; historically it would create a new focal point at the intersection of two key axes in the city; formally the sculpted tower element would act as a counterpoint to the deliberately monotone bass notes

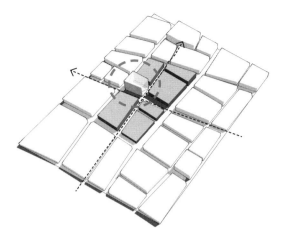

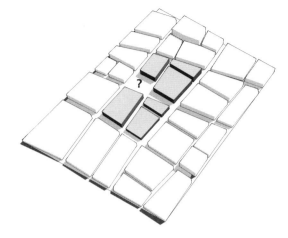

ORIGINAL DESIGN

PROBLEM

of the residential development surrounding it; and socially it would ensure that the development did not become a residential enclave dissociated from the city.

How could we respond to the changing terrain around us? It was tempting to just do as the client asked: carry on regardless and finish the submission as it was. Instead, we decided to review the project, and our crit posed the following questions:

— How can we retain public amenity without adding area and cost?
— How can we respect and signify the historic axes?
— How can we maintain a formal counterpoint: a taller more sculpted element to complement the residential elements?
— How can we retain an idea of social ambition within the scheme?

Each residential block had a covered central atrium from which all the apartments were accessed – an early client request to give the development more of a hotel feel. The problem with this central space was that it made the apartments technically single aspect, with one side being internal, as well as being an inefficient use of floor area. We proposed to remove this atrium and leave the internal space open like a large courtyard garden for the residents. This meant the apartments would now be accessed from the street and be dual aspect, and there would be a new shaded garden space. The area and volume of atrium space that was removed from the residential blocks would therefore form the basis of a new 'public' element to be funded by the developer with no additional overall project area. It would provide amenities for the residents such as a library, gym, swimming pool, events space and gallery. The increased complexity in

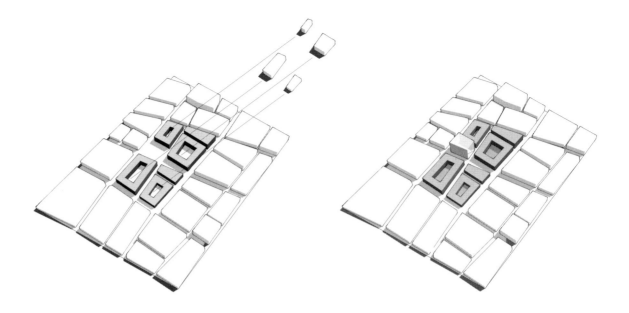

THE CRIT   **THE SOLUTION**

terms of function made it slightly more expensive to build, but the increased future revenue from providing for these facilities more than compensated for that. The client then approached the local government, who still could not fund any of the capital costs of the building, but suggested that they collaborate on the running of the facilities, thus opening the new amenity to the rest of the city as originally intended.

Through a collaborative design review we managed to retain public amenity, the overall form and layout, and the original social ambition of the scheme. In addition, the apartments were now more valuable because they were dual aspect and better ventilated, while a green space was provided at the heart of each residential block.

Example 2 – overcoming plant problems

Email after email went unheeded: *'We need a final and accurate indication of the cooling tower sizes, please.' 'The plant screen to the top of the building now needs to go into fabrication to meet the programme – the level of the screen is +23.130 based on our discussions 6 months ago. Can you confirm that the cooling towers will not protrude above this level?'* Still no reply. The office building we had designed and that was now being constructed had some fairly onerous heating and cooling requirements and required large cooling towers to be located on the rooftop. However, the size of these was never fully confirmed. A screen was introduced to the top of the building as a visual barrier to hide the plant, its height set at 300mm (11¾in.)above the height we had been given for the cooling towers.

With the screen constructed and put in place, the plant finally arrived on site. The cooling towers were now 1.3m (4ft 3in.) higher than originally stated – rising a metre

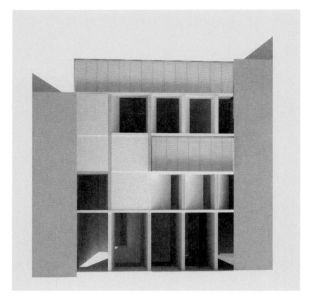

ORIGINAL DESIGN
2.3m-high (7ft 7in.) screen hides cooling towers behind

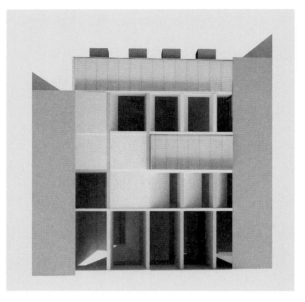

AS BUILT – PROBLEM
Cooling towers built 1m (3ft 3in.) higher than screen

(3 ft 3in.) above the screen. The item that had been added solely to hide the plant now wouldn't do its job, and was superfluous. More critically, the visible plant contradicted the terms of the planning consent. The local government official in charge of the project visited the site and recommended that the cooling towers be replaced at the height stipulated in the original approved design.

The building was built and due to open in less than a month. The services engineer explained that the plant was the correct size for the heating and cooling requirements of the building – removing and replacing it was not an option. The other potential solution was to increase the height of the screen by one metre. This would have been extremely costly and would have involved additional structure as well as pushing the building above the maximum height allowed.

We opened the problem up to the whole office in a desperate attempt to solve the conundrum. We puzzled over it until one member of staff produced a picture of a Donald Judd sculpture, rotated it by 90 degrees and pinned it to the wall. We all understood straight away the solution contained in the image:
— Remove the superfluous screen.
— Allow the cubic forms of the cooling towers to define the top of the building.
— Treat or paint the plant in a considered manner and strip it of unnecessary branding and structure to enable it to become part of the architecture.
This solution would solve the issue of the useless plant screen, while improving the look of the cooling towers. It would also be a more honest approach, expressing function –

THE CRIT
Building a screen up higher than the cooling towers was not an option, aesthetically or legally

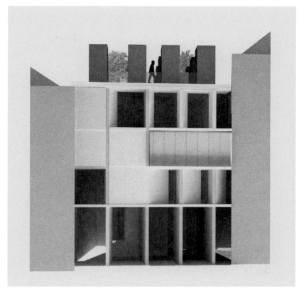

THE SOLUTION
The cooling towers, repainted and stripped of unnecessary structure to become a new, more honest formal element at the top of the building

the idea of exposing the plant appealed to our Modernist sensibilities more than an apologetic screen. The new cooling towers would also provide more of a dialogue with the varied roof forms of the neighbouring buildings than a flat horizontal screen. We could even use the spaces in between as a roof garden. All we needed was specialist paint and a new glass balustrade.

As the higher-than-approved height was not a consistent mass on top of the building, was more permeable and set back from the building line, the changes were accepted, and the resubmitted proposal was approved. Through collaborative design review we had managed to avert a disaster, and tease out hidden opportunities in the original design.

Harnessing the power of the crit

The review is one of the most fundamental tools an architect has at their disposal. Collaborative and objective evaluation, irrespective of the stage of the project, is essential to the success of our designs. The fleeting pause of the crit allows us to respond objectively to changing parameters that can affect a project in a considered and rational manner. Additionally, the collaborative nature of the crit allows for fresh perspectives on these issues, which can unlock hidden potential in our designs as well as identify unseen flaws. We should make time for the crit in practice regardless of time, money or office hierarchy. If not, our designs will suffer.

DIAGRAM

Complexity and confusion

diagram, *verb*
From Ancient Greek – *diagraphein*
(to mark out using lines)
1. To represent in a diagrammatic
way; to show in a diagram (an outline
or sketch that explains the operation
of something).

Clarity and directness are essential in architecture in order to demystify theories and substantiate claims (see 'Obscurity'). However, this need not apply to the actual designs, which can be complex, varied and rich. Take that holiest of architectural devices: the diagram.

As students we are often taught to ensure 'clarity of the diagram' in whatever we do. This precise depiction is intended to distil the architectural idea into a single vision. This can be a worthwhile pursuit, but it also limits the design to one outcome, one formal arrangement, one functional scenario, one relationship of space.

I think we should allow our diagrams to become more confused, offering multiple outcomes. In this way we can provide variety and tension, not sameness and sterility. Through tangling the diagram we can make richer, freer designs for our eyes to look at, our cities to receive, and end users to inhabit.

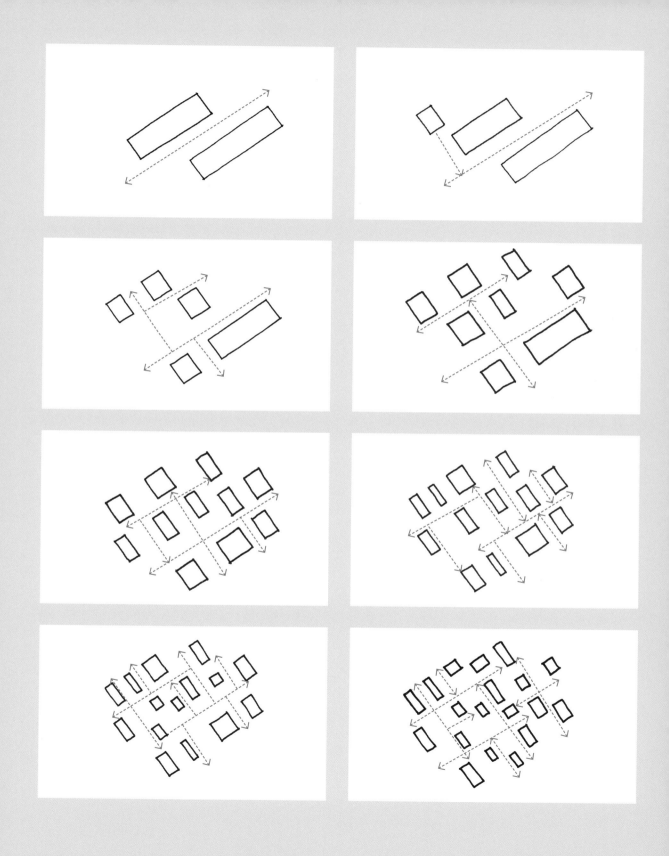

OPTIMIZE

Designing for speed

optimize, *verb*
From Latin – *optimus* (best)
1. (transitive) To make as perfect,
advantageous, effective as possible.
2. (transitive) To carry out a task or
activity with maximum efficiency.
3. (transitive) To find the best solution
when combining separate, often
conflicting, requirements.

Many styles of architecture seem to have encapsulated movement: Gothic, a tangled collection of grappling forms; Baroque, a languid, celestial upward sway; Neoclassicism, a regulated goose-step; Brutalism, the punishing crash of wave on rock; Deconstructivism, violent uncoordinated spasms. None, however, have truly captured speed.

Art Deco is often said to evoke speed with its streamlined curves and go-faster stripes, but this is an applied notion of speed – like putting a vest and running shoes on a lazy man and calling him a champion sprinter.

Why try to create an architecture of speed? Speed is attained through the optimization of form and function, whether by evolution or design. Unnecessary components are rejected, tailored forms are chosen over borrowed, recycled geometry, materials are selected for economy and performance, and colour and pattern are always useful, such as the feathers of a peacock, or the camouflage of a warship. All these are qualities to which I believe architecture should aspire, as shown in the following examples.

Peregrine falcon

A bird does not rely on engines to achieve speed, but on its structural qualities.

— *Keel – structure*
The large keel (breastbone) allows for a greater muscle area to generate the power required for high speed.
— *Wings – form*
The wingspan is more than double the total area of the bird, to power flight. During flight, the wings are tucked in and streamlined, creating an aerofoil effect like the wing of a plane.
— *Feathers – materiality*
The feathers are small and stiff, reducing drag and enabling much faster speeds than longer, looser feathers.

GRAPPLING Duomo, Milan, Italy

GOTHIC Diva Battle Royal, Texas, USA

SWAY L'Església de Santa Maria, Alicante, Spain

BAROQUE Tango dancers

REGULATED Mansudae Assembly Hall, Pyongyang, North Korea

NEOCLASSICAL Chinese Honour Guard

PUNISHING Nichinan Cultural Centre, Japan

BRUTALISM Wave on rock

SPASMS Disney Concert Hall, Los Angeles, USA

DECONSTRUCTIVISM Girl, freaking out

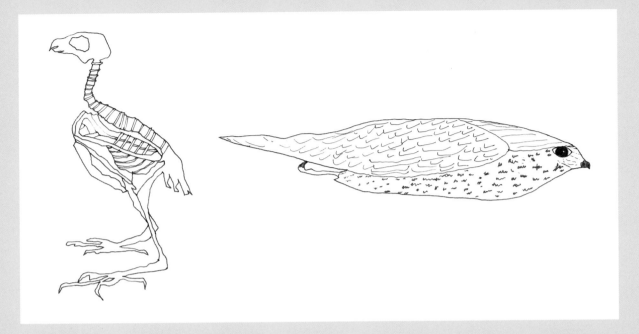

FALCO PEREGRINUS Structure, form, materiality

CUTTY SARK Structure, form, materiality

Cutty Sark
This is the original fast ship, or clipper.

— *Bow + stern – structure*
The long bow prevents water washing over the hull, while the square stern gives buoyancy, enabling the ship to cut through the water. The heavy iron hull provides mass to generate power.
— *Sails – form*
The sail area is more than four times the area of the boat. As in the falcon, the mass being carried is therefore significantly smaller than the mass carrying it.
— *Hull cladding – materiality*
The boat's hull is clad in a composite of brass and zinc, preventing the growth of barnacles and the onset of rust, which would slow the ship down.
What can we learn from these two examples to inform our architectural designs?

Restrict structure to essentials
There should be nothing extraneous, nothing redundant; every structural element should be essential. In architecture this translates as structural form and decoration being one and the same. Why have a steel frame, filled with insulation, if a skin is then applied? If we followed the example of the falcon, or the *Cutty Sark*, the skin would be an integral part of the structure, and vice versa. However, in the example of the bird or the ship, heavy mass is also required to generate the necessary power (provided by the oversized keel in the falcon, or the iron structure of the *Cutty Sark*). In architecture this translates as needing a solid mass or base to act as a counterpoint to the lighter elements.

Tailor the form
To retain a sense of dynamism, the mass should not dominate the overall form. As a rough guide, try a minimum ratio of 3:1 of light elements to solid mass. The form should not be wilful or haphazard; every element of the falcon or the ship is streamlined and tailored to enable it to achieve the maximum speed. In architecture this means, for example, that there should be no clumsy boxes on the roof to contain plant; there should be no stylistic additions that don't contribute to a fully functional form or relate to context; there should be nothing borrowed from other projects that isn't fully compatible with the needs of the project in question.

Use materials appropriately
Materials play a vital role: the feathers of the falcon and the brass hull of the *Cutty Sark* are perfect models for architecture. Both are undeniably beautiful, but more crucially they perform functions critical to the attainment of speed. True beauty is not about aesthetics alone; it must also be functional. In architecture this might manifest itself as pure white render to reflect heat from a building in a hot climate; sculptural metal fins that enable discreet ventilation; or in the use of perforated mesh cladding that provides both privacy and light in equal measures. Beauty and function must always be designed in tandem.

Through structural economy, tailoring of forms, and appropriate material selection we can create an architecture of speed, of optimization.

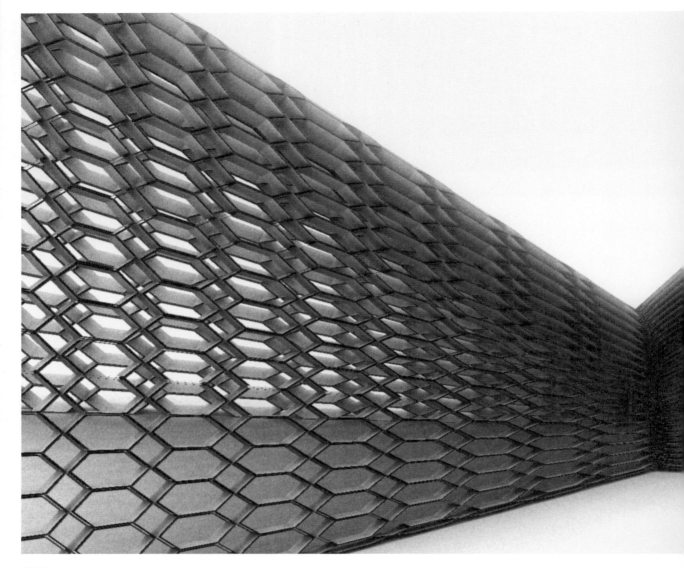

ARCH
Paris, J. Tait, 2012

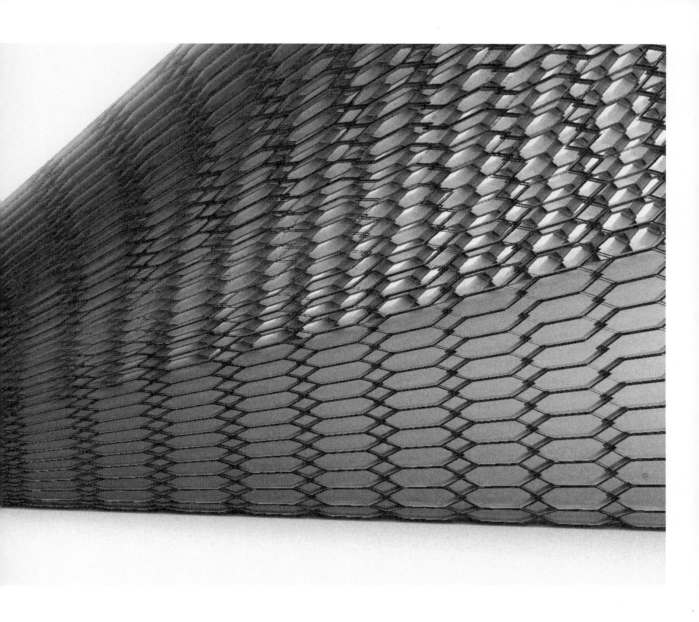

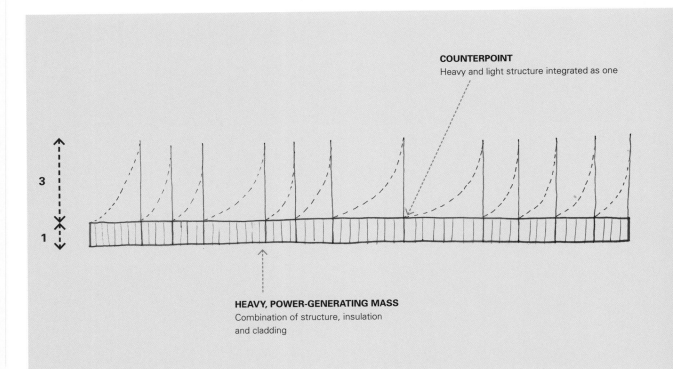

COUNTERPOINT
Heavy and light structure integrated as one

3

1

HEAVY, POWER-GENERATING MASS
Combination of structure, insulation
and cladding

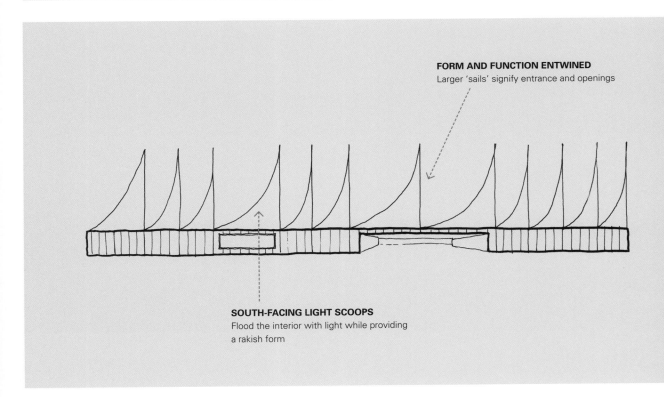

FORM AND FUNCTION ENTWINED
Larger 'sails' signify entrance and openings

SOUTH-FACING LIGHT SCOOPS
Flood the interior with light while providing
a rakish form

4 — Augment

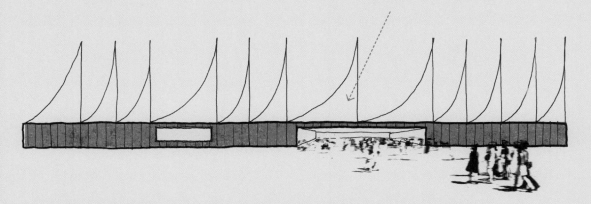

FUNCTIONAL BEAUTY
By means of a translucent skin the 'sails'
receive light by day and emit light at night.

ECONOMIZE

Finding flair in frugality

economize, *verb*
From Ancient Greek – *oiko-nomia*
(house – management)
1. (intransitive) To practise economy;
to manage resources carefully avoiding
extravagance or waste.
2. (transitive) To use frugally.

In architecture, extravagance is sometimes expected, even when it may not be required. It is often used as a tool by architects and their clients to achieve an effect. For example, local government might want an iconic museum to show that they are at the forefront of 'culture'; a corporation might want a grandly proportioned lobby to impress clients; a hotel might want exquisitely crafted interiors to project luxury; or a homeowner might want a gold tap for their new kitchen ... just because. Yet these projects are the exceptions; 99 per cent of the time the client simply wants a building built to schedule and on budget. While a lack of budget and time might at first appear to limit creativity, with the excesses of extravagance set aside we can find other ways to exercise flair.

A canny approach allows us to find inspiration in frugality. We can distil what is important, and filter out what is not. Focus on the design; fight for the inclusion or integrity of the salient points our buildings are making. This approach can elevate an ordinary project to a well-considered piece of architecture – at no additional cost.

Two low-cost social housing projects built six decades apart that achieved this combination of flair and frugality are the Hallfield Estate in London, designed by Tecton and completed by Lindsay Drake and Sir Denys Lasdun from 1949–1955, and Laurieston Phase 1 in Glasgow, by Elder and Cannon Architects, finished in 2015. Hallfield was designed in a time of post-Second World War austerity for the local Borough Council, while Laurieston was built for a Housing Association at £110,000 per unit (the average comparative unit cost £129,300).[1]

Crucially, to achieve this is a process of picking your battles – of fighting for what is important to the design and letting go what isn't. It would be naive to think that budget does not affect the quality of our architecture – it can. But we can always find ways to work cleverly within financial constraints, to eke out quality and beauty in our designs. Any architect who blames the lack of budget for their compromised designs either hasn't identified the areas where flair could present itself in the first instance, or didn't fight hard enough to retain them once they were found. If the success of our designs rests solely on the money available to build them, then they weren't good designs in the first place.

HALLFIELD

FLAIR

Care is taken by the architect to ensure that the transition from street level to building level is given importance. Access to a refuse area is via angular access steps – a simple, normally hidden function is given added flair via the means of a stair that is expressive in form and appears to float when viewed from some angles.

FRUGALITY

The staircase is fabricated from simple, low-cost materials such as concrete and steel. This floating illusion is created by the use of a discreet support of dark blue Staffordshire bricks.

LAURIESTON

FLAIR

A simple door canopy is not only a shelter from rain while you fumble for your key, but becomes a signifier through the careful choice of materials and expression of form. The material choice allows the canopy to share a consistency with the lintel above (and not appear as an afterthought), while the exaggerated form adds to the overall façade composition.

FRUGALITY

The canopy is in-situ concrete, a readily available and relatively cheap material and process. The canopy is not used throughout, but only where serving the ground-floor flats, which are accessed directly from the street. This signifies this particular flat type while reducing their overall number through use only where essential. The form of the entrance, and by extension the architecture, displays its function.

HALLFIELD

FLAIR

Knowing that the standardized floor plans and repetition of building layouts required by the typology and budget would create similarly standard and repetitious façades, Tecton broke away from Modernist convention and separated the function of the blocks from their façade. The façades were treated like abstract artworks of red and grey chequerboard and differing linear patterns of precast concrete panels. In the image on the left further attention to detail is paid by painting the railings between the panels black, contributing to the 'floating' effect; the screen appears completely detached from the structure of the building.[2]

FRUGALITY

The treatment of the façade as an artwork is done by minimal means. On the chequerboard façades a simple change in colour between panels was all that was needed to create the desired effect. For the concrete 'screens' both the vertical elements and the horizontal elements are not merely cosmetic – they are column locations and balustrade heights, which would have been required anyway. By unifying and abstracting these elements the façade becomes an 'artwork' through a few clever design moves.

LAURIESTON

FLAIR

Variety on the façades is achieved, despite the unified approach to materiality and proportion, by allowing the function and aspect of the apartments to dictate different approaches. The bedroom windows facing out from the east façade are narrow in proportion, reflecting the need to limit daylight and increase privacy. The west-facing façade is defined by deep balcony reveals, which provide a genuine external space to take advantage of views and sunsets in the evenings, as well its unique aspect on to an area of green space. The south façade has wider windows and projecting balconies to take maximum advantage of the increased sunlight and daylight, while providing additional outdoor space from the living areas.

FRUGALITY

By providing variation within consistency of proportions, materials and building components (precast concrete lintels, metal railings, timber handrails) the same building methods, suppliers and subcontractors can be used throughout. This approach means that the building responds to context and environment on all sides, but retains a coherency when read as a whole. As well as a visual and architectural consistency, this approach to the façade design creates an economy of scale across the 1500-unit project.

HALLFIELD

FLAIR

A flat, banal façade of red brick and flush steel windows is animated with the addition of sculptural balconies. These serve to provide visual interest, while also giving the occupants a small outdoor garden space and views across the development. A standard rectilinear balcony, or no balcony, would not have imbued the façade with the playfulness it now has.

FRUGALITY

These expressive balconies are only on the third and fifth floors to limit overshadowing, while also limiting the overall number. As with the stair, this expressive element is made from the relatively low-cost materials of concrete, render and steel.

LAURIESTON

FLAIR

The repetition of the north-facing façade is deliberately and skilfully disrupted by the introduction of a floating glass box projecting from the building mass. This serves to add an element of surprise to the façade, while creating a unique space for the inhabitants of the house.

FRUGALITY

The frugality is in the carefulness of its use. The glass box is used just once – to signify a unique house type in the block, a three-storey townhouse, and to provide a local way-finding device. By using it only where it signifies something different the integrity of its use is maintained and the additional cost associated with it is not scattered haphazardly around the building. Its scarcity piques a curiosity in anyone who views it, which would not be the case if it were ubiquitous.

HALLFIELD

FLAIR

A hierarchy of materials is employed according to location, visibility and function. The corner columns supporting the block are tapered, fluted and made from poured and shuttered concrete, suggesting a higher level of care and attention to detail – and thus importance. The gable façades are clad in white tiles in a carefully detailed grid of grey cement, while the brick underneath the overhang – least visible – is unadorned and simply built.

FRUGALITY

By ascertaining which elements of the building need to be shown by their material expression to be of higher importance, less important elements can be made from lower-cost materials to compensate. Through material choices the columns and gables dominate and the rear wall recedes, as is appropriate to the function of these elements.

LAURIESTON

FLAIR

The dominant material throughout is relatively expensive handmade brick, which presents a warm and textured appearance to the street. The roof profile similarly allows for a linear roof profile to the street, removing any domestic clichés and giving the building a more civic, formal feel, akin to the Georgian and Victorian terraces which once dominated the area.

FRUGALITY

Knowing that it was important to retain the texture and warmth at all costs, the architect made the decision to use a machine-made brick to the rear, which is not visible from the street. At face value this might have seemed like an exercise in cost-saving, but the reflective nature of the brick allows light to reflect among the back courts and gardens. Similarly, the pitch of the roof becomes visible only from the residents' rear garden area, presenting a more domestic feel when not addressing the street.

COLOUR
The careful use of red

colour, *verb*
From Latin – *color* (tint, hue)
1. (transitive) To apply a colour (a hue,
tinge, shade) to something.
2. (transitive) To give a distinguishable
quality to something.
3. (transitive) To influence in a
distorted manner.

Deriving from the Latin word *rubrica*, for red ochre or red chalk, the process of rubrication was used in medieval manuscripts to highlight key text in red ink. This picked out the salient points of an impenetrable text, while also adding a layer of decoration to delight the eye. Rubrication therefore made the manuscript legible to the general public and contributed to its commercial success.[1] Architecture too, can make use of rubrication.

Uses of red
Red is an emotive colour that has various meanings across different cultures: passion, intensity, strength, love, hatred, anger, power, warning, sex, romance, blood, revolution … There are few colours that evoke so many concepts.

In Spain, for example, red is used to antagonize the bull in the ancient sport of bullfighting; various revolutionaries from French republicans to Soviet Bolsheviks have used the red flag as a symbol of rebellion; in the UK, postboxes are painted bright red to heighten visibility; originating in the USA, fast-food outlets have long used the colour to promote impulse buying and stimulate appetite;[2] across the world red's urgency is literally used to stop traffic.

The use of red is very much alive in architecture too. In ancient Chinese architecture red combined with black symbolized happiness; in Sweden houses were painted red to imitate the grandeur of brick buildings in environments where that material was unavailable; many traditional Indian buildings, particularly temples and forts, are made from local red sandstone.

The most successful use of red in contemporary architecture is perhaps when it is used honestly: when the material the building is made from is inherently red, where it is not applied, such as in Gillespie, Kidd and Coia's St Bride's Church near Glasgow, where red brick gives the solid monoliths warmth and forms a stark marker in a landscape dominated by grey rendered buildings; the Caixa Forum in Madrid by Herzog & de Meuron, which uses an oxidized iron roof object as a 'tactile and lively complement'[3] to the existing bricks below; or Souto do Moura's Casa das Histórias in Cascais, Portugal, where the deep red concrete evokes the vernacular coloured render of the area while vividly contrasting with the surrounding greenery.[4] In these examples it is clear that the red colour was an essential part of the overall building design, conveying texture, enhancing form, contextual relevance, and the effect of sunlight.

4 — Augment

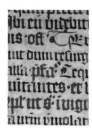     

HIGHLIGHT **ANGER** **REVOLUTION** **LEGIBILITY** **HUNGER** **WARNING**

RED BRICK
St Bride's, East Kilbride, UK, G, K + C

RED IRON
Caixa Forum, Madrid, Herzog & de Meuron

RED CONCRETE
Casa das Histórias, Cascais, Souto de Moura

But what about architectural rubrication, where the architect *applies* red, usually by way of a bright painted finish, to highlight a key aspect of the building? Here the careful use of red is critical. Too much, and the building risks being read as an architectural one-liner. Do we want our buildings to be defined solely by their colour, or do we want them to be remembered for their form, the spaces they create, their response to context, and how they are used?

If the use of red becomes too dominant, it is in danger of being used as an apology for the dull, sterile architecture it masks. If overused, this colour can lose all its power. Consider if it were removed from a building – would it be better or worse? We should aim to use red carefully and sparingly, to highlight salient features of the architecture and draw attention to its key principles.

— *Reinforcement of ethos*
At the PA Technology Industrial Park in Princeton, USA, Richard Rogers used red as a symbolic device to reinforce the continuing theme of his work – the celebration of structure. To reinforce the physical manifestation of this ethos, the external tension structure was painted red to highlight its importance to the overall design and elevate this perfunctory building type from a simple steel shed.

— *Promoting legibility*
Bernard Tschumi's vast Parc de la Villette in Paris was described by the architect as 'as one of the largest buildings ever constructed – a discontinuous building but a single structure nevertheless'.[5] In order to make this vast 'building' legible, Tschumi devised a series of twenty-five 'dispersed points', which allow park users to navigate towards the different cultural and leisure facilities within. These coloured steel points become markers within the vastness of the park, discernible from a distance by their colour.

EXPRESSION OF ETHOS
PA Technology Laboratory, Princeton, NJ, USA

If no colour is used, the key functional element of the design – the cable structure – is not expressed visually.

LEGIBILITY
Parc de la Villette, Paris, Bernard Tschumi

If no colour is used, the 'dispersed points' become illegible.

DIALOGUE
Olympic Energy Centres, London, John McAslan

If no colour is used, the staircase recedes into the water tank behind, weakening the eastern end of the overall building composition.

FORCED IDENTITY
GMW Building, Berlin, Sauerbruch Hutton

WEAK METAPHOR
Serpentine Pavilion, London, Jean Nouvel

PERSONAL PREFERENCE?
Winnett House, Los Angeles, USA, KDA

The lower images show that if no colour is used the overall building design is otherwise unaffected.

— *Fostering dialogue*

At John McAslan + Partners' Olympic Energy Centres in London the building composition is dominated by the 45m-high flue tower. In order to balance the composition of the building, a staircase becomes a 'feature' by being expressed as a coloured steel sculptural element adjacent to black-painted water tanks. This allows the eastern end of the building to share a formal dialogue with the flue tower, and a chromatic dialogue with the earthy hues of the Corten steel mesh façade.

Conclusion

Colour in architecture should be used as an outcome of the natural hue of the building materials selected. Or, when rubricating (applying colour to highlight elements), you should do so carefully and thoughtfully. If not, the colour use might appear arbitrary and wilful – and any message intended by its use risks being lost.

CONTRAST

A tapestry of differences

contrast, *verb*
From Italian – *contrastare* (to stand against)
1. (transitive) To compare in order to reveal differences; opposing forms, natures, functions, etc.
2. (intransitive) To display dissimilar or opposite qualities in comparison with something else.

'There is no quality in this world that is not what it is merely by contrast. Nothing exists in itself.'[1]
— Herman Melville

Architecture thrives on contrasts: light/dark, curved/rectilinear, order/disorder, rough/smooth, clear/opaque, solid/void. Each of these qualities would be meaningless without its opposite. Darkness seems darker when contrasted with a piercing shaft of light from above; a curve becomes more elegant, more pronounced when juxtaposed with a rectilinear element; the proportions of a piazza seem more pure when juxtaposed with the chaos of the surrounding city, a window's transparency is obvious when set into an opaque wall.

The need for contrast is a balancing act. Not enough contrast results in blandness. Too much contrast, however, and clashing elements will compete with one another. Either way, individual architectural elements may become indistinguishable, and the sense of overall composition will be lost.

Contrast can be achieved through a building responding to its context as well as within an individual building design. For example, at the city level, does your building contrast with the existing grid? Does your façade design mimic or contrast with the building's neighbours? Or, in a landscape, does your building ape the landforms or proudly differ from them? Does your building plan accommodate a sequence of contrasting spaces that accentuate each other, or treat space as a regular, static construct? Is the building a riot of form and competing contrasts, or is it a composition of carefully positioned contrasts?

We can look at contrasts found in three aspects of architecture: its *character* – how it responds to other buildings around it, and to what degree it contrasts with them; its *rhythm* – how the plan or form of a building heightens interest and sensation through varying contrasts; and *grain* – the impression the building gives through its approach to embedded or created textures, and whether the grain of the building is fine or coarse.

Contrasting character

Woody Allen's 1983 comic film *Zelig* might be interpreted as an instructive allegory of contrast in architecture. Protagonist Leonard Zelig mimics the people around him, with an incessant desire to fit in. He poses as a Republican, a Democrat, a baseball player, an Italian gangster and an African American trumpet player, among many others.

CONTRAST IN ARCHITECTURE

LIGHT AND DARK
Fort Dunree, Ireland

RECTILINEAR AND CURVED
National Congress, Brasília, Oscar Niemeyer

ORDER AND DISORDER
Piazza San Marco, Venice, Italy

SOLID AND VOID
Fundação Iberê Camargo, Porto Alegre, Spain, Alvaro Siza

CLEAR AND OPAQUE
Whitney Museum of Modern Art, New York,
Marcel Breuer

NO CONTRAST

This building becomes a 'Zelig' chameleon by copying its surroundings. It is weak, apologetic and lacks confidence.

TOO MUCH CONTRAST

This building squeezes as much of itself into the site as it can. It disrespects all aspects of its surroundings. It is greedy, selfish and aggressive.

BALANCE OF CONTRAST

This building respects certain key factors of its surroundings – storey heights, roof forms, façade rhythms – but does so in its own way. It is confident, assured and well adjusted.

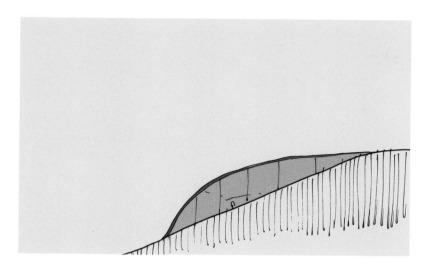

NO CONTRAST
This building becomes a 'Zelig' chameleon by copying its surroundings. It is weak, apologetic and lacks confidence.

TOO MUCH CONTRAST
This building squeezes as much of itself into the site as it can. It disrespects all aspects of its surroundings. It is greedy, selfish and aggressive.

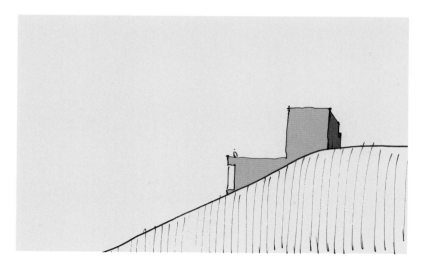

BALANCE OF CONTRAST
This building respects the topography, but does so in its own way. It is confident, assured and well-adjusted.

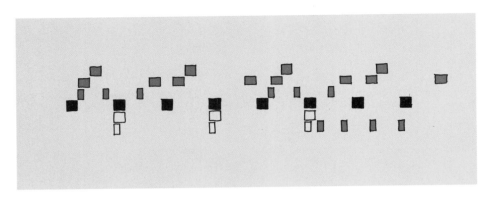

TYPICAL TECHNO BEAT SEQUENCE

KEY

  Syncopated backbeat / walls off grid

  Unsyncopated backbeat / walls on grid

  Bass Drum/Structural Grid

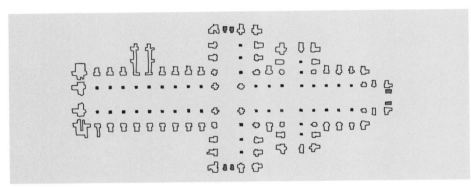

SALISBURY CATHEDRAL Plan

NOT ENOUGH CONTRAST

Walls and openings occur always on the grid, creating a constant, relentless unsyncopated rhythm.

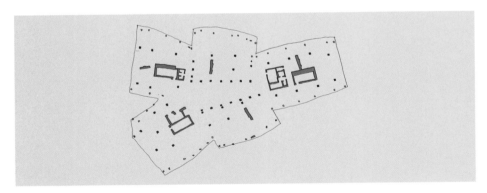

NOVARTIS CAMPUS
Frank Gehry

TOO MUCH CONTRAST

The structural grid deviates, meaning there is no consistent base from which the syncopation can stand out. The plan becomes random, and the syncopation is lost.

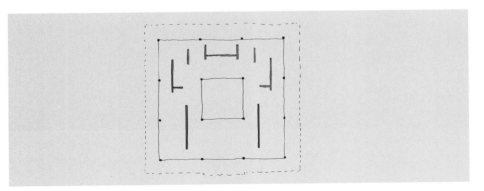

SCHAEFER MUSEUM
Mies van der Rohe

BALANCE OF CONTRAST

The structural grid remains constant throughout, providing the framework for the whole plan composition. Syncopation is carefully placed between the grid to add variety, surprise and a feeling of movement

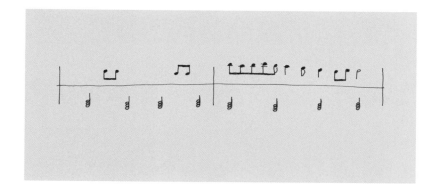

DEEP COVER Sheet music, Dr Dre

ACCENTS

BASS

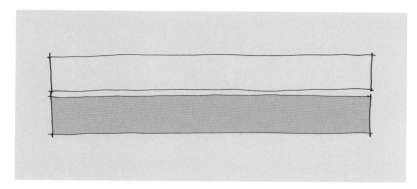

NO CONTRAST
Bass and accent combine into one boring form.

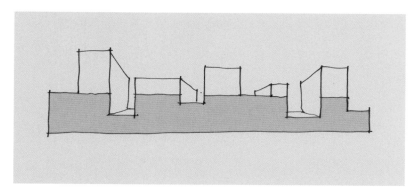

TOO MUCH CONTRAST
An inconsistent datum means 'accent' and 'bass' compete for the same space.

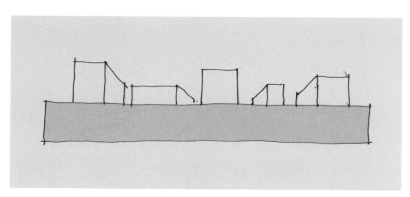

BALANCE OF CONTRAST
A consistent datum allows the more expressive forms above to become more distinct.

FINE GRAIN Sand dunes

FINE GRAIN Amman, Jordan

NO CONTRAST
New buildings assimilate into the urban
grain, with no contrast or layering

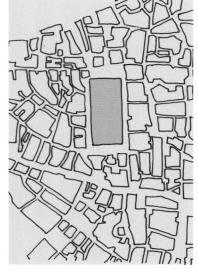

TOO MUCH CONTRAST
New building takes no account of existing
street patterns and block sizes

BALANCE OF CONTRAST
New buildings take account of existing
street patterns while contrasting in size
and form

Dr Eudora Fletcher, played by Mia Farrow, eventually confronts Zelig with some reverse psychology to allow him to admit that he is unhappy in his own skin: 'Who am I, I'm nothing?'[2] His desire to be all things to all men is really a desire not to be himself. The same might be said of architecture that mimics its surroundings.

In cities there is much pressure to produce 'Zelig' architecture that fits with its surroundings; an architecture of no contrast. This is often to appease planning departments or heritage organizations, but it can reflect a lack of confidence and reluctance to explore the extent to which contrast could successfully be used. Conversely, there are also commercial pressures to produce 'anti-Zelig' architecture – buildings

COARSE GRAIN Rocky beach

COARSE GRAIN Manhattan, New York

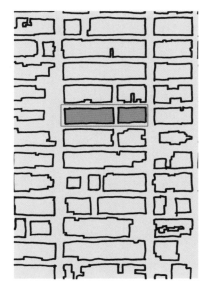

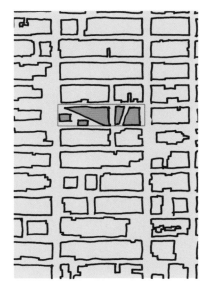

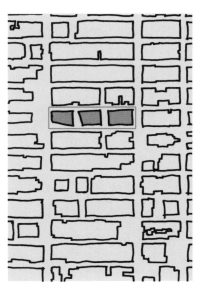

NO CONTRAST
New buildings assimilate into urban grain, with no increase in block permeability or navigability

TOO MUCH CONTRAST
New buildings are too fragmented, clashing with the rigid block pattern and ignoring street frontages

BALANCE OF CONTRAST
New buildings respect the block by maintaining frontages and not becoming too fragmented

that squeeze as many floors and as much lettable area on to a site as possible, with little regard for context, resulting in an architecture of too much contrast. Architecture should be of its time, made to fit specific concerns, designed to add another layer of memory to the city. To achieve this, maintaining a balanced level of contrast is essential.

The same issues can affect single buildings in a landscape. We may try to mimic the landforms surrounding our buildings such that landscape and architecture become one: a lack of contrast. Or conversely, again often due to commercial pressures, inappropriate one-size-fit-all solutions are employed in unique landscapes. Perhaps the answer lies in Alvaro Siza's observation: 'What is made by men is not natural ... more and more I think that there must be a certain distance between the natural and the man-made. But there must also be a dialogue between the two. Architecture comes from natural forms, but it also transforms nature.'[3] By introducing a dialogue of contrasts between our manmade building and the natural landscape, we can celebrate both.

Contrasting rhythm

We can look at the structure of music to see how to introduce contrasting rhythms into our architectural designs.

— Syncopation

Techno music thrives on the syncopation of its standard 4/4 rhythm. Syncopation is a musical sleight of hand that brings a beat ahead of or behind where it is expected in order to introduce variety and surprise. In techno (or house) music this makes the mechanical beat more elastic, more of an organic rhythm. This is achieved by a 'backbeat' of contrasting percussive elements carefully placed before and after the main 4/4 bass drum, producing a complex sonic tapestry of contrasts.

In an architectural plan, if we treat the structural grid like the 4/4 beat, we can then syncopate it with other elements to provide the necessary backbeat: a parallel wall might be staggered slightly from the grid to provide a sense of movement; a shorter, sharper, perpendicular wall just after the grid could allow for a momentary pause. A series of distinct elements combine to provide a sense of movement and contrast of form and space. If all the walls are placed on the structural grid, no syncopation occurs; if they are arranged randomly the building plan will be incoherent with no overall structure. A master of syncopation in the plan was Mies van der Rohe, who allowed the grid to march on in a regular manner while introducing walls and openings before and after to syncopate the composition. Like the techno producer, he created a balance of contrast between the regular beat (the grid) and the more expressive accents (the walls).

— Bass line

Meanwhile, in hip hop, the song is almost always driven by a consistent bass line; the vocals, strings or horn samples, and various other effects, come to the fore against this underpinning element. The consistency and economy of the bass line (often just one or two notes) provides an anchor against which the contrasts play.

This approach can also apply to the design of architectural form. When designing a building we often have a datum line – a consistent level derived from the surrounding context – that we use to accommodate particular functions or proportions in the building. This datum line is our bass line. Above this, we can then introduce more expressive elements such as additional sculpted blocks or tapered roof forms, which work in contrast to the bass line. There is a balance of contrast and unity between the two elements. For an example see Le Corbusier's Villa Savoye, near Paris, or Alvar Aalto's Finlandia Hall. In both cases, expressive roof forms are accentuated by a consistent 'bass line' below. Again, achieving the right balance between the base block and the expressive elements is vital.

4 — Augment

Contrasting grain

Sand is recognized as having a fine grain: a collection of tiny particles that on their own seem insignificant combine to form a homogeneous golden carpet. Fine sand is easy to traverse – it has little contrast. Meanwhile, rocks, stones and rubble have a coarse grain – they are large, sharp and wildly varied. Rocks are not easy to navigate – they have an excess of contrast. These principles of fine and coarse grain can also be applied to architecture.

— *Urban grain*

At an urban level, 'fine grain' is characterized by cities of multiple small blocks competing with each other – little differences in form go unnoticed, as buildings are so close together that they almost read as one. Fine-grained cities include Amman, Rome and Copenhagen. These cities are relatively permeable, offer plentiful chances for spatial interaction and allow for quick navigation through the regular arrangement of their small blocks. Coarse-grained cities include New York, Glasgow and Buenos Aires, made up of larger blocks that are more easily distinguished. The grid appears as a series of distinct islands, not a carpet of little differences. However, they do not enable as much permeability through buildings or as much potential for social interaction.

By introducing a larger, orthogonal element to the fine grain of a city plan such as Rome, we can provide a contrast which enables the creation of a new layer of history, as well as providing an element of careful contrast with the tightly packed plan. If, however, this introduction of orthogonality is too sweeping, too drastic, the excessive contrast will create a visible and physical disjuncture between the new proposal and the existing buildings surrounding it.

In a coarse grid block, the opposite problem presents itself. Not enough contrast in any new proposals would have the effect of replicating the same large block, further amplifying the existing level of high contrast. Conversely, breaking the block into tiny pieces reminiscent of the fine-grain city jars with the unity and scale of the urban blocks surrounding it. A balance of contrast could be achieved by breaking up the block, but in a restrained manner referencing key elements of context (urban grid, sight lines, surrounding building heights) while providing increased permeability through the site.

Contrast is integral to architecture, but we must use it carefully in order to harness its full potential. Not enough contrast, and our buildings risk becoming historicist, sterile and static. Too much and they may seem aggressive, staccato and jarring. Achieving the right balance of contrast should enable us to generate buildings of confidence, movement and variety through their character, rhythm and grain.

SCALE

Reveal new possibilities through manipulation

scale, *verb*
From Latin – *scala* (ladder)
1. (transitive) To form, render or draw (plans, models, representations) in accordance with a specific ratio of proportionate reduction.
2. (transitive) To adjust proportionately in size or amount.

'All social systems we've put into place are a mere sketch: "one plus one equals two", that's all we've learned, but one plus one has never equalled two – there are in fact no numbers and no letters, we've codified our existence to bring it down to human size, to make it comprehensible, we've created a scale so we can forget its unfathomable scale.'[1]
— Lucy, *Lucy* (2014)

Scale is how we perceive something in relation to something else. It is a human construct for comparing one thing to another in order to understand its size; it is pure relativism. Scale is understood by mathematical measurements derived from perception.

The primary – and most natural – aspect of understanding scale is in relation to ourselves. Humans first developed a scale of measurement based on what was most available and known to them – themselves. For example, the inch is derived from the breadth of the average man's thumb;[2] the foot is based on the length of an average man's foot;[3] the ancient measurement of the cubit is based on 'the length of the arm from the elbow to the tip of the middle finger and was considered the equivalent of 6 palms or 2 spans'.[4] Many imperial measurements are based on the human body, and the metric system was only universally adopted in the second half of the twentieth century.

This notion that 'Man is the measure of all things'[5] also applies to architecture. From the height of a handrail or the ergonomics of a door handle, to the dimensions of a kitchen, the rise of a flight of stairs, or the width of a corridor – all are designed relative to the scale of the human body and how we use these elements and spaces. This anthropometry is critical to ensure that buildings are functional, and easy to navigate and use.

Another consideration is visual scale. Visual scale is not concerned with the actual physical size of elements, but rather with how large or small an element of architecture appears in relation to its typical size, or to other elements around it.[6] Visual scale can be manipulated by the architect so large buildings appear small, or small buildings appear enlarged. Historian Geoffrey Scott remarked on how the curves and undulations that mimic the human body in Baroque churches give them a more intimate scale, while the small Renaissance Tempietto in Rome appears enlarged in comparison, by virtue of its less human attributes.

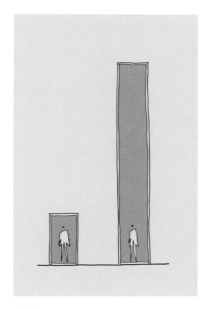

SCALE
Door to 'entrance slot'

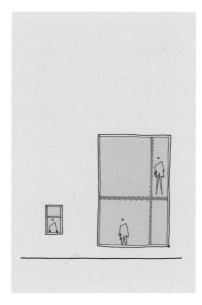

SCALE
Window to 'transparent wall'

SCALE
Standard brick to 'elemental block'

Visual scale can range from the macro to the micro. For example, we talk of the 'urban scale', which is architecture at the scale of masterplans and urban grids, where the relative scale of open space to built form, and of street width to building height affects the quality of the environment. We also refer to 'street scale', which is architecture experienced at ground level as a collection of buildings whose variation or uniformity, regularity or irregularity provide a sense of the scale of the street. Finally, we talk of 'building scale', which is the scale of the individual elements of a building that combine to form the overall composition.

The scale of these individual building elements – doors, windows, walls – in relation to one another ensures legibility. The familiarity of elements – the dimensions of a brick, the height of a doorway, the height to length ratio of a window – also allows us to measure space with our eyes. How elements in a building design relate to one another is something we learn to expect.

This familiarity can also become predictable and sterile. A door 1 metre by 2 metres (3ft 3in. x 6ft 7in.) will always be perceived as a door; a window will always be a window if it begins 1 metre above ground level and stops 300mm (11¾in.) below the ceiling; a brick is always a brick if made 215mm long, 65mm high and 100mm deep (8½in. x 2½in. x 4in.). However, these standardized elements can be transformed into architectural devices – elements that contribute to the overall concept and define the architecture by their presence, challenging our notions of scale and what a building should be.

A stretched door becomes an entrance slot; an enlarged window becomes a glazed wall spanning multiple floors and dividing walls; supersized bricks become elemental building blocks. When the scale of these elements is altered, they can be used to express hierarchy and importance, openness and increased light, solidity and firmness – or to challenge perceptions of normality in architecture.

TREE   **POLLEN**   **WOOL**   **YOGURT**

The true wonder of scale is perhaps most vivid when an everyday object is placed under a microscope. A simple, legible object immediately becomes complex and illegible, infinitesimal and abstract, revealing hidden worlds within. No material change has affected it, no rearrangement of their matter; it is simply a question of scale. Under the microscope the true structure of an object is revealed: a tree becomes a complex matrix of Lamé curves; pollen dust from a flower becomes a collection of spiky spheres; a woolly jumper becomes an intricate mass of rough strands; yogurt becomes a fluorescent mass of squirming organisms. By the shifting of scale, our perception of these familiar, everyday objects is challenged. As mathematician Michael Barnsley notes: 'Never again will your interpretation of these things be quite the same.'[7] It is the limitations of the human eye and our notions of visual scale that have prevented us from seeing their true composition.

Not only can scale be manipulated by the architect as a physical device to achieve a spatial or formal effect, it can also be used to reimagine familiar objects, as if seen under a microscope. By playing with scale via photomontage, for example, we might see new possibilities in the banal reality: a rusted metal wall becomes a collection of coastal seaside towers; a concrete bench, a hilltop viewing gallery; a ventilation outlet becomes a polar research station; or a brick pattern, a rusticated Brutalist monument.

The purpose of playing with scale should not be to produce architecture by clumsily copying and scaling, but instead to find hidden possibilities in the world around us. By taking elements or objects out of context and out of scale, new forms and relationships can show themselves, and reveal exciting architectural possibilities.

By taking these elements or objects out of context and out of scale, new forms and relationships show themselves in the world around us. By playing with scale we can break away from stereotypes to allow existing banal realities to reveal exciting new architectural possibilities.

RUSTED METAL SHEET PILING
Reality

RE-SCALE
(Copy, paste, cut, stretch)

SEASIDE TOWERS?
Possibility

CONCRETE BENCH
Reality

RE-SCALE
(Copy, paste, duplicate, stretch)

MOUNTAIN VIEWPOINT?
Possibility

4 — Augment

J.TAIT
City, Fascicle City, 2011

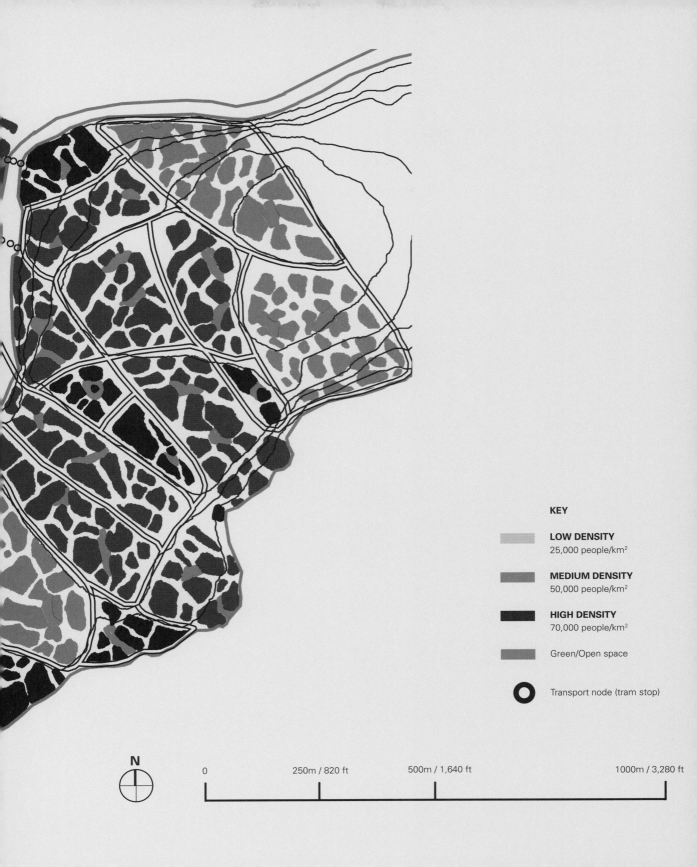

KEY

LOW DENSITY
25,000 people/km²

MEDIUM DENSITY
50,000 people/km²

HIGH DENSITY
70,000 people/km²

Green/Open space

Transport node (tram stop)

N

0   250m / 820 ft   500m / 1,640 ft   1000m / 3,280 ft

CRAFT

A new timelessness

craft, *verb*
Germanic – *kraft* (strength, skill)
1. (transitive) To make or manufacture
(objects, products, components) with
particular skill and heightened attention
to detail.

In the pursuit of perfection we seek imperfection. Despite all the technological advances of our modern age, we still seek out the handmade, the tarnished, the unfinished, the blemished – materials that display the process of their birth and ageing.

We see this in the traces of timber formwork, or the holes formed from the use of form ties during construction visible on cast concrete; the imperfections of the tree are directly translated in the knots and imperfections in timber cladding and panelling, which weathers from a brown hue to a muted grey; the metamorphosis undergone by oxidized metals – copper turned green, iron rusted from grey to orange; of the timelessness of stone with its indentations telling the story of the effort required to extract it from the ground and the weathering it later undergoes in repose; or the uniqueness of each handmade brick – its sparkle, texture and the way it absorbs the grime of daily life.

Craftsmanship

This reverence for the process of making and the ageing of materials reflects a yearning for craftsmanship. The materials that require crafting are generally solid and timeless: metal, wood, stone or concrete, and they age gracefully, their inherent imperfections crystallizing and resolving throughout their eternal life span. If material gives life to form, then craftsmanship imbues our materials – and by extension our buildings – with life, human touch and its associated complexities and imperfections.

However, industrial, mass-produced materials are now the norm, such as medium-density fibreboard, paperboard, high-pressure laminates, polyvinyl chloride, polyurethane, silicone, sheetrock, phenolic resin and fibreglass, among other examples. These do not require craftsmanship. They are assembled and machined behind closed doors, in a process rarely seen or understood by the architect. They tend to be lightweight materials with a limited life; simple in appearance though complex by nature. They are perfect, smooth and shiny – not imperfect, textured and lustred. They do not age, remaining constant, only to die prematurely: none will live past the age of forty.[1]

These materials have become our reality – they are inexpensive and quickly made; crafted materials are more expensive and take longer.[2] Our timescales, our budgets and our attitude towards disposability rarely allow space for craft. Yet we still yearn for the qualities that craft embodies, and so perform a repertoire of tricks. We anodize bare metal sections to give them the sheen and lustre of patinated or burnished metal; we use prematurely aged green copper; we create functionally redundant shadow gaps that mimic wooden jointing techniques; we lay wood-effect vinyl flooring; we make stone

CONCRETE	TIMBER	NATURAL COPPER	SANDSTONE	HANDMADE BRICK
vs	vs	vs	vs	vs
FIBREGLASS	FIBRE CEMENT CLADDING	PRE-AGED COPPER	SANDSTONE RAINSCREEN	BRICK SLIPS

rainscreen – slivers of this noble material – and glue it on to something else. We also use reclaimed materials because the new ones are no longer up to the job.

Of course, modern craft is still possible in architecture. There are still capable concrete workers, companies that specialize in real timber cladding, skilled metalworkers and stonemasons, and they still make their mark in modern construction. However, their numbers have been falling since the 1970s, primarily due to the rise of industrialization and prefabrication.[3] There are certain countries, like Switzerland, where a 'material consciousness'[4] is still apparent, but they are exceptions. Switzerland has a unique tradition of engineering and building excellence fostered by institutions such as the Swiss Federal Institute of Technology in Zurich (ETHZ), strong regional identities that protect notions of local craft, and its architecture is characterized by precision of execution and economy of concept.[5] Perhaps most significantly, it is one of the richest countries in the world: Swiss architecture is a luxury product.

Disposability

The shift in the production and use of materials in architecture is not simply the fault of the architect, but a symptom of a wider societal shift towards a more disposable culture.[6] Our most prized possessions are made of plastic and paper-thin metal, and become obsolete within months. Materialist culture, not material culture, dominates.

Presently we place the notion of self – in the collective sense of our own time, our fashions, our concerns – ahead of the notion of timelessness. It is no coincidence that the design life of our buildings is often less than our own life expectancy. We no longer build buildings for the future; 'we don't leave pyramids'.[7] Instead, we build for ourselves, not those who will follow us. But why do we make buildings with lifespans of four to six decades,[8] when those built 400 years ago endure? This lack of timelessness can largely be attributed to the materials we now use.

FORM

DETAIL

SPACE Rolex Learning Center, Lausanne, Switzerland, SANAA, 2010

A new timelessness

Architects once led the shift from craftsmanship to the use of industrialized materials. We could now lead the re-introduction of craftsmanship through technology, to harness the potential of concrete, wood, metal, brick, stone and timber for the digital age. This would not be craftsmanship in a nostalgic, fetishized sense, but would forge a new approach to materiality, craft and timelessness: as sociologist Richard Sennett puts it 'to engage with the tools of our time'.[9] This would allow us to use natural materials in new ways, which could democratize and economize craft, making it a viable alternative to mass production. This process of mass-digitized commercially viable bespoke craft is already underway in the automotive, aerospace, healthcare and fashion industries – but has not yet been fully taken up by the construction industry.

The use of digital fabrication in architecture is not new, having been pioneered by architects such as Greg Lynn and Frank Gehry in the 1990s, and further developed by Zaha Hadid Architects among others in the twenty-first century. However, it has usually been confined to small-scale experimentation or unique commissions. Crucially, digital fabrication is often used in conjunction with industrialized, artificial, temporary materials such as glass-reinforced plastic, polyurethane, laminated plywood, acrylic or other plastics – and tends to place the creation of self-consciously digital forms (parametric architecture) above all else, which can limit conceptual approaches.

Yet other possibilities for digital craftsmanship of ancient materials have emerged. SANAA used a CNC router at their Rolex Learning Center in Lausanne, Switzerland, to cut the complex double curves of the formwork required for the concrete building,[10] while Herzog & de Meuron's sculptural brick façade at the Tate Modern extension prompted the contractors to invent new 3D setting-out tools, to ensure that tolerances of +/-

FORM

SPACE Tate Modern Extension, London, Herzog & de Meuron, 2016   **DETAIL**

2mm were maintained over the 65m height. Both examples used digital technology in tandem with contractors (who are re-embracing craft through technology), to express the possibilities of architecture – not to use architecture to express the possibilities of digital technology.

These projects may lead the way, but they still represent luxury, not the everyday. However, like SANAA and Herzog & de Meuron, if we reject the false, artificial materials of standardization, and fully engage with the people who build our buildings, we now have an opportunity to make digitally crafted, ancient materials the new norm. The more contractors that buy CNC machines or develop new 3D setting-out tools, the more their competitors will take note. If the majority of contractors see this as the direction of travel for the industry they will follow – and many have invested already in the BIM software that allows them to access and build directly from 3D models.[11] 'Digital craftsmanship' will cease to be simply a risk taken for a high-profile project. These methods could become as cost-effective as mass-produced, artificial materials are now.

Of course, digital fabrication is not a prerequisite for good architecture, far from it – but it could give us the means to take control of the gap between the design and construction of our buildings; the gap between what we want our buildings to be made from and what budgets and timescales currently allow. It might enable us to eschew composite, finite, temporary materials and instead return to materials that endure and express their age in all of our projects, not just the chosen few, to be enjoyed by future generations. We might use the tools of our time to reconnect with the metamorphosis that matter undergoes to become a building material; create a new timelessness based on appreciation of materiality, not materialism. Let's leave pyramids again.

NOTES

INTRODUCTION

[1] James Williamson, *Kahn at Penn: Transformative Teacher of Architecture* (Abingdon: Routledge, 2016), page 142.

WONDER

[1] Rudolf Otto, translated by John W. Harvey, *The Idea of the Holy: An inquiry into the non-rational factor in the idea of the devine and its relation to the rational* (London: Oxford University Press, 1923), p 18.

[2] Immanuel Kant, translated by John T. Goldthwait, *Observations on the Feeling of the Beautiful and Sublime* (Berkeley: University of California Press, 1965), p 47.

[3] Otto, *The Idea of the Holy*, p 68.

[4] Kant, *Observations on the Feeling of the Beautiful and Sublime*, page 46.

[5] Otto, *The Idea of the Holy*, p 42.

[6] http://www.arup.com/projects/china_central_television_headquarters

[7] Otto, *The Idea of the Holy*, p 43.

[8] Ibid., page 43

[9] Otto, *The Idea of the Holy*, p 43.

[10] Ibid., p 36.

[11] Ibid., p 69.

[12] Ibid., p 71.

[13] Ibid., p 71.

[14] Juhani Pallasmaa, *The Eyes of the Skin: Architecture and the Senses* (New York: John Wiley & Sons, 2005), p 51.

[15] Pallasmaa, *The Eyes of the Skin*, p 52.

[16] Richard Saul Wurman (ed.), *What Will Be Has Always Been* (New York: Rizzoli, 1986), pp 56–59.

[17] Otto, *The Idea of the Holy*, p 72.

[18] Wurman, *What Will Be Has Always Been*, pp 56–59.

ENVIRONMENT

[1] http://engineering.mit.edu/ask/why-does-structural-behavior-change-different-types-soil

[2] Lee D. Jones and Ian Jefferson, *Expansive Soils* (Institution of Civil Engineers, 2012), Chapter 5.

[3] Jancis Robinson (ed.), *The Oxford Companion to Wine*, 3rd edition (Oxford University Press, 2006).

DISORDER

[1] Le Corbusier, translated by Frederick Etchells, *Towards a New Architecture* (Thousand Oaks: BN Publishing, 2008), p 67.

[2] James Gleick, *Nature's Chaos* (New York: Little, Brown and Company, 2001), p 39.

[3] *Architectural Theory: From the Renaissance to the Present* (Cologne: Taschen, 2006), p 154.

[4] Le Corbusier, *Towards a New Architecture*, p 31.

MEMORY

[1] Gaston Bachelard, translated by Daniel Russell, *The Poetics of Reverie: Childhood, Language, and the Cosmos* (Boston: Beacon Press, 1971), p 104.

[2] Chris Marker (dir.), *La Jetée* (France: Argos Films, 1962).

[3] Marc Augé, translated by John Howe, *Non-Places: Introduction to an Anthropology of Supermodernity* (London: Verso, 1995), pp 77–78.

[4] Italo Calvino, translated by William Weaver, *Invisible Cities* (Orlando: Harcourt Brace and Com-pany, 1974), pp 10–11.

[5] Calvino, *Invisible Cities*, pp 10–11.

[6] Ibid.

[7] Gaston Bachelard, translated by Maria Jolas, *The Poetics of Space* (Boston: Beacon Press, 1994), p 4.

[8] Bachelard, *The Poetics of Space*, p 8.

[9] Ibid., p 15.

[10] Ibid., p 146.

[11] Friedrich Nietzsche, *Philosophy in the Tragic Age of the Greeks* (Washington, DC: Gateway Editions, 1996), p 62.

[12] http://www.toyhalloffame.org/toys/alphabet-blocks

[13] George Hersey, *Architecture and Geometry in the Age of the Baroque* (Chicago: University of Chicago Press, 2000), p 205.

FUNCTION

[1] Hilde Heynen, *Architecture and Modernity: A Critique* (Cambridge: MIT Press, 1999), p 108.

[2] Michael H. Mitias, *Philosophy and Architecture* (Boston: Brill, 1994), p 96.

[3] Heynen, *Architecture and Modernity*, p 108.

[4] Rem Koolhaas, *Delirious New York: A Retroactive Manifesto for Manhattan* (New York: The Monacelli Press, 1994), p 100.

[5] Kenneth Frampton, *Modern Architecture: A Critical History*, 3rd edition (London: Thames & Hudson, 1992), p 228.

[6] Kenneth Frampton, *Modern Architecture: A Critical History*, 3rd edition (London: Thames & Hudson, 1992), p 190.

[7] http://www.designcurial.com/news/jail-breaker-4403655

[8] http://hosoyaschaefer.com/wp-content/uploads/2013/03/2006_Design-for-Shopping_Print.pdf

[9] Lisa Scharoun, *America at the Mall: The Cultural Role of a Retail Utopia*, (Jefferson: McFarland & Co, 2012), p 113

[10] http://www.promontorio.net/userfiles/practice/2014_11_11_PROMONTORIO_Retail_LowRes.pdf

[11] http://libeskind.com/work/crystals-at-citycenter

[12] Heynen, *Architecture and Modernity*, p 123.

FORM

[1] *Architectural Theory: From the Renaissance to the Present* (Cologne: Taschen, 2006), p 476.

[2] Kenneth Frampton, *Modern Architecture: A Critical History* (London: Thames & Hudson, 1980), p 248.

[3] Karen Forbes, *Site Specific* (San Francisco: ORO Editions, 2015), p 142.

IRONY

[1] https://www.youtube.com/watch?v=u4RJcNHWu7Y

[2] http://www.tate.org.uk/context-comment/articles/architecture-and-sixties-still-radical-after-all-these-years

[3] Anthony Vidler, *The Architectural Uncanny: Essays in the Modern Unhomely* (Cambridge: MIT Press, 1994), p 193.

[4] http://oma.eu/projects/zeebrugge-sea-terminal

[5] http://oma.eu/projects/irish-prime-minister-residence

[6] Robert Venturi, Denise Scott Brown and Steven Izenour, *Learning from Las Vegas*, revised edition (Cambridge: MIT, 1977), p 3.

POLITICS

[1] David Kilcullen, *Blood Year: Islamic State and the Failures of the War on Terror* (London: Hurst Publishers, 2016), pp 198–199.

[2] Patrik Schumacher, 'Where is the architecture?', ICON, August 2016, p 126.

[3] http://www.wsj.com/articles/tax-breaks-for-twitter-bring-benefits-and-criticism-1461947597

[4] Charlie LeDuff, *Detroit: An American Autopsy* (New York: Penguin, 2013), p 68.

[5] CABE, *Design quality and the private finance initiative* (London: CABE, 2005), p 4.

[6] https://www.theguardian.com/money/2009/nov/07/landbanking-investment-scheme

[7] http://www.building.co.uk/architects-and-recession-battered-bruised-and-broke/5012558.article

[8] Communities and Local Government, *Safer Places: A Counter-Terrorism Supplement* (London: Home Office, 2009), p 18.

[9] Anna Minton, *What Kind of World are We Building? The Privatisation of Public Space* (London: RICS, 2006), p 6.

[10] Roy Coleman and Lynn Hancock, 'Culture and Curfew in Fantasy City: Whose Time, Whose Place?', *Nerve*, (14) 2009, pp 12–13.

[11] http://www.jfklibrary.org/Exhibits/Permanent-Exhibits/The-Space-Race.aspx

[12] Edward J. Blakely and Mary Gail Synder, *Fortress America: Gated Communities in the United States* (Washington: Brookings, 1997), p 28.

[13] Oscar Niemeyer, *The Curves of Time: The Memoirs of Oscar Niemeyer* (London: Phaidon, 2000), p 170.

[14] Ibid., p 169.

[15] Ibid., pp 175–176.

[16] http://nytimes.com/2016/05/23/t-magazine/pritzker-venice-biennale-chile-architect-alejandro-aravena.html?_r=0

[17] Ibid.

[18] Niemeyer, *The Curves of Time*, p 175.

[19] Bill Berkeley, *The Graves Are Not Yet Full: Race, Tribe and Power in the Heart of Africa* (New York: Basic Books, 2002), pp 239–240.

WALK

1 Walter Benjamin, *The Arcades Project* (Cambridge, MA: The Belknap Press of Harvard University Press, 1999), p 99.
2 Rainer Bauböck, *Integration in a Pluralistic Society: Strategies for the Future* (Vienna: Institut für Höhere Studien, 1993), p 12.
3 Charles Jencks, *Bartlett International Lecture Series: Generic Individualism – The Reigning Style of Our Time – and its Discontents* (2015). Available at: https://vimeo.com/152598975 Accessed: 6 February 2016).
4 http://www.coop-himmelblau.at/architecture/projects/bmw-welt/
5 http://www.zaha-hadid.com/architecture/cma-cgm-headquarters/
6 http://www.rmjm.com/portfolio/capital-gate-adnec-development-phase-3-abu-dhabi/
7 http://www.hok.com/design/type/commercial/baku-flame-towers/
8 http://www.civicarts.com/titanic-belfast
9 http://www.calatrava.com/projects/palau-de-las-artes-valencia.html
10 Jencks, *Bartlett International Lecture Series*.
11 http://www.toureiffel.paris/images/PDF/all_you_need_to_know_about_the_eiffel_tower.pdf
12 Ibid.
13 Walter Benjamin, *The Arcades Project* (Cambridge, MA: The Belknap Press of Harvard University Press, 1999), p 168.
14 http://www.lonelyplanet.com/france/paris/introduction
15 Charles Baudelaire, *The Flowers of Evil* (Oxford: Oxford University Press, 1993), p 207.
16 Benjamin, *The Arcades Project*, p 422.
17 Ibid., p 417.
18 Ibid., p 422.
19 Ibid., p 423.
20 Timothy R. Gleason, 'The Communicative Roles of Street and Social Landscape Photography', *Simile* vol. 8, no. 4 (2008), pp 1–13.
21 Jean-Claude Gautrand, *Robert Doisneau* (Cologne: Taschen, 2003), p 97.
22 Eleonore Kofman and Elizabeth Lebas, *Writings on Cities: Henri Lefebvre* (Oxford: Blackwell Publishing, 1996), p 214.
23 Kofman and Lebas, *Writings on Cities: Henri Lefebvre*, p 219
24 Ibid., p 221
25 Ibid., p 213
26 Rebecca Solnit, *Wanderlust* (London: Verso, 2001), p 176.
27 http://www.theguardian.com/cities/2015/feb/24/private-london-exposed-thames-path-riverside-walking-route
28 Solnit, *Wanderlust*, p 14.

INFLUENCE

1 Linda A. Henkel, 'Point-and-Shoot Memories: The Influence of Taking Photos on Memory for a Museum Tour', *Psychological Science*, February 2014 (25), pp 396–402, first published on December 5, 2013.
2 http://www.scottisharchitects.org.uk/architect_full.php?id=100095
3 Patrick Nuttgens, *The Story of Architecture* (Oxford: Phaidon, 1983), p 125.
4 Glasgow City Council, *Walmer Crescent: Conservation Area Appraisal* (Glasgow: DRS, 2006).
5 http://www.historic-scotland.gov.uk/memorandum-app3.pdf
6 Ali Davey, *Short Guide: Maintenance and Repair Techniques for Traditional Cast Iron* (Edinburgh: Historic Scotland, 2013).
7 http://portal.historic-scotland.gov.uk/designation/LB32608

RECLAIM

1 http://ngm.nationalgeographic.com/2014/02/il-duomo/mueller-text

RESPECT

1 James W.P. Campbell, *Building St Paul's* (London: Thames & Hudson, 2007), p 21.
2 Ibid., p 21.

OBSCURE

1 https://www.youtube.com/watch?v=zG2WMVkD5dw
2 Ibid.
3 Ibid.
4 Ibid.
5 Ibid.
6 Ibid.
7 Ibid.
8 Ibid.
9 Ibid.
10 Ibid.
11 Ibid.

HEROIZE

1 Aristotle (trans. Anthony Kenny), *Poetics* (Oxford: Oxford University Press, 2013), p 29.
2 Sophocles, *The Three Theban Plays: Antigone, Oedipus the King, Oedipus at Colonus* (London: Penguin Classics, 1984), p 160.
3 Le Corbusier (trans. Frederick Etchells), *Towards a New Architecture* (Thousand Oaks: BN Publishing, 1923), p 13.
4 Ibid., p 3.
5 Sophocles, *The Three Theban Plays*, p 162.
6 http://www.econ.nyu.edu/dept/courses/gately/DGS_Vehicle%20Ownership_2007.pdf
7 Kenneth Frampton, *Modern Architecture: A Critical History* (London: Thames & Hudson, 1992), p 155.
8 Stefi Orazi, *Modernist Estates: The Buildings and the People Who Live in Them Today* (London: Frances Lincoln Limited, 2015), p 9.
9 Ibid., p 10.
10 Frampton, Modern Architecture, p 281.
11 Ibid., p 308.
12 http://www.pritzkerprize.com/2000/bio
13 Rem Koolhaas and Bruce Mau, *S, M, L, XL* (New York: The Monacelli Press, 1995), p 959.
14 Rem Koolhaas, 'From Bauhaus to Koolhaas', *Wired*, July 1996: https://www.wired.com/1996/07/koolhaas/.
15 Rem Koolhaas, *Content* (Cologne: Taschen, 2004), p 162.
16 Ibid, p 163.
17 http://www.smithsonianmag.com/arts-culture/why-is-rem-koolhaas-the-worlds-most-controversial-architect-18254921/?no-ist=
18 Ibid.
19 http://www.nytimes.com/2005/04/10/arts/design/rem-koolhaas-learns-not-to-overthink-it.html?_r=0
20 Ibid.
21 Koolhaas, *Content*, p 118.
22 http://oma.eu/projects/universal-headquarters
23 Koolhaas, *Content*, p 512.

IMPROVE

1 Peter Jones, *Ove Arup: Master Builder of the Twentieth Century* (New Haven: Yale University Press, 2006), p 214.
2 http://www.dezeen.com/2012/10/11/basket-apartments-student-housing-by-ofis-arhitekti/
3 Oscar Niemeyer, *The Curves of Time: The Memoirs of Oscar Niemeyer* (London: Phaidon, 2000), p 176.

IMPROVISE

1 Ajay Heble and Rebecca Caines, *The Improvisation Studies Reader* (London: Routledge, 2015), p 4.

3   ASSEMBLE

WALL

[1] Francesco Cacciatore, *The Wall as Living Place: Hollow Structural Forms in Louis Kahn's Work* (Siracusa: Lettera Ventidue Edizioni, 2014), p 3.

[2] Gaston Bachelard, *The Poetics of Space* (Boston: Beacon Press, 1994), pp 217–218.

[3] Slavoj Žižek, 'Aesthetics and Architecture' (presentation, 2010).

[4] https://en.wikipedia.org/wiki/Border_barrier

[5] Rory Kennedy, *The Fence* (HBO, 2010).

[6] *Fourth report of the Secretary-General on the threat posed by ISIL (Da'esh) to international peace and security and the range of United Nations efforts in support of Member States in countering the threat* (United Nations, 2017), pp 8–12.

STRUCTURE

[1] Edward R. Ford, *The Architectural Detail* (San Francisco: Chronicle Books, 2012), p 145.

[2] Hanif Kara, Adams Kara Taylor, *Design Engineering AKT* (Barcelona: ACTAR, 2008), p 10.

[3] Rem Koolhaas, *Content* (Cologne: Taschen, 2004), p 164.

DOOR

[1] http://www.etymonline.com/index.php?term=salvo

FAÇADE

[1] Musei Civici Veneziani, *The Doge's Palace in Venice: Guide* (Milan: Mondadori Electa, 2004).

STAIR

[1] Franz Kafka, (ed. Nahum N. Glatzer), *The Penguin Complete Short Stories of Franz Kafka* (London: Penguin Books, 1983), p 451.

SERVICES

[1] Kenneth Frampton, *Modern Architecture: A Critical History* (London, Thames & Hudson, 1992), p 244.

[2] John Donat, *World Architecture 1* (London: Studio Books, 1964), p 35.

ECONOMIZE

[1] Glasgow City Council, *Glasgow's Affordable Housing Supply Programme: Performance Review* (Glasgow: Glasgow City Council, 2015).

[2] City of Westminster, 2008. *Conservation area audit: Hallfield Estate, consultation draft*, March 2008

COLOUR

[1] http://www.hrc.utexas.edu/educator/modules/gutenberg/invention/illuminations/

[2] https://udel.edu/~rworley/e412/Psyc_of_color_final_paper.pdf

[3] http://www.iconeye.com/404/item/3368-caixa-forum

[4] http://www.architectural-review.com/today/casa-das-histrias-paula-rego-by-eduardo-souto-de-moura-cascais-portugal/8600562.fullarticle

[5] http://www.tschumi.com/projects/3/

CONTRAST

[1] Herman Melville, *Moby-Dick or the White Whale* (Eighth Impression, 1922) (Boston: The St Botolph Society, 1892), p 55.

[2] Woody Allen, *Zelig* (USA: Warner Bros., Orion Pictures, 1983).

[3] Philip Jodidio, *Alvaro Siza* (Cologne: Taschen, 2003), p 12.

SCALE

[1] Luc Besson, *Lucy* (USA: Universal Pictures, 2014).

[2] Lord John Swinton, *A Proposal for Uniformity of Weights and Measures in Scotland* (Edinburgh, 1779), p 134.

[3] Oswald Ashton Wentworth Dilke, *Mathematics and Measurement* (Berkeley: University of California Press, 1987), p 23.

[4] https://www.britannica.com/science/cubit

[5] Benjamin Hall Kennedy, *The Theaetetus of Plato* (Cambridge: University Press, 1881), pp 116–117.

[6] Francis D. K. Ching, *Architecture: Form, Space and Order* (3rd Edition) (New Jersey: John Wiley & Sons, 2007), p 330.

[7] Michael F. Barnsley, *Fractals Everywhere* (3rd Revised Edition) (Mineola, New York: Dover Publications, 2012), p 1.

CRAFT

[1] AECB, *Typical Life Expectancy of Building Components*, accessed at: https://www.aecb.net.

[2] Richard Sennett, 'Craftsmanship' (Presentation), Harold M. Williams Auditorium, Getty Center, 2009.

[3] Graham J. Ive and Stephen L. Gruneberg, *The Economics of the Modern Construction Sector* (New York: Springer, 2000), p 60.

[4] Richard Sennett, *The Craftsman* (London: Penguin, 2009), pp 119–120.

[5] Steven Spier, *New Architecture from Switzerland* (London: Thames & Hudson, 2003), pp 8–9.

[6] Anna Moran and Sorcha O'Brien, *Love Objects: Emotion, Design and Material Culture* (London: Bloomsbury, 2014), p 140.

[7] Rem Koolhaas, *Content* (Cologne: Taschen, 2004), p 162.

[8] Anderson, J., Shiers, D. 2009. *The Green Guide to Specification*. Oxford: Wiley-Blackwell.

[9] Richard Sennett, 'Craftsmanship' (Presentation), Harold M. Williams Auditorium, Getty Center, 2009.

[10] Pedro Felipe Martins et al., *Digital Fabrication Technology in Concrete Architecture Fabrication* (Volume 1) – eCAADe 32.

[11] http://www.sir-robert-mcalpine.com/about-us/our-expertise/expertise_bimexperience/

FURTHER READING

- Architecture isn't everything – get a life.
- Never think you know it all.
- Play with wooden blocks again.
- Remember that every architectural element should celebrate space and light.

READ PHILOSOPHY (it is the foundation of humanity; architecture is the setting for humanity):

Marc Augé, translated by John Howe, *Non-Places: Introduction to an Anthropology of Supermo-dernity* (London: Verso, 1995)

Gaston Bachelard, translated by Maria Jolas, *The Poetics of Space* (Boston: Beacon Press, 1994)

Walter Benjamin, *The Arcades Project* (Cambridge, MA: The Belknap Press of Harvard University Press, 1999)

Immanuel Kant, translated by John T. Goldthwait, *Observations on the Feeling of the Beautiful and Sublime* (Berkeley: University of California Press, 1965)

Eleonore Kofman and Elizabeth Lebas, *Writings on Cities: Henri Lefebvre* (Oxford: Blackwell Publishing, 1996)

Rudolf Otto, translated by John W. Harvey, *The Idea of the Holy: An inquiry into the non-rational factor in the idea of the divine and its relation to the rational* (London: Oxford University Press, 1923)

Richard Sennett, *The Craftsman* (London: Penguin, 2009)

- Create, don't just facilitate.
- Always question, never settle.

FIND OUT WHAT MAKES YOUR HEROES TICK (maybe some of it will rub off):

Alex Ferguson with Michael Moritz, *Leading* (London: Hodder and Stoughton, 2015)

Rem Koolhaas, *Content* (Cologne: Taschen, 2004)

Oscar Niemeyer, *The Curves of Time: The Memoirs of Oscar Niemeyer* (London: Phaidon, 2000)

Richard Saul Wurman (ed.), *What Will Be Has Always Been: The Words of Louis I. Kahn* (New York: Rizzoli, 1986)

- Spend clients' money as if it were your own.
- Don't use other people's buildings to generate a design response.
- Let the supports sing.

READ ABOUT THE PAST (it will inform the future):

Brian Dillon, *Ruins* (London: Whitechapel Gallery and Boston: MIT, 2011)

Kenneth Frampton, *Modern Architecture: A Critical History* (London: Thames & Hudson, 1980)

Rem Koolhaas, *Delirious New York: A Retroactive Manifesto for Manhattan* (New York: The Monacelli Press, 1994)

Patrick Nuttgens, *The Story of Architecture* (Oxford: Phaidon, 1983)

Times Atlases, *History of the World in Maps: The Rise and Fall of Empires, Countries and Cities* (London: HarperCollins UK, 2016)

- Dream.
- Play with the landscape, don't fight it.
- Listen more than you talk.

WATCH FILMS (the right ones will blow your mind and influence your buildings):

Thom Andersen, *LA Plays Itself* (USA: Thom Andersen, 2003)

Woody Allen, *Zelig* (USA: Warner Bros., Orion Pictures, 1983)

Stanley Kubrick, *The Shining* (USA: Warner Bros., 1980)

Chris Marker, *La Jetée* (France: Argos Films, 1962)

Ridley Scott, *Blade Runner* (USA: Warner Bros., 1982)

Andrei Tarkovsky, *The Stalker* (Soviet Union: Dom Kino, 1979)

Spike Lee, *Do the Right Thing* (USA: Universal Pictures, 1989)

- Inhabit dead space.
- Remember that walls create space, not division.
- Find inspiration everywhere.
- Add your own layer of memory to the city, but don't destroy other memories in the process.

READ FICTION (escapism will inform your architecture and its predicted futures may become your setting one day):

Any works by J.G. Ballard

Charles Baudelaire, *The Flowers of Evil* (Oxford: Oxford University Press, 1993)

Ray Bradbury, *Fahrenheit 451* (London: Harper, 1953)

Italo Calvino, translated by William Weaver, *Invisible Cities* (Orlando: Harcourt Brace and Company, 1974)

W.G. Sebald, *Austerlitz* (London: Penguin, 2001)

Sophocles, *The Three Theban Plays: Antigone, Oedipus the King, Oedipus at Colonus* (London: Penguin Classics, 1984)

- Think before you design.
- If you need air conditioning, you've designed it wrong. Open a window.
- Don't make broccoli in the staff kitchen.
- Scale is only ever relative.

KEEP UP TO DATE (but don't follow fashions, they are fleeting):

bldgblog.com
dezeen.com
iconeye.com
monocle.com
theguardian.com
wired.com

- Never build with a material that will die before you do.
- Colour is not to be scared of, just to be used properly.
- Spend as much time as possible with children. Their enthusiasm and curiosity is infectious.

LEARN TO DRAW BY HAND (it is the only way of directly connecting our brains with our architecture):

Antonio Angelillo, *Alvaro Siza: Writings on Architecture* (Milan: Skira, 1997)

Francis D.K. Ching with Steven P. Jurosek, *Design Drawing* (New York: John Wiley and Sons, 1997)

Luigi Ficacci, *Giovanni Battista Piranesi* (Cologne: Taschen, 2001)

Atelier Hoko, *Science of the Secondary: Door / Window / Pipe (bundle)* (Singapore: Atelier Hoko, 2015)

- Walk more. Your surroundings will surprise you if you allow them.
- Learn from nature: it is infinitely more complex and interesting than the manmade world.

ACKNOWLEDGMENTS

Dedicated to my family – a constant source of inspiration, strength and support.

This book developed from a series of private thoughts and sketches, started in the depths of the Great Recession, into a published work with the help of the following people:

My beautiful daughters Alexa and Theia, who provided the original inspiration and daily drive to write this book. You surprise and delight me every day.

My incredible wife Joanne, who has been there from the beginning, providing support and advice each day. Your belief in me is a constant source of strength.

My parents Jim and Isobel, whose guidance has been invaluable in this process. I am forever grateful for the grounding and opportunities you have given me.

Lucas Dietrich for believing in an unpublished, unknown quantity and distilling the scope and purpose of the book.

Fleur Jones and Liz Jones for guiding me through the process of writing my first book with patience and diligence.

The original Strathy Arch, nothing's changed in over fifteen years!

Everyone at the Mitchell Library, Glasgow, whose shelves are a continual font of knowledge.

All my family, friends and colleagues, who have shown an interest in and support for this work.

For more about the author, please vist www.jtait.com.

PICTURE CREDITS

INDEX

Page numbers in *italics* refer to captions